Chicano Studies Reader

A Bridge to Writing

Edited by
Roberta Orona-Cordova

KENDALL/HUNT PUBLISHING COMPANY
4050 Westmark Drive   Dubuque, Iowa 52002

Cover photo: Yreina D. Cervantez © 2003 "THE HEART OF THE SKY, THE HEART OF THE EARTH/
ELIZABETH AND MARY O MAIRA Y VIRGINIA" Watercolor, 20″ × 14″

For my best friend Vincent

Contents

Chapter 5 *Chicana/o Queers Speak Their Minds*   121

Chapter 6 *A Fresh Look at Chicano/a-Themed Films*   143

Preface

I came of age during the Chicano/a Movement: first as a student at the University of California, Berkeley, and later as a volunteer student-worker in the nearby Mexican barrio in East Oakland. When I first stepped onto Sproul Plaza at U.C. Berkeley in 1970, my daughter was 18 months old. I was wearing a miniskirt, go-go boots, false eyelashes, and a hair extension that folded into a French twist. I pushed my baby's stroller across Sproul Plaza and found my way to the Associated Student Union for an EOP (Economic Opportunity Program) orientation. That same day we walked into a student meeting where the group's leaders welcomed us to a new organization they called MECHA,** and therein began my transformation.

When I started Berkeley I was "Spanish." I was not aware of the "politics" or the historical significance of the term. On the other hand, while growing up in Albuquerque I was asked if I was Mexican, and the answer was always "yes," without my realizing the "politics" of this identity. It was during my years at Berkeley that I shaped and formed myself into a Chicana. This was a timely and much needed turning point in my life. Today and always I am a Chicana (born and raised in the United States and politically conscious of sex, class, and racial discrimination against Mexicans and Mexican-Americans, and dedicated to working to improve social and economic conditions within this community).

While growing up, and for many years as a young adult, I was deeply insecure and suffered from low self-esteem. Naturally, this affected my self-image. The Chicano/a Movement gave me a "self": a self-possessed and proud Mestiza, not Spanish nor Mexican, but Chicana. In spite of its own disorder at times, the Movement created order in my life, as well as in many of our communities through educational opportunities created by our revolution. After graduating from Berkeley, I knew I wanted to become an educator and hopefully make a small contribution to students who followed a similar path as mine.

During the Chicano/a Movement the one-word mantra we used to describe our lives was "lucha" (from luchar, to struggle). The goal of the Movement was to overcome struggle through education, self-determination, political action, and leadership. Although struggle continues in our communities, we have through the years added "success" to our process. We will never forget our struggles or those who come from there and find their own paths, nor do we begrudge any one of our people his or her success.

**Movimiento Estudiantil Chicano/a de Aztlán
   (Chicano/a Student Movement in Aztlán)

The contributors in *A Bridge to Writing* experienced their own unique challenges and struggles. They are scholars, students, teachers, colleagues, friends, and a musician. You will read essays, testimonials, research papers, reviews, and song. The writers here are Chicano/a warriors, young and younger ones—the latter are our new heroes and heroines today.

Acknowledgments

I would like to thank all the contributors in the *Chicano/a Studies Reader: A Bridge to Writing*, many of whom teach in the Department of Chicano/a Studies at Cal State University, Northridge (CSUN). Also, I wish to thank Professor Gerald Resendez for his contribution on the history of Chicano/a Studies. I am especially grateful to Dr. Karin Duran who was always available to answer questions, and offer assistance and support. Also, thank you Karin and Theresa Montaño for helping me decide on the title. Dr. Juana Mora, always a champion supporter of Chicanas and Chicanos in the academy, was particularly encouraging during the process of putting this anthology together. I cannot thank her enough for her generous spirit and sincere support.

Senior Editor Joseph D. Wells at Kendall/Hunt Publishing Company, I am happy you found me; thank you. I am also grateful to you for echoing a mother's words of advice to my daughter. Stefani DeMoss, Developmental Editor, and Colleen Zelinsky, Permissions Editor, your assistance is greatly appreciated. I hope one day we meet in person.

It was a pleasure to participate in a workshop at CSUN led by Professor Irene Clark in the English Department, and sponsored by the Center for Excellence in Learning and Teaching (CELT). It was in one of these sessions that I learned from colleagues how to develop an anticipation guide, a helpful tool for students to respond to before they begin reading an essay. I am also grateful to Jane Hancock, Faye Peitzman, and my classmates in the UCLA Summer Writing Invitational, 2003, for all their excellent ideas on pedagogy, especially strategies for writing and responding to poetry. Students Javier Morelos, and Julie Monroy, thank you for your assistance with research and typing in the early stages of this project.

Diana Delgado, you will always be an excellent resource regarding poetry—thank you. Elizabeth Rodríguez Kessler, it is wonderful to have a colleague and friend I can call for counsel in the early hours of the morning, and the late hours of the night.

Every woman needs a *compañero* as fabulous as my Vincent. I would be lost without your unconditional support.

To the models who cheerfully agreed to participate in the photo sessions; and to my daughter Paulette Maria, for her and Judah's photo contributions: thank you all.

Fabiola Torres-Reyes, behind every working-woman is a WOMAN. You are my heroine, my Macintosh queen—*un millón de gracias*. I owe you one. Please do not collect too soon.

Yreina Cervántez, your watercolor is filled with symbolic beauty; the beauty of our heritage. Gracías

A Brief History of Chicano/a Studies

*C*hicano/a Studies is a relatively recent development in higher education. In the late 1960s, universities in the Southwest responded to the call from student and community groups for the need to establish Chicano academic departments on college campuses. As a result, interdisciplinary academic departments were established on various campuses in California. They were called Mexican-American or La Raza Studies. Subsequently, some became Chicano Studies, and even later they became Chicano and Chicana Studies. Changes occurred as these departments understood more clearly the academic nature of the discipline and the purpose for their existence.

Early founders of Chicano/a Studies recognized that it would be impossible to transform universities to meet the needs of the times because historically, academic departments were organized according to traditional academic disciplines and they were steeped in a culture that was exclusionary, racist, sexist, and Eurocentric in its perception of knowledge and learning. They did not deal adequately with Mexicans or other minorities in the United States. The experiences of Mexicans, of other minorities, and of women were not part of the content of higher education courses and programs, nor were they part of the faculties and administrations of institutions of higher learning. Universities were not prepared to incorporate learning from the perspective of peoples that had been excluded from mainstream American society, and furthermore, they were not prepared to bring those minorities into the university and ensure their success. It was also clear that traditional departments were not prepared, nor willing to hire minority faculty. Changing curricula to incorporate the experiences of minorities and their contributions to knowledge and to learning would also not come about easily.

It was soon obvious that the only solution would be to establish new departments, with a Chicano/a Studies curricula, and with faculty that would be well-grounded in the experience of minorities, and academically prepared to teach them. It was essential that this faculty know the content of the materials that they would teach, understand the educational experiences of the students, and be prepared to provide the necessary support to ensure success in the university. Furthermore, it was abundantly clear that Chicano/a Studies needed to be a multidisciplinary "area" studies department that would focus on multidisciplinary subjects: social sciences, humanities, education, culture, the performing arts, and community studies.

Chicano/a Studies was to ensure the success of students, many of whom had negative experiences in elementary and high schools. These experiences seriously damaged their self-image and motivation. Chicano/a Studies was to provide a relevant course of studies; a faculty that was sensitive, knowledgeable, and competent; an environment that would foster learning; and textbooks and materials that would be meaningful, motivating, and that would make students excited about higher education.

Today, while Chicano/a Studies departments demonstrate their academic legitimacy, some struggle to survive; but the precedent and possibilities for these programs is established. The future will provide the challenge not only to survive, but also to continue to meet the needs of an ever-increasing and culturally diverse population.

Professor Gerald Resendez

Introduction

Many years ago a Chicana undergraduate who was preparing to enter Boalt Hall Law School, at the University of California, Berkeley, approached her instructor at San Francisco State University. She expressed her insecurity about embarking on three years of training alongside white, wealthy classmates that she felt were smarter than she. The wise and experienced professor offered the following words of encouragement: "Never forget that they are not smarter than you; they only have more information." For the last 30 years this Chicana has been a successful attorney and political activist. Today, she is a Democratic Party county chair in northern New Mexico.

*T*he *Chicano/a Studies Reader: A Bridge to Writing* is a collection of articles, essays, personal narratives, and poems that represent writings by Chicanos and Chicanas as they traveled many roads of knowledge and many miles of information since the early days of affirmative action in the late 1960s when the first flood of Chicanos and Chicanas enrolled in universities across the nation. Having many years of education, training, and knowledge they are now as informed, trained, and always as smart as those classmates who unwittingly challenged young college-age Chicanos and Chicanas to excel in college. In addition, the collection offers a few selections by the next generation, sons and daughters of the pioneers; a new generation that speaks with courageous, affirming *voices* about how they see their/our world today.

The topics and themes in *A Bridge to Writing* were selected because they are important issues that impact and affect the community of Chicanos and Chicanas. They are subjects that are both social and political in nature and provoke social and political action. They are designed to motivate students to think critically about their own lives so they can become active and proactive citizens, and ultimately influence and affect change in their personal lives, in their families, and in their communities.

Chicano/a Studies is an interdisciplinary department. Scholars offer expertise in several disciplines: behavior and social science, humanities, art, literature, education, field studies, music, theatre, and dance. Selected essays, thus, represent different styles in research documentation: *The Modern Language Association* (MLA), *The American Psychological Association* (APA), and *The Chicago Manual of Style* (Chicago). The intention here is to introduce students to different documentation methods, and to prepare them for expectations faculty will have of them when it is time to write a research paper. For instance, in English composition and in literature, professors ask students to use MLA; history and political science and education generally use one of two styles, APA or Chicago. Instructors should require students to purchase a writer's handbook that reflects all three documentation styles.

At least one essay in each chapter is academically challenging, and based on theory representative of a specific discipline. Students are not to expect professors to do the thinking for them. They are to first read and re-read the essay, discuss it, and record their responses. After students complete the reading and journal writing process, it is recommended that instructors interpret difficult concepts, and explain the author's thesis and intention in a challenging essay.

There is ample source material in libraries and on the Internet for students to read "beyond" the text. Encourage students to conduct research on any one of the themes in chapter headings, especially when it is time for them to explore a topic leading to a final paper.

How to Use the Anticipation Guide

The purpose of the anticipation guide at the beginning of each chapter is to encourage students to discuss ideas presented in the essays before they begin to read. They are to respond to each statement in the guide by answering the following: (4) Strongly Agree, (3) Agree, (2) Disagree, (1) Strongly Disagree. Once they write down their answers, they are to write a short paragraph about any one of the statements. Of course, this activity can be adjusted depending on the interest and inclination of each professor. One suggestion, however, is to instruct students to take one of the ten ideas in the guide and write freely about it. Free-writing does not have to be structured—just writing is enough at the beginning. An excellent way to stimulate ideas is to ask students to form groups of three to four people, after they complete the short writing activity. Remember, keep it short; and no more than one paragraph. They can then take turns reading their paragraphs and ask for ideas, input, and feedback. This works much better if the groups are small in number. Students can use this opportunity to take notes about what their classmates have to say about their ideas, and/or record notes regarding ideas other people have.

Next, students should read the entire chapter over a period of one to two weeks, keeping in mind the goal is to complete all the readings. The selections are varied and themes represent different points of view and unique approaches to thinking about the topics. Ideas for discussion and writing activities are listed under *Writing Prompts* at the end of each chapter, which will help students analyze the text and encourage them to freely express their ideas.

Suggested Writing Activities Following the Poems

The poets' contributions reflect their emotional responses to themes in the chapter they introduce. Instructors may find unique ways for students to respond to the poems; however, the text offers a few ideas to consider. Students often write in free verse; that is the intention in this section. At times it is easier for students to respond to a topic in short phrases, single words, or with rhyme and rhythm. There may even be budding poets in the class. Let them roam free to explore their own emotional terrain.

Journal Writing

Students often think of a journal as a diary. Most certainly it is for some; however, for students who read *A Bridge to Writing*, journals are for responding to issues raised in the *Writing Prompts*. It is always helpful to keep these ideas in a notebook. Later students can refer to their journal entries when they have to begin writing a paper for a letter grade. Students should be held accountable for journal writing. Consider placing the same value on journal assignments as that of a final essay, or assign a significant number of points for journal writing.

The Writing Prompts

There is a set of prompts following each essay. Use the prompts to initiate class discussions; however, students benefit most by doing their thinking on paper and in their journals. Journal writing requires thoughtful and analytical writing about the reading. The strategy described below is free flowing and sometimes scattered, but it also leads to focused, specific writing at the end of the reading-thinking-journal writing process.

The Three-Page Technique

This is one of the most helpful exercises for overcoming writer's block. It is best to give students class time to practice this activity. Ask them to use lined, loose-leaf paper, *or* they may write in a notebook. The principle at work here is to write whatever comes to their minds about the essays after completing the reading in each chapter. What is most important is that they write non-stop. The exercise is not effective if they stop to think. THINKING COMES LATER. Here is a sample paragraph considering the readings in Chapter 2, "Revolution in the Classroom."

> *I never thought I'd end up in college myself. I wonder what I'll end up doing. My sister went to college, but then she's the smart one in the family. Here I am and I have to follow in her footsteps. Yeah, I want to be successful, but I don't know where to start. Everyone I know says college isn't the answer, except my parents, of course. They say an education is the only way. I didn't know so many Chicana women had so much trouble planning to go to college, or faced so many obstacles about it either. What else should I write about? Let's see, I'm supposed to keep this up non-stop. What a stupid exercise. I hate to write. I really do, but here goes. I'll keep it up because the teacher said so. I wonder how many other people have trouble in high school? Maybe I should find out more about it. Where do I start? I'll ask the teacher where to start my research if I don't come up with my own ideas.*

Note that the student wrote whatever came to her mind, on or off the subject. That is the purpose of this exercise. The student explores her ideas and raises questions. This exercise helps all students get started and will help them develop the first or final draft of a thesis statement. By the time students start the three-pages they have completed the anticipation guide, read the chapter readings, and participated in exploring ideas from class discussions and through *Writing Prompts,* at the end of each chapter. When they start the three-page technique they will approach writing without inhibitions. Try it; they'll like it. You may want to ask or require them to practice this as homework before and every time they start to work on the writing assignment they will eventually turn in for a final grade. It is especially useful each time they sit at their computer to work on their research papers. By the way, students can also practice this technique by doing the writing directly on the computer. There is something about doing it the old-fashioned way in long hand that is more appealing for some. Either way, it still works like "magic," for the mind works in wondrous ways, and no matter how much students resist focused, specific, controlled thinking, this process will bring them around and to the point of a thesis. A final note: If a student ends up writing a love letter, or some other kind of prose, poem, etc. (it often happens), that is acceptable, too. They needed to get that out of the way. Encourage the student to start all over again. Warning: This process is not as successful if students stop to contemplate their ideas. They have to write, write, write NON-STOP.

To the Student—What Is Active Reading?

Active reading means responding to what you read either on paper, in the margins of a book or article, or simply thinking about what you read, and definitely talking about your ideas with classmates, friends, and professors. I often tell my students to listen to their ideas. "Trust your thinking," and, of course, "record your responses." Recently, for example, a friend offered to let me borrow a book. "No thank you," I said. "I write all over my books." A book is yours once you read it; cherish what is inside; relish what you learn; discuss it; and of course, in class you are given many opportunities to share your ideas. What is most important is that you value what you think. Listening is the key. An idea you scribble in a book or on paper is the "meat" and the building blocks of analysis. Reading is an adventure; it stimulates your mind to think, act, and write. I majored in rhetoric and writing because I was afraid to speak in front of one person, much less a crowd. Now you cannot shut me up, and I write down just about everything. Years ago, I had to finally discipline myself to stop writing what my friends said to me during a phone conversation. Too bad—some of those stories and dialogue were grist for great characters.

If you want to write, you must read. If reading provides knowledge, writing is the tool to transmit and communicate that knowledge, *but* active reading must come first; it is the *bridge* one crosses that leads to writing; the process that stimulates writing. Prominent Chicana writer Sandra Cisneros, for instance, offered students sound advice when she visited Cal State University, Northridge, in April of 2003. A student in the audience asked her what she recommended to someone who aspired to be a successful writer. Ms. Cisneros told the student(s) to visit the library and check out several books, read them, and go back to the library and check out several more books. This is the best advice any writer or professor can offer students. Plan to read this entire anthology.

Chapter 1—Who Am I and How Do People See Me?

Students often say, "I'm a person, a human being before I'm anything else." Of course, we all want to be seen as human beings first; however, people, racist or not, categorize and too often judge people according to skin color. Remember Rodney King offered a simple, idealistic solution following the L.A. riots, which broke out in 1992: "Why can't we all just get along?" Unfortunately, the reality is we do not all get along; we live in a society where religion, gender, culture, class, and race still separate people. Many of us "walk through life" believing that we are human beings first, but the fact is in our world today, and more so since 9/11, people see skin color first, before they see a "person."

The readings in "Who Am I and How Do People See Me?" ask students to explore their own identities: to "own," and embrace who they are, and to be proud to express that difference. Through these readings students are inspired to explore their heritage, to think about it, to talk about it in and out of the classroom, and to write about it, for in writing they reinforce culture and heritage. What then is the outcome, the result? Hopefully, as they meet, work, and share common spaces with people in other cultures they will respect black, white, gay, other Latinos, and any others who are culturally different, and expect and receive the same from them.

Walk the walk, tall and proud, for brown is beautiful.

Chapter 2—Revolution Is in the Classroom

This chapter opens with a powerful poem by Naomi Quiñonez, a Chicana poet and professor who earned a doctorate degree from Claremont Graduate University. "When You Look At Me" tells her detractors you only see a "maid," "waitress," or "nanny," but in fact "It is difficult for you to say 'Dr. Quiñonez.'" She represents many Chicanos/as who relate countless tales about racial profiling. For instance, recently, another university professor, a Chicana returning from an academic conference in Mexico, was stopped by a white male, INS officer (standing with three other officers—a Latina, a black male, and an Asian female), after having passed through two customs checkpoints. The white officer did not believe the Chicana when she (1) told him she was returning from a professional meeting, and (2) was on her way to the university where she was employed as a professor. After over 10 minutes of inquiry, and running a check on the legitimacy of her passport, he let her go.

The first essay, "Message from the borderlands to Chicana/o educators: Seeking peace, social justice, and quality schools in unjust times," is a call to all teachers: primary, secondary, and college educators to take responsibility to educate students about social justice, and discuss media propaganda that feed the same to students. Educators must introduce discussions that critically evaluate, for example, JROTC on college campuses, and the war on Iraq, especially now, during what Theresa Montaño refers to as "these unjust times."

In "Chicana Resistance: Fostering College Aspirations," by Valerie Talavera-Bustillos, students will read an essay that demonstrates how she adapted educational theory to field study principles. Valerie's work illustrates in her study the many obstacles Chicanas face when they seek a college education, and how they manage to overcome these road blocks.. This essay will help students learn how to bridge theory and practice. Students may recognize a common theme in their educational process: negative voices from counselors, teachers, and sometimes even family members, that they were "under-prepared"; they were "setting their goals too high"; or they "could not afford a college education so don't even try."

Replace the 'S' in struggle for an 'S' in Success.

Chapter 3—9/11: Its Impact on the Chicano/a Community

The afternoon of September 11, 2001, two friends drove along Reseda Blvd. in Northridge, California. One friend said to the other, "Something is bothering me, but I'm not sure what it is." Several minutes later she blurted out, "I know what it is! I look around me and everything looks the same, yes looks the same; but no, sadly nothing is the same. Our world as we knew it here in this country will never be the same." Since 9/11, streets, buildings, homes, shopping malls, theatres, schools, public places of gathering appear physically the same; however, the infrastructure shook, and cracked, when terrorists brought down the Twin Towers in those early hours of the morning.

Larry Littwin's essay reminds readers about the "promise" of improved relations between Mexico (under President Fox) and the United States (in the first phase of George W. Bush's administration). Littwin's essay discusses "the death of a promise" following 9/11.

David Rodríguez does not mince words as he tells his readers the only reason Bush sent U.S. troops to war in Iraq was to secure the treasures of Iraq's oil fields.

Chapter 3 encourages students to think critically beyond local and regional politics; to question the United States' involvement in foreign countries, and to consider, analyze, and critique how it affects Chicano/a issues, problems, and concerns.

"What did we do to people to make them hate us so much?"

Chapter 4—Addiction: Fiction, Fact, and Recovery

Alcoholism is a universal disease that crosses racial and cultural boundaries. However, it often strikes close to home in Chicano/a and Latino families. More and more people need to see this as an illness that can be cured, rather than a problem hidden away "in the family closet." Alcoholism is an illness family members commonly deny, neglect, or when they recognize it, fail to take steps to seek help.

College students often bring family problems and frustrations with them from home. The university environment is an ideal place to "party," and indulge in too much drinking. Is is a place to release unresolved family issues that students carry inside themselves because problems often start within the family network. For instance, students often do not recognize that they have a proclivity for heavy drinking because one or both of their parents were drinkers.

"Addiction: Fiction, Fact, and Recovery" is intended to raise the consciousness of young students regarding how they are specific targets by national liquor campaign ads. The intention here is that by making students aware they are manipulated by liquor ads, young Chicanos and Chicanas will think twice before they indulge in excessive drinking, hopefully.

In this chapter, students also read about two Chicanas who were victims of alcohol and drug abuse, and who after many years of pain and suffering, successfully turned their lives around, and today they both teach and work assisting others in recovery.

Another Chicana talks about how she lived for many years with an alcoholic, and today admits to being an enabler; yet, as she came of age through a university education and personal counseling, she came to terms with her husband's drinking problem, and ended a long-term relationship.

Don't be afraid to tell, help, or leave.

Chapter 5—Chicano/a Queers Speak Their Minds

A white lesbian in her mid-thirties enrolled in a course where ninety-eight percent of the students were from Spanish-speaking backgrounds. Barbara was planning to teach in secondary school and she wanted to learn about "Chicano culture." She actively participated in class discussions; she attended class regularly; and she obviously came to class with an "open mind and heart." Near the end of the semester students took a turn at giving an oral report on a Chicana or Mexicana who had made a significant contribution through history, politics, art, and so on. One student began a presentation on Frida Kahlo. The student showed slides of Kahlo's artwork; when Frida's 1939 painting *The Same Earth* came on the screen, the student informed the class that Frida had had sexual relationships with women. There was a loud gasp from several people in the classroom. Chicanos and Chicanas were clearly surprised and displeased.

At the end of class, Barbara approached the front of the classroom and confided in the professor. Her eyes filled with tears, she said, "I've never experienced such strong homophobia in my life." The instructor asked Barbara if she would agree to a discussion regarding homophobia during the next class meeting. She readily agreed.

When the class met again, the instructor asked the students to candidly discuss how they felt about gays and lesbians There was no way to determine if students became more understanding and accepting of homosexuals; however, Barbara felt somewhat better that the teacher and several students spoke in support of gay and lesbian rights.

What was apparent, however, was the common homophobic attitudes among Chicano/a students in the classroom. The teacher reminded students of the discrimination and racism they also faced daily from the moment they leave a safe and comfortable classroom in Chicano/a Studies, and the safe environment of their homes. "If you expect respect and acceptance as a Chicano or a Chicana, you must also respect other people," the instructor reminded the class. Later individual students approached the teacher and said "Thank you for providing space to air our true feelings."

"Queer Chicanas/o Speak Their Minds" is designed to give students an opportunity to discuss and write about, and ultimately, understand and be more accepting and nonjudgmental about gays and lesbians.

> *Never a cliché—apply the Golden Rule.*

Chapter 6—A Fresh Look at Chicano/a-Themed Films

In the spring of 2002, Cal State Northridge's cinema and television department sponsored an informative, stimulating series of workshops on screenwriting. One of these was titled "Minority Writers in Hollywood." During the question-and-answer segment, a Chicana student walked up to the podium and announced she would not see a film just because it was a Latino movie.

> *"I am going to see a movie if it's a good film. I don't see movies just because they have a Latino cast. I didn't go see* Tortilla Soup *just because it had a Latino cast. Besides why would I need to see this film when I already eat tortillas everyday?"*

Naturally, the student received hearty laughter from the audience. Of course, *Tortilla Soup* was not about tortillas, but about three daughters and the conflict they experienced trying to express their independence from their traditional father.

Chicano/a students will routinely watch *Friends, The Practice, The Drew Carey Show,* and *Sex and the City,* and the films *Terminator, Titanic, Charlie's Angels,* and *Legally Blonde.* They watch television shows that do not cast Chicanos or Chicanas and Mexicans, except for the barmaid or nanny, of course. Moreover, Mexican and Latino parents with two to four children in tow form lines from the box office window at a movie theater, all the way around the corner, waiting to see a Disney film that offers the classic formula of good against evil. Guess the skin color of the evil characters?

The Hollywood industry makes over $500 million dollars a year on movie tickets purchased by all Latinos/as, according to the Tomas Rivera Policy Institutes (TRPI), 1999 report (sponsored by the Screen Actor's Guild). $500 million dollars! Imagine the Chicano/a and Latino community holding a national boycott against prime time television programming (except for the George Lopez show, of course). Also, imagine the Latino/a community boycotting the opening weekend of a film like *Matrix.* Next, imagine parents and children standing in line to see a Disney animation film at the El Capitan theatre on Hollywood Blvd. in Los Angeles; they stand holding picket signs protesting a Disney film that promotes negative stereotypes about Chicanos/as and Mexicans. Now that's economic power!

The purpose of Chapter 6 is to teach students how to analyze films critically. Screen at least one of the films in class and ask students to see another one on their own. Numerous film reviews are available on the Internet. Require students to find at least four reviews (two positive and two negative). They can summarize the pros and cons in a short paper assignment. Do not forget to ask for a Works Cited page. This will give students a chance to practice how to arrange and format electronic citations.

Essays in this chapter are analytical, and offer a fresh look at contemporary films. The theses of each essay will generate spirited class discussions. In "Mainstreaming the Dream: *Spy Kids,* The Messenger," Gutiérrez examines how Robert Rodríguez introduces Mexican culture in his blockbuster film. Fabiola Torres-Reyes compares the adaptation of the play *Real Women Have Curves* to the film; she critiques the director's distortion of Lopez's play, which portrays Carmen, the protagonist's mother, strongly opposing her daughter (Ana), going away to college, even though she won a scholarship to Columbia University. Gabriel Gutiérrez uses theoretical principles to demonstrate how *The Lion King* promotes "homogenization of dominant ideals and marginalization of non-dominant ideals." Students will view a Disney film with a critical eye after reading this essay. Gerard Meraz introduces a fresh interpretation of *Viva Chocolat* by drawing a parallel between Chicana/Mestizas and Vienne, the main character, who is Mayan and European. Orona-Cordova, in "Salma's *Frida:* A Visual Feast, But Not Without Its Disappointments," argues that the performance by

Salma Hayek, and the screenplay are sorely lacking in quality; although the visual imagery is beautiful, and rich in color and texture.

> *If you care—boycott prime time television and Disney films that exclude Chicanos/as or that depict negative images of them.*

Identity: Who Am I and How Do People See Me?

"Reading is the gift you give yourself. This gift keeps on giving because it allows you the freedom to educate yourself not only because we are exposed to the ideas of others through their writing, but also to the beautiful, insightful, powerful ways ideas can be expressed so that we can make sense of our world and make our contribution to it."

Karin Duran

"Learning to write is much like learning to ride a bicycle. At some point you get brave enough to take off the training wheels. Then your instructor lets go of the bike, and you're on your own. At first the ride is a little wobbly, but once you let go, and you find that balance, the neighborhood, heck the whole world is yours to explore. It's true what they say, too, once you learn how to ride a bike, you never forget. It's the same way with a pen and paper."

Lorenzo "Toppy" Flores

Chapter 1—Anticipation Guide

Directions: Rate each statement below according to the following:

4—Strongly Agree   *3—Agree*   *2—Disagree*   *1—Strongly Disagree*

1. Recognizing your racial and cultural identity is important.

2. Individual experiences define different Chicano/a and Latino groups.

3. Chicanos/as and Central Americans share the same economic and political concerns.

4. People from mixed cultures have an advantage because they are able to move in and out of two cultures.

5. People from two cultures find it difficult to relate to one group or the other.

6. Children do not need to know or understand racism early in life.

7. It is better for a parent to confront school officials about problems their children have at school rather than discussing problems at home.

8. People have a difficult time understanding the term Chicano/a so it should be changed to Latino/a.

9. The term Chicano/a represents an historical, cultural, and political experience in the United States so it should be a term used by all people of Mexican and Mexican-American descent.

10. People who think and talk too much about race and identity are separatists.

Why Am I So Brown?

Trinidad Sánchez, Jr.

For Raquel Guerrero

A question Chicanitas sometimes ask
while others wonder: Why is the sky blue?
or the grass so green?

God made you brown, *mi'ja,*
color bronce—color of your *raza,* your people
connecting you to your *raices,* your roots
your story/historia
as you begin moving towards your future.

God made you brown, *mi'ja,*
color bronce, beautiful/strong,
reminding you of the goodness.
de tu mamá, de tus abuelas, your grandmothers
y tus antepasados, your ancestors.

God made you brown, *mi'ja,*
to wear as a crown, for you are royalty—
la raza nueva—the people of the sun.
It is the color of Chicana women—
leaders/*madres* of Chicano warriors
luchando por la paz y la dignidad
de la justicia de la nación Aztlán!

God wants you to understand . . . brown
is not a color . . . it is:
a state of being, a very human texture
alive and full of song, celebrating—
dancing to the new world
which is for everyone . . .

Finally, *mi'ja*
God made you brown
because it is one of HER favorite colors!
1986/1993

Suggested Writing Activities

1. Listen carefully as the professor reads the poem and take notes. Next write about any ideas that come to mind. Afterward, students take turns reading aloud.

2. Each of three students reads the poem in front of the class.

3. Students can also read silently, and ask questions after they read.

Are You Mexican?

Oriel María S. Bernal

People in the United States often ask me, "Where are you from?" When I first arrived in the United States four years ago, I would answer "I am from Honduras, but my mother is a Salvadoran-Guatemalan, and my father a Chinese Nicaraguan," as if explaining my origins in full detail would assure me and others of my own identity. Following my reply I would often hear: "Oh, so you speak Mexican," or "What part of Mexico is that from?" "Is it southern Mexico?" After hearing these comments, I did not know whether to defend my nationality or laugh. One time I deliberately snapped, "No, I am not Mexican!" and then patiently explained the geography of what Europeans termed "America." I have tried many explanations, yet still feel the need to clarify misconceptions people have about Latinos. I am not Mexican. My identity has undergone wide and narrow turns.

To begin to define my identity, I first want to discuss Mexicans. They are not easily defined because of their diversity. There are indigenous Mexicans, mestizo Mexicans, black Mexicans, and white Mexicans. There are Mexico-born people who do not even consider themselves Mexicans; some consider themselves Spanish, others identify with purely indigenous ways of life. Then there are non-native Mexicans who consider themselves Mexican until they die. There are southern Mexicans and northern Mexicans who have different regional customs. There are also *"Chilangos,"* and there are *Zapatistas*. Then, there are hundreds of regional and cultural mixes within Mexico itself. In sum, the Mexican experience is truly diverse and unique.

Since the beginning of the twentieth century, Mexican migration to the United States increased heavily: Entire families were escaping war-torn Mexico and the worst of *unstable* economic conditions in their country. As a result of this *influx* of Mexicans into the United States and the mingling of both cultures, the Chicano experience emerged, adding one more experience to the meaning of being, becoming, or deriving from another country.

Central Americans, as a people and migrant community, are also diverse in nature. There are black, mestizo, mulatto, Chinese, Arabic, and white Central Americans. There are Misquito, Maya, Lenca, Pipiles, and many other indigenous groups of Central Americans as well as many diverse mixes of all of the above groups. The Central American experience is also truly diverse. Over 100 different languages are spoken in the region. Only a low percent of these languages, however, are recognized.

Like Mexicans, Central Americans struggled for centuries and resisted the injustices of *colonization*. Five hundred years of colonization and decades of oppressed independence, as well as recent policies of *globalization* and the *penetration* and expansion of capitalist "First World" interests throughout the region, caused chaos and daily suffering, but also inspired daily resistance. Many are the reasons that caused Central Americans to migrate to other parts of the regions and world, especially during the last four decades. Unlike the Mexican community in the United States, however, the Central American community in the United States is much more recent.

Throughout the 1970s, '80s, and '90s, Central America experienced bloody wars between military governmental powers and civilian guerrilla forces. The 1980s in particular, the decade of my birth, was characterized by such *turmoil*. Central American governments, heavily funded by the United States, were spending millions of dollars trying to *impede* social revolutions from succeeding. These revolutions were comprised of working class people, indigenous communities, peasants, the poor, the *marginalized*, the discriminated and ignored. In other words, these people made up a great majority of the Central American population. These social movements demanded better living conditions from their governmental regimes, respect for human rights, education for their children, water and electricity, a government that would attend to their socio-economic and political needs, liberation from oppressive forces, and above all, justice. Over 300,000 innocent civilians throughout the regions (including entire indigenous communities), were killed or disappeared in the 1980s alone. The governments of El Salvador, Guatemala, Honduras, and Nicaragua, with great financial and logistical aid from the United States, committed among the worst human atrocities ever in the history of human kind. To this day, hundreds of *clandestine* graves of victims of governmental *repression* are still being found.

A heavy *influx* of Central Americans started to pour into the United States beginning in the early 1980s. The wars and unstable social, political, and economic conditions of Central American regions caused many individuals and families to *migrate*, ironically, to the country that was greatly responsible for their torment. Central American migration was driven by a complex series of factors: political, economical, and social. Central Americans were escaping war, political repression, human rights violations, ethnic cleansing, a violence that only *escalated* even after the signing of the Peace Accords, and an economy that did not serve the needs of the majority of the population. In my case, I left Honduras because of the increase in crime and violence in the region. I also left because my educational opportunities were limited.

Once in the United States, Mexicans and Central Americans become one. The "push and pull" factors that made us come to the Untied States were different, but difficulties we encountered living here were the same. We, Mexicans and Central Americans, face the same obstacles, the same discrimination, and the same limited opportunities to healthcare, education, and jobs. We are forced to survive within a system that uses us for hand labor to make the country more stable, yet does not want to give us the benefits of citizenship. We are forced to face a system that does not want us to go to college, yet it is constantly recruiting us for the front lines of the U.S. military. We are forced to face a society that treats the gang problem among Latino youth as a crime, and not as a product of a society that is not creating enough after-school programs. We are treated as "aliens," some of us "illegal," others "legal," as if human beings stopped being human after crossing a border.

Throughout the four years that I have been in the United States, people continue to ask the same question: "Where are you from?" and continue to think that being Central American means I "speak Mexican." No longer, however, am I offended or irritated because people do not understand our distinct experiences. I now take the time to explain the geography of the American continent in order to explain that I am a Central American migrant. Nationalities only divide us. Enough physical borders have already been placed between countries for us to be creating more nationalistic borders between Latino immigrants: Mexican, Central, or South American. We have all undergone economic, social, and political struggles. Many of us came to the United States in search of better living conditions, yet we found that racial discrimination is among the most defining characteristics of this country. Having said all this, I maintain that I am an Hondureña (born and raised in Honduras), half Chinese, partly Nicaraguan (from my father's side), half Salvadoreña, partly Guatemalteca (from my mother's side), a Central American indeed; one who migrated to the United States and has since learned much from the Mexican and Chicano communities.

Writing Prompts

1. Bernal writes about diversity between Mexican and other Latino/a groups. What is the point of this discussion?

2. Do you think there are similarities between the experiences of Mexicans, Chicanos/as, and Central Americans who live in the United States? Explain and develop your answer.

3. The author demonstrates common difficulties and obstacles that challenge Chicanos/as and Central Americans in the United States. Discuss the origin of these obstacles.

4. Why do you think the author was "irritated" at first, when she came to the United States and people asked her if she "spoke Mexican"?

5. According to the author, what were the reasons so many Central Americans came to the United States?

En las Mañanitas

Elizabeth Rodríquez Kessler

I.

I know you weren't always
Proud of me—
My shyness,
My darkness,
My bloodied cuticles
From biting nails and tender skin,
My extra pounds,
Rounding out hips and breasts,
Not petite and delicate,
Graceful and slim-ankled,
A conversational extrovert
Like you.

I went home to Houston recently, home to the bed of my youth, home to my family. Mi familia? No, my family. Actually, my familia. How do I describe us? As I tried to sleep in my old twin bed, next to the soft, nasal breathing of my mother sleeping in the other twin, memories flooded my mind: my education, *Mexico Bello* dances, summers in Mexico and Indiana, Rodriguez vs. Listenberger, *mi abuelita*, WeeWee. Secure in her *hybrid* identity, my mother slept peacefully beside me as I *probed* the definition of my being and tossed uncomfortably as the sun began to stream in through white lace curtains onto a bed I had outgrown.

Much like Richard Rodriguez, who had heard the nuns pronounce his name in the hard clanging syllables of English, I, too, heard my principal, a young Incarnate Word nun from Ireland, turn the softness of Rodriguez into something foreign, unintelligible: Ra (a as in father)-dri (i as in it)-geze (e as in cheese) with the accent on the last syllable. "Elizabeth Ra-dri-geze?" Sister Brendan called roll from her *perch* on the landing at the first set of stairs the builders had forgotten to enclose and therefore left outside. I stood *mute*. I had no idea she was calling my name as I stood in the sixth grade line outside the school. My first day at Annunciation School started out badly. I couldn't recognize my own identity. No one called me by my first name at home, and that certainly wasn't my last.

When did the term "inner city school" get such a bad reputation? Little, red brick, three story Annunciation School, run by Sisters of the Incarnate Word prepared us well, even though we were surrounded by Union Station, the World Trade Building, warehouses, and slum housing beyond the tracks. The city bus took me there, a seven-cent, fifteen minute ride with a four-block walk. We weren't "inner city kids"; we didn't even know the term. But most of us had one thing in common: our parents wanted us to go to Catholic school near their workplace so they could have parent-child time driving in from and back to suburbia. And most of us were white—except for Sammy Freund, the Jewish kid who went to Mass daily, and Anthony Russo, the Italian idol all the girls adored, and Elizabeth Radrigeze, the shy short dark girl who lived with her grandmother. But nobody knew, that I, too, took the car ride with my mom, thirty minutes away where I could see Houston's skyline as I rode my Schwin down neighborhood streets with *manicured* lawns. On weekends—

II.

I used to cry
On Saturday nights
In my bedroom all
Alone.
On Sundays
You'd take me back,
Back to Wee,
Away from you—
Until one fine day
Sunday meant
I'd stay.
No longer a visitor,
I wasn't ready,
Nor was Wee.
And then
I used to cry
On Saturday nights
In my bedroom all
Alone.

Growing up Mexican-American wasn't the awful experience so many claim it to be, that is if you don't know you're "different," other. Surrounded by mainly white students in high school—Incarnate Word Academy was built next door to Annunciation School so the *transition* was *minimal,* just more white girls from farther away with more money—we were one. No longer wearing the plaid, pleated skirts of little kids, we wore straight, navy-blue skirts with a kick pleat, white blouses, and blue blazers. Only the three Dominguez sisters stood out distinctly because they stayed together, accented voices—when they spoke—but *conspicuous* in their seemingly comfortable clan. The nuns successfully homogenized us, making us all equal among equals—all God's children in blue and white, with voices of angels *indistinguishable* in our hymns. We weren't white, brown, and black (two black girls were in my class and no Asians); we were white, even the Dominguez sisters, and we were being *prepped* for our *destiny;* strangely enough, it was similar to the traditional Mexican-American destiny: marriage and motherhood, service to men.

During my freshman year, my world changed drastically. Those ten-minute bus rides changed to thirty, and I would have a new home. But what about Wee, my gentle, kind, soft-spoken grandmother? Alone. Left all alone because my mother reclaimed me. I moved, *paradoxically,* further away from my connection with Mexico. The summer trips Wee and I used to take to visit my grandfather's family suddenly stopped, and Wee would board the Greyhound Bus alone, carrying boxes of old clothes to "the poor people" in Mexico. For a year prior to her trips, she'd collect my out-grown dresses, clothes my mom didn't wear and my step-dad didn't want, and she'd take bags and boxes across the border to give to the children and to her "relatives." Every summer she'd go visit her Spanish in-laws who were now no longer immigrant Spaniards but Mexican citizens and no longer in-laws because my grandfather had died very young. But Tía Lupe, Tío Librado, Tía Josefina, and my great-abuelita Magdalena were always glad to see her and grateful for the gifts. And for a woman with British-American ancestry, she spoke Spanish without hesitation but always spoke English to me.

"Stay out of the sun. You don't want to get dark."

Ironically, I was *la güerita* in Montemorelos, a town without paved roads where children played outside all day and most adults worked as citrus pickers for the orange and grapefruit growers surrounding the town. My Tía Josefina, however, had a small neighborhood store, and my Tía Lupe was the principal of *la escuela secundaria.* She was also the dutiful daughter who never married but took care of her mother.

One summer when I was twelve, I got sick, and the doctor couldn't determine what was wrong. After three days, my Tía Lupe decided to take things into her own hands, *diagnosing* me with a case of *"el ojo."* On the third night, a hot, breezeless night, she closed the *shutters* and doors to the room, lit candles—partly from necessity as they had no electricity and partly for ritual—placed me on the bed, and rubbed a fresh chicken egg over me from head to sole, accompanied by *Padre Nuestros* and *Ave Marias* recited by all the women present. Tía Lupe mumbled other prayers as she broke the egg into a saucer and placed it under the bed. After a few more prayers, they blew out all but one candle and left me to sleep peacefully. No one disturbed me, and I woke up naturally the next morning without *symptoms*. Tía Lupe removed the egg and discovered the yolk had ruptured. I was released from the spell of *"el ojo"* and allowed to play with my cousins again.

That was my last visit to Montemorelos. In the summer between my seventh and eighth grades, the trips took a new destination: Indiana. For the next eight years, August was no longer the time for oranges and limes picked from trees, making tamales—pork, bean, coconut—in the *patío*, killing a goat and draining its blood, or visiting *el escusado* outside at Tío Librado's home. Now Mom, Floyd, my step-father, and I drove across the country to visit Mark Twain's home, the construction of the Arch in St. Louis, Bourbon Street in New Orleans, cornfields and wheat fields in Oklahoma and Kansas, the Great Lakes, and Marshall Field in Chicago. Instead of tamales, my grandmother Hattie made noodles from scratch. Instead of gathering eggs from the chickens in the backyard or lemons and limes from the trees, we'd pick blueberries, gather mushrooms, and harvest *rhubarb*. And instead of swimming in the river, we'd go fishing on the beautiful lakes surrounded by elegant summer homes in Culver or go to the county fair in the baseball field a block away. We could go to the Kandy Kitchen for pop and ice cream but the local theater on Main Street was off limits because the "wet backs" who picked the fields went there on the weekends. And so it was that I discovered slowly, but painfully and conclusively, that I was not only not a Listenberger, but that I was other.

I have never lost contact with my Rodriguez family, but its influence has never been direct. Instead, my contact with the Latino social clubs in Houston re-introduced me to my heritage. As I grew older, my mother decided it was time to introduce me to society. Most of her friends were Mexican American, and they, too, had daughters my age. When the social season began with the rounds of dances and parties, I slowly became acquainted my mother's friends and their children, my peers. As young girls we weren't allowed to date, but we went with our parents to the dances where we would meet sons of the families, also without dates. Finally, Virginia, the doctor's daughter, Dolores, the dentist's daughter, Rose Marie, the restaurant owner's daughter, and I hit the magical age of fifteen. Instead of a *quinceañera*, we were all *debutantes*, introduced to society, with dates and dressed in white formals, under the proud eyes of our parents at the *Mexico Bello* Debutante Ball. After that, we could officially take dates to the Christmas Dance, the *Familias Unidas'* Mother's Day Dance, the Azalea Club Hawaiian Dance, and the *Mexico Bello* Black and White Ball. Ballrooms in all the major Houston hotels—the Shamrock, the Rice, the Shereton—as well as the Houston Club, the Pinemont Country Club, and other *venues* sparkled with formal attire, orchids and roses, Latino music, and the wealthy, educated, politically involved, and socially rising middle class Mexican Americans.

However, education sent me back to the world of whiteness, as most of my fellow classmates were white, and *mis amigas* went to other universities. The young blood needed to *promote* the social clubs found other career-oriented *outlets* for their free time. With the *waning* interest, the deaths of the senior club members, and time, the clubs gradually *disbanded,* and many of us were Mexican in name only.

Richard Rodriguez seems to believe that education is the *culprit* that created the *chasm* between himself and his father. I wish I could say that that is the case between my mother and me. Sometimes we talk for long periods of time on the phone, other times, we can't find anything to say to each other. But education didn't do that. That's just the way it's been between us all our lives. Is this the age-old mother-daughter conflict? Is it a conflict of a generation gap in ethnic standards? Or is it an unconscious consequence of putting career development and life with a new husband before raising me until I had become a budding teenager? At a time when identity formation and attachments are developing, I turned to Wee for guidance, and my personality developed from hers not from Mom's. Then my role model, my maternal figure, and my roots to my lower socio-economic Mexican-American culture were displaced, replanted, suddenly, immediately, and with no opportunity for me to say goodbye. I became a *hybrid*—raised in the educational influence of Anglo goals and in the upper middle class Mexican-American social expectations for young women. Thus, growing up as a hybrid woman is not quite the same as being raised as a hybrid flower. The beauty and exotic qualities are not always appreciated by observers, especially when they are the people who created you.

No, education didn't separate me from my heritage even though I chose to major in English and teach it for thirty-three years. Being an administrator in *predominantly* white schools certainly didn't help me *embrace* my otherness. But teaching and studying in universities of diverse populations for the last thirteen years have made me aware and proud of my ethnicity. We all make decisions and whether I'm seen as a tan Anglo or *una güerita* by Mexicanos, ultimately, it's my decision to determine my identity and to live accordingly.

> *En las mananitas*
> *Cantan los pajaritos,*
> *Y las canciones que cantan*
> *Pueden ser mios.*
>
> (Early in the morning
> The birds sing,
> And the songs they sing
> Can be mine.)

Writing Prompts

1. Rodríguez Kessler opens her essay with a poem. Who is she talking to and why does she set this up at the beginning of her essay?

2. During long periods of time the author lived with her Grandmother Wee Wee, who introduced Rodríguez Kessler to her Mexican heritage. Identify and discuss one or two examples of this experience.

3. When the author moved back home with her mother, how was her life different from her life with her grandmother?

4. Trace the author's entrance into Mexican culture and her return to Anglo culture. Discuss in detail.

5. The author starts Part II of her poem with the words, "I used to cry on Saturday nights in my bedroom all alone," and she ends the stanza with, "And then I used to cry on Saturday nights." Is she crying for the same reason both times she writes these lines? Explain.

6. Kessler writes, "The beauty and exotic qualities ('of being a hybrid flower') are not always appreciated by observers, especially when they are the people who created you." Explain how this line refers to the poem at the beginning of the essay.

The Scholarship Jacket

Marta Salinas

Marta Salina's stories have appeared in the Los Angeles Herald Examiner *and in* California Living. *Historically, bilingual students have been punished for speaking Spanish, and often have not been given the opportunities afforded to those whose native language is English. The difficulties of transcending the stereotypes, as well as the real economic limitations, of one's class are also described in this story of a young girl's struggle for recognition.*

The small Texas school that I attended carried out a tradition every year during the eighth grade graduation; a beautiful gold and green jacket, the school colors, was awarded to the class *valedictorian,* the student who had maintained the highest grades for eight years. The scholarship jacket had a big gold S on the left front side and the winner's name was written in gold letters on the pocket.

My oldest sister Rosie had won the jacket a few years back and I fully expected to win also. I was fourteen and in the eighth grade. I had been a straight A student since the first grade, and the last year I had looked forward to owning that jacket. My father was a farm laborer who couldn't earn enough money to feed eight children, so when I was six I was given to my grandparents to raise. We couldn't participate in sports at school because there were registration fees, uniform costs, and trips out of town; so even though we were quite *agile* and athletic, there would never be a sports school jacket for us. This one, the scholarship jacket, was our only chance.

In May, close to graduation, spring fever struck, and no one paid any attention in class; instead we stared out the windows and at each other, wanting to speed up the last few weeks of school. I *despaired* every time I looked in the mirror. Pencil thin, not a curve anywhere, I was called "Beanpole" and "String Bean" and I knew that's what I looked like. A flat chest, no hips, and a brain, that's what I had. That really isn't much for a fourteen-year-old to work with, I thought, as I *absentmindedly* wandered from my history class to the gym. Another hour of sweating in basketball and displaying my toothpick legs was coming up. Then I remembered my P.E. shorts were still in a bag under my desk where I'd forgotten them. I had to walk all the way back and get them. Coach Thompson was a real bear if anyone wasn't dressed for P.E. She had said I was a good forward and once she even tried to talk Grandma into letting me join the team. Grandma, of course, said no.

From *Nosotras: Litana Literature Today* by Marta Salinas. Reprinted by permission of Bilingual Press/Editorial Bilingue, Arizona State University, Tempe, Arizona.

I was almost back at my classroom's door when I heard angry voices and arguing. I stopped. I didn't mean to *eavesdrop;* I just hesitated, not knowing what to do. I needed those shorts and I was going to be late, but I didn't want to interrupt an argument between my teachers. I recognized the voices: Mr. Schmidt, my history teacher, and Mr. Boone, my math teacher. They seemed to be arguing about me. I couldn't believe it. I still remember the shock that rooted me flat against the wall as if I were trying to blend in with the graffiti written there.

"I refuse to do it! I don't care who her father is, her grades don't even begin to compare to Martha's. I won't lie or falsify records. Martha has a straight A plus average and you know it." That was Mr. Schmidt and he sounded very angry. Mr. Boone's voice sounded calm and quiet.

"Look, Joann's father is not only on the Board, he owns the only store in town; we could say it was a close tie and—"

The pounding in my ears drowned out the rest of the words, only a word here and there filtered through. ". . . Martha is Mexican . . . resign . . . won't do it. . . ." Mr. Schmidt came rushing out, and luckily for me went down the opposite way toward the auditorium, so he didn't see me. Shaking, I waited a few minutes and then went in and grabbed my bag and fled from the room. Mr. Boone looked up when I came in but didn't say anything. To this day I don't remember if I got in trouble in P.E. for being late or how I made it through the rest of the afternoon. I went home very sad and cried into my pillow that night so Grandmother wouldn't hear me. It seemed a cruel coincidence that I had overheard that conversation.

The next day when the principal called me into his office, I knew what it would be about. He looked uncomfortable and unhappy. I decided I wasn't going to make it any easier for him so I looked him straight in the eye. He looked away and *fidgeted* with the papers on his desk.

"Martha," he said, "there's been a change in policy this year regarding the scholarship jacket. As you know, it has always been free." He cleared his throat and continued. "This year the Board decided to charge fifteen dollars—which still won't cover the complete cost of the jacket."

I stared at him in shock and a small sound of *dismay* escaped my throat. I hadn't expected this. He still avoided looking in my eyes.

"So if you are unable to pay the fifteen dollars for the jacket, it will be given to the next one in line."

Standing with all the dignity I could *muster,* I said, "I'll speak to my grandfather about it, sir, and let you know tomorrow." I cried on the walk home from the bus stop. The dirt road was a quarter of a mile from the highway, so by the time I got home, my eyes were red and puffy.

"Where's Grandpa?" I asked Grandma, looking down at the floor so she wouldn't ask me why I'd been crying. She was sewing on a quilt and didn't look up.

"I think he's out back working in the bean field."

I went outside and looked out at the fields. There he was. I could see him walking between the rows, his body bent over the little plants, hoe in hand. I walked slowly out to him, trying to think how I could best ask him for the money. There was a cool breeze blowing and a sweet smell of mesquite in the air, but I didn't appreciate it. I kicked at a dirt clod. I wanted that jacket so much. It was more than just being a valedictorian and giving a little thank you speech for the jacket on graduation night. It represented eight years of hard work and expectation. I knew I had to be honest with Grandpa; it was my only chance. He saw me and looked up.

He waited for me to speak. I cleared my throat nervously and clasped my hands behind my back so he wouldn't see them shaking. "Grandpa, I have a big favor to ask you," I said in Spanish, the only language he knew. He still waited silently. I tried again. "Grandpa, this year the principal said the scholarship jacket is not going to be free. It's going to cost fifteen dollars and I have to take the money in tomorrow, otherwise it'll be given to someone else." The last words came out in an eager rush. Grandpa straightened up tiredly and leaned his chin on the hoe handle. He looked out over the field that was filled with the tiny green bean plants. I waited, desperately hoping he'd say I could have the money.

He turned to me and asked quietly, "What does a scholarship jacket mean?"

I answered quickly; maybe there was a chance. "It means you've earned it by having the highest grades for eight years and that's why they're giving it to you." Too late I realized the significance of my words. Grandpa knew that I understood it was not a matter of money. It wasn't that. He went back to hoeing the weeds that sprang up between the delicate little bean plants. It was a time consuming job; sometimes the small *shoots* were right next to each other. Finally he spoke again.

"Then if you pay for it, Marta, it's not a scholarship jacket, is it? Tell your principal I will not pay the fifteen dollars."

I walked back to the house and locked myself in the bathroom for a long time. I was angry with Grandfather even thought I knew he was right, and I was angry with the Board, whoever they were. Why did they have to change the rules just when it was my turn to win the jacket?

It was a very sad and withdrawn girl who dragged into the principal's office the next day. This time he did look me in the eyes.

"What did your grandfather say?"

I sat very straight in my chair.

"He said to tell you he won't pay the fifteen dollars."

The principal muttered something I couldn't understand under his breath, and walked over to the window. He stood looking out at something outside. He looked bigger than usual when he stood up; he was a tall *gaunt* man with gray hair, and I watched the back of his head while I waited for him to speak.

"Why?" he finally asked, "Your grandfather has the money. Doesn't he own a small bean farm?"

I looked at him, forcing my eyes to stay dry. "He said if I had to pay for it, then it wouldn't be a scholarship jacket," I said and stood up to leave. "I guess you'll just have to give it to Joann." I hadn't meant to say that; it had just slipped out. I was almost to the door when he stopped me.

"Martha—wait."

I turned and looked at him, waiting. What did he want now? I could feel my heart pounding. Something bitter and *vile* tasting was coming up in my mouth; I was afraid I was going to be sick. I didn't need any sympathy speeches. He sighed loudly and went back to his big desk. He looked at me, biting his lip, as if thinking.

"Okay, damn it. We'll make an exception in your case. I'll tell the Board, you'll get your jacket."

I could hardly believe it. I spoke in a trembling rush. "Oh, thank you, sir!" Suddenly I felt great. I didn't know about *adrenaline* in those days, but I knew something was pumping through me, making me feel as tall as the sky. I wanted to yell, jump, run the mile, do something. I ran out so I could cry in the hall where there was no one to see me. At the end of the day, Mr. Schmidt winked at me and said, "I hear you're getting a scholarship jacket this year."

His face looked as happy and innocent as a baby's, but I knew better. Without answering I gave him a quick hug and ran to the bus. I cried on the walk home again, but this time because I was so happy. I couldn't wait to tell Grandpa and ran straight to the field. I joined him in the row where he was working and without saying anything I *crouched* down and started pulling up the weeds with my hands. Grandpa worked alongside me for a few minutes, but he didn't ask what had happened. After I had a little pile of weeds between the rows, I stood up and faced him.

"The principal said he's making an exception for me, Grandpa, and I'm getting the jacket after all. That's after I told him what you said."

Grandpa didn't say anything, he just gave me a pat on the shoulder and a smile. He pulled out the crumpled red handkerchief that he always carried in his back pocket and wiped the sweat off his forehead.

"Better go see if your grandmother needs any help with supper."

I gave him a big grin. He didn't fool me. I skipped and ran back to the house whistling some silly tune.

Writing Prompts

1. What did Marta learn about herself (her identity) when she overheard Mr. Boone, her math teacher, say that he wanted the scholarship jacket awarded to Joann's father who was on the school board?

2. What is the lesson Marta's grandfather taught her?

3. Do you think Marta's grandfather should have talked to Mr. Boone, or to the principal? Explain why, or why not?

4. Describe the grandfather's physical demeanor when he responds to Marta. Why is this significant?

5. Would Marta's grandfather have made a stronger impression on her if he had expressed anger? Explain why, or why not.

Chicana Identity Matters

Deena J. González

What is involved in the taking of a name, suggests the Chicana lesbian *feminist theoretician* Gloria Anzaldúa (1987), unites our search for a Chicano/a identity in this century. Some searches *defy categorization. Disunited* in our self-labeling—"Hi"-spanic, Latino, Mexican-American, even Chicano-American—our *ruminations* constantly project a homecoming that *eludes* us. This also unifies our condition in this century and is instructive. "They caught us before we had a chance to figure it all out," Chicana/o activists protest. Our laments are ongoing proclamations, as enduring as José Vasconcelos's concept of *"La Raza Cosmica,"* which he *espoused* in the 1920s. His concept of an enduring race was one thing; our self-identification is another. The word Chicana has always been difficult to use, especially if applied to women living in the previous centuries. *Illusory* even today, many Spanish-surnamed, Mexican-origin women refuse the term.

Still, we Chicana historians make an effort to apply the concept. Why? Our *contemporary* conditions are as *illustrative* as our histories, particularly the histories of the unnamed, of women. For women who have no name, Anzaldúa (1987) suggests this: "She has this fear / that she has no names / that she has many names / that she doesn't know her names / She has this fear that / she's an *image* / that comes and goes / clearing and darkening" (43). For women who remain faceless despite their *consistent* presence in documents, this business of acquiring identity is the basis for living and for life, is the basis of the struggle for selfhood—in our (Chicana) present but also in "their" (Aztec/Native or mestizo) pasts (Hernández, 1992).

We find tremendous *consolation* in tracing the sources of our *empowerment*—the struggle for identity and for recognition is one, but only one, struggle in a long history of finding or locating identity. Lending identity, as historians do, is another important task, but it is often undiscussed although it lies on the flip side of the identity coin. Identity is both *assumed* and given; some people have "more" identity, some less. Every day, historians lift out of the records, or find in the records, or situate persons in records—our fundamental task is to organize this information in selective categories, and this is not easy. Who is *denigrated* one century is *reified* in the next. Malinche (of Mexico, translator to the Spanish conqueror, Hernán Cortes) and Doña Gertrudis Barceló (of New Mexico, nineteenth-century businesswoman) are examples. For mainstream historians, ignoring a group—say women of Mexican descent, as many have done—is part of a selection process; not naming women *constitutes* including them by *omission*. For the most part, in *mainstream* history texts and in the works of Chicano historians, Chicanas are absent. It is in these omitting spaces that Chicanas have found a place in the debates raging through the historical profession, and there, we occupy a *pivotal* if uncomfortable role because we *resurrect* images and real persons from the past. Our task as Chicana historians is twofold—to resurrect and to *delineate/revise*. How do we do justice to both, and then translate our findings into languages that majority or *dominant* societies understand? Do we even want to do that? Our choices are neither simple nor clear. Here are examples from our very ordinary *existences* as historians and as self-identified Chicanas.

To the new generation of Western American historians—the *revisionist brigade;* as they have been called—the "West" is a place, a region, a state of mind, a culture; *wide-ranging;* long, far, distant, pockmarked by the *dynamics* of contest and conflict, *consensus* and contradiction. Not an easy place to reside, in other words. But to Chicana/o historians, the West is really the Mexican North.[1] The concepts we use and the *configurations* we bring to our work, whether of class (upper and working) or of the *sexualized, gendered, racialized* systems (in *matrices* traced like virgin, martyr, witch, or whore; or Native, mestiza, or Chicana) are different.[2] Never has the *sunbonneted* helpmate, *sturdy homesteader,* or *ruddy* miner or rancher been less useful to our projects. For us, teaching a class in Western American history, then, makes no sense. We ask, why not call it a history of the Mexican North? Why not call it a history of many names, of places termed by Native historians, as far back as they can remember, the Dancing Ground of the Sun, or by Chicano/a historians, Aztlán? You see our *dilemmas* and the new directions we are *plotting*. Add to this that few, except the most recent professionally trained historians, were schooled in Chicano/a history. We are self-trained. Where do we begin, what do we name our *undertaking*, what organizes our *chronology*? The questions link our investigations with the *preoccupations* of other historians.

These issues reflect my themes for this article: Chicana is a *contemporary* term, but can be applied to Spanish-speaking and Mexican-origin women in any area presently considered territory of the United States. Historians may well be bothered by the renaming, although established courtesies indicate that people should be known by their preferred terms. In 1980, the United States government ignored the *protocol* and *lumped* us together under the *generic* "Hispanic," rewriting history, so to speak, by suggesting that the tie to Spain was greater than the tie to our indigenous heritage. This may have suited other Latino groups living in the United States, but it caused a new wave of dissension among Chicano/as. As Luis Valdez (1994) postured, "Why be an adjective, and not a noun? Why Hispanic? It doesn't *compute*. Why not Germanic, a Germanic?"

For Chicanas, one dilemma in self-identification set in not because we do not know who we are or are *misguided* in applying labels, but because, like many other terms,

Chicana has always been *problematized* as an identity in waiting, as an incomplete act. Philosophically, spiritually, or politically, Chicanas do not all look at the world in the same way, or even in ways Euro-Americans might understand. It is not true that we do not know who we are. If anything, we should suffer the accusation that we know too much who we are, have too much identity.

Add to this the internal, embattling ideological wars dominating our newly created spaces in the *academy*. Chicanas most agree on the name we have selected for ourselves; problematized, discussed, and assessed, it provided the point of departure, but everything since then has spun away from an assumed "core" of understanding. The fractures are rampant and also hidden from the mainstream. (Unless you have followed the recent Chicano Studies debates at University of California at Santa Barbara, where at least one conclusion can be drawn—Chicanas and Chicanos do not agree on all issues.) Mainly, we least discuss our differences in favor of presenting a united front in the academic theater that would most often like to get rid of us all. To say *fracture* is to speak of secrets or to name lies. In our conferences of the past years, we have begun to witness that a *resurgent* Chicano/a nationalist student movement contradicts Chicano/a faculty agendas. Among Chicanas, lesbian/*feminist pedagogies* and *scholarship* parted ways with other types of Chicana (feminist) practices long ago. The majority of Chicana lesbian-feminist scholars do not feel comfortable operating within the *confines* and structures of the overwhelmingly male-identified, even "minority," organizations that exist within *the academy*. The majority of Chicana lesbian academics are not out, and many fear being outed. At one Ford Foundation Fellows gathering, gay/lesbian Chicano, African-American, and Native American academics discussed the policies of *revelation,* with one group decidedly arguing for secrecy, while those of us with tenure urged our colleagues to consider that in most departments, very little is truly secret—least of all who pairs up with whom.

Continuing with the practices and politics of identifying, of self-identification, and the *constructions* of identity, mixed-race Chicana and Native/Chicana women decry the *implicit* racism that *parades* a Native/Othered guest lecturer before a Chicana conference not much interested in exploring this old division, but that would rather project a falsely *unified consciousness* by listing the speakers as *"foremothers."* These are also examples from our daily lives as Chicana academics.[3]

Probing such politics and policies of identity and *location, contemporarily* as I have just done, or historically as I intend next, is difficult because *self-designation* is a twentieth-century exercise full of *self-consciousness*. Locating the identity of subjects long since dead, in the case of my work on nineteenth-century Nuevo Mexicanas, is equally problematic because the people I write about exist in the cultural and *collective* memories of the Chicano/Hispano families of Santa Fe. *Ancestry* remains exceedingly important in the lives of Northern Nuevo Mexicans. The twin processes of naming and revealing *engender* further responsibilities and *prerogatives* and have been *contextualized* for that reason in these opening passages.[4]

Some might want to search the past for clues about how we came to our contemporary *ideological impasses* over the significance of our identities. Identity today, our autobiographical *anecdotes* reveal and the documents *detailing* the lives of nineteenth-century Spanish-Mexican women suggest, is not the same as identity once was. Nineteenth-century Spanish-speakers named themselves as village residents first, as members of particular families second, then as (Catholics) parishioners, and, continuously, as non-Indians. Without Native people—against whom they would identify—the Spanish-speaking *mestizo* and non-mestizo might not have chosen specific identities at all, adopting instead a more *colonialist* attitude that *rendered* indigenous residents nonexistent.

As we know today, *identity formulations* have as much to do with what one carries inside as with what one *encounters* outside. Indigenous people thus existed as opposites to the Spanish, and then, in the case of the majority mestizo population (that is, after the first twenty-five years of conquest and colonization by the Spanish), their ongoing presence *delineated* a clearing space within which a small but *tenacious,* conquistador class could continue to *roam, relocate,* and define itself, if uneasily. Physical appearance—or *phenotype* as *geneticists* might say—by itself helped identity concerns hardly at all, as we see in the present when we must piece together color, speech, dress, and many other *"markers"* to situate or locate one (an-other's) identity.

Mexico and the Southwest witnessed various color representations. After the first phases of conquest between Natives and Europeans, Indian actually began signifying non-Spanish-speaking, not non-Spanish, as very few Spanish-speaking residents of the northern frontiers could label themselves pure-blooded Spanish, even if they were of the *criollo* class (that is, were descendents of people self-designated as Spanish but born in the New World), even if color supported their sense of superiority. In the early part of the nineteenth century, in the midst of creating and adopting a *criolloized* existence, many used their labels not simply to *delineate* an ethnic identity, but to *designate* their classes primarily. This *fragile* existence as frontierspeople *transcended* other *ponderings* over and beyond their quests for specific, regional identities—as Santa Feans, as Tucsonenses, as Tejanos. The *migrations* northward on mixed-race peoples, some studies suggest, signaled among the migrants an improved class status. *Resettlement* they imply, hastened social and economic *mobility,* but were best considered locale by locale. The resulting identity *formations* were *lodged* in a *hodge-podge* system that was best understood by residents of a region, by insiders, and only loosely by those living throughout the distant territories of the former Spanish Empire (Morner, 1967).

Categorization primarily on the basis of any single identifying characteristic—that is, skin color, language skill, religious devotion, or birthplace—would be a mistake. Finally, on the question of the origins of the identity models I am *asserting* here, or on the origins of Chican*a* identity, it is important to bear in mind that insider/outsider concerns operated on a *multitiered* and in a multidirectional social system; a conquistador class may have sought to *assert* its power through identity *manipulations*. Wannabes—those seeking upper class status or non-lowest class status—in Tucson, Santa Fe, and San Antonio, determined that *harkening* back to a conquistador heritage was better than to claim mestizo or indigenous ethnicity. The state, or empire in this case, supported the denials readily enough: identity cards were common, and rules and regulations from both Church and State *dictated* marriage choices, to name only two examples of how race or ethnicity were also *determined or ordained.*

From the beginning of Spanish contact, then, the search for identity *hinged* around questions of status and social location, as well as on the relationship to the state or empire, which is to say, pro-Crown; or later, pro-Spain or pro-Mexico; or later still, pro-Revolution.

In New Mexico, whose Spanish-Mexican women I speak about next, the *hyphenations* and terms were equally complex. "Spanish-Mexican" appeared as early as the colonial period (Castañeda, 1990). It was used interchangeably with gente de habla español, at times to *connote* a criollo heritage, and otherwise to signify Spanish-Catholic background and Spanish *linguistic* dominance.[5] By 1820, a new sense of Mexicanness *pervaded,* with even criollos picking up the label, "Mexican." Thus, Mexican still was recognized for the indigenous, Aztec word that it was (Me-shi-can), but it was Hispanicized sufficiently (Me-ji-cano/a) that it also came to be recognized as the basis for an *evolving national identity.* Mexico (the country) would not name itself until later, but already politicians, officials, criollos, mestizos, and Natives used the word and applied Mexican, if infrequently, to themselves. In the independence movements, adaptation of an indigenous word, of course, marked the *severed* bonds to Spain, and Mexico and Mexicanos continue to this day to glorify and uphold the concept of an indigenous, mixed-race inheritance. Unfortunately for us Mexican/Chicano residents of the Southwestern United States, the federal government is *abysmally* ignorant of this rich heritage about naming and identity formations.

Notes

Reprinted from *Culture and Difference: Critical Perspectives on the Bicultural Experience in the United States,* ed. Antonia Darder (Westport, CT: Bergin and Garvey, 1995).

1. For examples of the newer, revisionary work, see Milner 1996.

2. For a review of this literature, see Castañeda 1992.

3. The example comes from a MALCS conference, 1993, and was made by observers and participants at the gathering. MALCS is one of the only national Chicana academic organizations in the country.

4. For a more complete review of the historical practice of revelations, see also González, forthcoming.

5. On another label, see Miranda 1988.

References

Anzaldúa, G. 1987. *Borderlands/La Frontera: The New Mestiza.* San Francisco: Spinsters/ Aunt Lute Press.

Castañeda, A. 1992. "Women of Color and the Rewriting of Western History: The Discourse, Politics, and Decolonization of History." *Pacific Historical Review,* p. 501–533.

———. 1990. "Gender, Race, and Culture: Spanish-Mexican Women in the Historiography of Frontier California." *Frontiers* 11: 8–20.

Hernández, I. 1992. "Open Letter to Chicanas: On the Power and Politics of Origin." In Without Discovery: A Native Response to Columbus, ed. R. González. Seattle: Broken Moon.

Morner, M. 1967. *Race Mixture in the Hisotry of Latin America.* Boston: Little Brown.

Valdez, L. 1994. "The Hemispheric American." Lecture delivered at Claremont Mckenna College, Athaneium, Claremont, CA.

Writing Prompts

1. González ends the opening paragraph by saying "Mexican-origin women refuse (to use) the term" Chicana/o. Why do these women reject the term? If you have no idea, ask a friend, family member, or a Chicana.

2. Consider the question, "What's in a name?" How would you answer this? Do you think "naming" is important? Why, or why not?

3. The author says that Chicanas must "locate" their identity. Explain what she means. What does she say about women's (Chicana's) place or role in history?

4. Explore and discuss why González proposes that re-naming Western American history to "a history of the Mexican North" is more appropriate?

5. Spanish, Hispanic, Latino, Mexican, Mexican-American, Chicano/a are many names we give ourselves. Does this suggest we are confused? Who are you? Which term applies to you, and why?

6. The author reveals that Chicanas, though united on issues of gender (and race), have conflicts and differences in the academy. What does she mean? Give a few examples of these differences.

7. González describes how Spanish-speakers began "to name" and identify themselves. What group did they attempt to negate, and why?

8. González writes that people use "markers" to situate or locate one ("an-other's") identity. Think of someone who is completely opposite you in appearance. How would you describe this person's "markers"? What impressions or ideas do you form by that individual's appearance?

9. The author argues that after the conquest between Native Americans and Europeans (in the United States), Spanish-speakers started labeling themselves "Spanish," which suggested they were a better class of people. Describe two ways in which these settlers were able to manipulate their identity to appear superior to the indigenous people.

Words to Learn

"Why Am I So Brown?"

mi'ja—shortened form of *mi hija,* "my daughter"

color bronce—bronze color

raza—the people

raices—roots

de tu mamá, de tus abuelas—of your mother, of your grandmothers

y tus antepasados—and your ancestors

la raza nueva—the new race

madres—mothers

luchando por la paz y la dignidad de la justicia de la nación Aztlán—fighting for peace and dignity of justice in the nation of Aztlan

"Are You Mexican?"

Chilango—a Mexican from Mexico City

Zapatistas—an indigenous revolutionary group in Chiapas, Mexico

unstable—unsteady or unsure in purpose or intent

influx—a sudden arrival of a large number of people or things

diverse—made up of many different elements and very different or distinct from one another

colonization—the act or state of being subjugated or captured

globalization—the process by which a business or company becomes international or starts operating at an international level

penetration—the action of penetrating, entering, or passing through something

turmoil—a state of great confusion, commotion, or disturbance

impede—to interfere with the movement, progress, or development of something or somebody

marginalized—to take or keep somebody or something away from the center of attention, influence, or power

clandestine—secret or underground

repression—the process of suppressing somebody or the condition of having political, social, or cultural freedom controlled by force

migrate—to move from one region or country to another, often to seek work or other economic opportunities

escalated—to become or cause something to become greater, more serious, or more intense

"En las Mañanitas"

Mexico bello—beautiful Mexico

mi abuelita—my grandmother

hybrid—something made up of a mixture of different elements

probed—to conduct a thorough investigation of something

perch—any temporary resting place for a person or thing

mute—silenced and speechless

manicured—a treatment that usually involves shaping, polishing, and treating something that is rough

transition—a process or period in which something undergoes a change and passes from one state, stage, form, or activity to another

minimal—smallest possible in amount or least possible in extent

conspicuous—attracting attention through being unusual or remarkable

indistinguishable—impossible to tell apart from somebody or something else

prepped—to study, prepare, or train for a particular examination, sporting event, or other activity

destiny—the apparently predetermined and inevitable series of events that happen to somebody or something

paradoxically—it seems to be absurd or contradictory, but in fact is or may be true

la güerita—the little white skinned girl

la escuela secundaria—junior high school

diagnosing—the identifying of the nature or cause of something, especially a problem or fault

shutters—a hinged cover for a door or window, often with louvers and usually fitted in pairs

symptoms—a sign or indication of the existence of something, especially something undesirable

el escusado—the toilet

rhubarb—a perennial plant, found in the wild and cultivated, with green or pink leaf stalks that are edible when cooked

quinceañera—a rites of passage celebration given to young women on their fifteenth birthday symbolizing adulthood

debutantes—young women who are being introduced formally into society by appearing at a public event such as a dance

familias unidas—united families

venues—a place where an event is held

mis amigas—my girlfriends

promote—to encourage the growth and development of something

outlets—a way of releasing emotions or impulses

waning—to decrease gradually in intensity or power

disbanded—to break up as a group or organization, or to cause a group or organization to break up

culprit—somebody who is responsible for or guilty of an offense or misdeed

chasm—a wide difference in feelings, ideas, or interests

predominantly—most common or greatest in number or amount

embrace—to hug, to welcome, to include or take up something, especially a belief or way of life

"The Scholarship Jacket"

valedictorian—the highest ranking student who delivers the valedictory address at graduation

agile—able to move quickly and with suppleness, skill, and control

despaired—somebody or something that makes somebody feel hopeless or exasperated

absentmindedly—to be preoccupied or forgetful

eavesdrop—to listen to a conversation without the speakers being aware of it

fidgeted—to move around in a restless, absentminded, or uneasy manner

dismay—a feeling of hopelessness, disappointment, or discouragement

muster—any gathering of people or collection of things

mesquite—the wood of a mesquite tree or shrub, often burned in a barbecue to flavor food

shoots—the point a seed begins to grow

gaunt—extremely thin and bony in appearance

vile—extremely unpleasant to experience

adrenaline—a hormone secreted in the adrenal gland that raises blood pressure, produces a rapid heartbeat, and acts as a neurotransmitter when the body is subjected to stress or danger

crouched—to squat down on the balls of the feet with knees bent and body hunched over

"Chicana Identity Matters"

feminist—somebody who believes in the need to secure rights and opportunities for women equal to those of men, or somebody who works to secure these rights and opportunities

theoretician—somebody who is inclined to or skilled in speculative contemplation or theorizing, or is learned in the theoretical aspect of a subject

defy—to challenge openly somebody's or something's authority or power by refusing to obey a command or regulation

categorization—the defining and grouping of people or things into categories

disunited—divided into separate groups or factions because of a disagreement or difference of opinion

rumination—inclined to be thoughtful and reflective

elude—to escape from or avoid somebody or something by cunning, skill, or resourcefulness

la raza cosmica—the cosmic race

espoused—to adopt or support something as a belief or cause

illusory—produced by, based on, or consisting of an illusion

contemporary—in existence now

illustrative—serving to illustrate or explain something

image—a picture or likeness of somebody or something, produced either physically by a sculptor, painter, or photographer, or conjured in the mind

consistent—able to maintain a particular standard or repeat a particular task with minimal variation *consolation*—comfort to somebody who is distressed or disappointed

empowerment—to have a sense of confidence or self-esteem

assumed—taken for granted

denigrated—to disparage or criticize somebody or something, to lower somebody's self-esteem or to make something seem unimportant

reified—to think of or treat something abstract as if it existed as a real and tangible object

constitutes—the parts or members of something, or the way in which they combine to form it

omission—something that has been deliberately or accidentally left out or not done

mainstream—the ideas, actions, and values that are most widely accepted by a group or society

pivotal—vitally important, especially in determining the outcome, progress, or success of something

resurrect—to bring back into use something that had been stopped or discarded

delineate—to describe or explain something in detail

revise—to amend a text in order to correct, update, or improve it

dominant—more important, effective, or prominent than others

existence—the state of being real, actual, or current, rather than imagined, invented, or obsolete

revisionist brigade—a group of people organized to achieve a particular goal, or characterized by a common trait such as attitude, background, appearance, or activities

wide-ranging—dealing with a great variety of matters

dynamics—the forces that tend to produce activity or change in any situation

consensus—general or widespread agreement among all the members of a group

configurations—to set up, design, or arrange the parts of something for a specific purpose

sexualized—to impose a sexual interpretation or perception on something or somebody

gendered—relating to or appropriate to one gender rather than the other

racialized—relating to or characteristic of races or a particular race of people

matrices—(plural for matrix) a situation or set of circumstances that allows or encourages the origin, development, or growth of something

sunbonnet—a hat with a wide brim and a flap at the back, worn by babies and, in the past, by women to protect the face and neck from sun

sturdy homesteader—a determined home owner whose house is adjoined to land and buildings and declared as the owner's fixed residence and therefore exempt from seizure and forced sale for the recovery of debts

ruddy—a healthy reddish glow

dilemmas—a form of reasoning that, though valid, leads to two undesirable alternatives

plotting—making secret plans, especially to do something illegal or subversive with others

undertaking—a promise, agreement, or responsibility to do something

chronology—the order in which events occur, or their arrangement according to this order

preoccupations—constant thought about or persistent interest in something

protocol—the rules of correct or appropriate behavior for a particular group of people or in a particular situation

lumped—to consider people, ideas, or objects as a single group, often without good reason

generic—usable or suitable in a variety of contexts

compute—to calculate an answer or result

misguided—motivated by or based on ideas that are mistaken, heedless, or inappropriate

problematized—made into a problem

academy—an educational institution devoted to a particular subject

fracture—a split or division in something such as a system, organization, or agreement

resurgent—rising or becoming stronger again

feminist pedagogy—the science or profession of teaching from a women-centered point of view

scholarship—a body of learning on an academic subject

confines—to keep somebody or something from leaving an enclosed or limited space

the academy—the academic community, especially scholars at colleges and universities

revelation—information that is newly disclosed, especially surprising or valuable information

constructions—structures or things that have been built or created

implicit—not stated, but understood in what is expressed

parades—showy or ostentatious exhibitions or display of something

unified consciousness—a collective awareness of or sensitivity to issues in a particular field or ideology

"foremothers"—women of an earlier generation from whom traditions, values, or ideas have been inherited

location—the positioning or siting of something or somebody in a particular place

contemporarily—currently

self-designation—a name, label, or description given to oneself

self-consciousness—feeling acutely and uncomfortably aware of failings and shortcomings when in the company of others and believing that others are noticing them too

collective—made or shared by everyone in a group

ancestry—direct descendents, especially somebody more distant than a grandparent

engender—to arise or come into existence, or cause something to do so

prerogatives—an exclusive privilege, right, or choice enjoyed by a person or group occupying a particular rank or position

contextualized—to place a word, phrase, or idea within a suitable circumstance

ideological impasses—an ideal at which no further progress can be made or agreement reached

anecdote—short personal accounts of an incident or event

detailing—to describe or explain something in detail

mestizo—somebody who has parents or ancestors of different racial origins, especially somebody in Latin America of both Native American and European ancestry

colonialist—a person belonging to a country or area that is ruled by another country

rendered—to give help or provide a service

identity formulations—the creation of characteristics that somebody recognizes as belonging uniquely to himself or herself and constituting his or her individual personality for life

encounters—to be faced with somebody or something, or come up against somebody or something

delineated—to describe or explain something in detail

tenacious—tending to stick firmly to any decision, plan, or opinion without changing or doubting it

roam—to move over a large area, especially without any particular purpose or definite destination

relocate—to move or be moved to a new place on a long-term basis, especially to change the location of a business or a residence

phenotype—the visible characteristics of an organism resulting from the interaction between its genetic makeup and the environment

geneticists—a person in the branch of biology dealing with heredity and genetic

variations—different kinds

markers—objects or signs that indicate the position or presence of something or the direction in which somebody or something is to go

criollo: creole—Spaniards born in the colonies who claim not to be mixed with other races, especially with the indigenous races

delineate—to describe or explain something in detail

designate—to formally choose somebody for a job, position, or duty

fragile—not strong, sound, or secure and unlikely to withstand any severe stresses and strains that may be put on it

transcended—to go beyond a limit or range, for example, of thought or belief

pondering—thinking about something carefully over a period of time

migrations—the act or process of moving from one region or country to another

resettlement—a group or population with a new place to live and transfer it there

mobility—the ability to move from one level or location to another

formations—the process by which something develops or takes a particular shape

lodged—become jammed or embedded somewhere, or in something

hodge-podge—a mixture of several unrelated things

categorization—to place somebody or something in a particular category and define or judge the person or thing accordingly

asserting—starting to have recognition

multitiered—many series of layers or levels placed one above the other

assert—to start to have an effect or become noticeable

manipulations—to control or influence somebody or something in an ingenious or devious way

harkening—to listen and pay attention

dictated—to rule over or make decisions for others with absolute authority, or attempt to do so

determined—feeling or showing firmness or a fixed purpose

ordained—to order or establish something formally, especially by law or by another authority

hinged—something on which a subsequent action or an outcome depends

hyphenations—belonging to a group of people identified in two ways that may be joined as one term

connote—to imply or suggest something in addition to the exact meaning

linguistic—the systematic study of language

pervaded—to spread through or be present throughout something

evolving—to develop something gradually, often into something more complex or advanced, or undergo such development

national identity—the status of belonging and identifying to a specific nation by origin, birth, or naturalization

severed—separated or pulled apart, or to become separated or put apart

abysmally—profoundly or extremely

Revolution Is in the Classroom

Chapter 2—Anticipation Guide

Directions: Rate each statement below according to the following:

4—Strongly Agree   *3—Agree*   *2—Disagree*   *1—Strongly Disagree*

1. Chicano/a families place a high value on a college education.

2. Poverty influences parents' and students' attitudes about education.

3. Teachers are to blame when students do not learn skills expected of them.

4. Parents are to blame when students do not learn skills expected of them.

5. If teachers and counselors have low expectations of students, there is a greater chance students will not attend college.

6. Parents in Chicano/a-Latino families who expect women to follow traditional expectations and place marriage before education are common today.

7. The *JROTC* plays a significant role in convincing young Chicanas and Chicanos to join the military.

8. As Chicano/a educators we must teach our children and youth their historical roots/background.

9. Parents sometimes discourage their children from attending college only because parents cannot afford tuition costs.

10. The negative stigma attached to affirmative action policies suggests that some students in colleges are not as intelligent as other students.

When You Look at Me

Dr. Naomi H. Quiñonez

I.

When you look at me
you see motel maids
changing sheets
in the pink and gray rooms
your parents stay in.

You see dark brown women
on their knees scrubbing floors
in Baja restaurants
or standing with a blue-eyed child
on each hip.

It doesn't matter if I wear
tweed suits and pace the floor
on Givenchy heels
in front of busy chalk boards.

You see Lupita the nanny
in your T.V. mind.
She wears mismatched clothes
and slides heavily on leather huaraches
towards her unwashed children.

To you I am an aberration
that confuses your senses
and blurs your vision.
It is difficult for you to
say "Dr. Quiñonez."
You want me to remain nameless
silent, invisible.

But I stand before you
speaking your language
and teaching you things
you are not sure of.

Now you must either change
your misguided notions of who I am
Or kill the me
that cannot live in your world.

II.

When you look at me
you see educated nipples
intelligent legs
a brilliant ass.

You chica, mija, chula me
until you get beyond the fact
that I have a PhD.

In department meetings
I call for broad visions
and student needs.
You envision a broad
who can meet your needs.

You are unfamiliar
with a woman
who can see through
your veneer.
My loud clear voice
threatens your ears.

To you I am expendable
like the woman who keeps
taking you back
like the mother who is
always there to feed you.

Like that part of yourself
that you thought you destroyed
when you decided to become
A thin worn metallic chair . . .
A conflict without a resolution.

Suggested Writing Activities

1. Write a poem as though you are writing a letter to someone you would like to know, or create an imaginary person. Start with Dear _____ .

2. Write a "question poem." Write a series of questions that you do not have the answers for; or, you may want each stanza to start with a question, and then create and write the answers.

Message from the Borderlands to Chicana/o Educators: Seeking Peace, Social Justice, and Quality Schools in Unjust Times

Theresa Montaño

We are teaching in a political era of intense scrutiny when educators are under tremendous pressure to *conform* to educational policies intended to silence our righteous *indignation* at an unjust, unequal, and undemocratic political system. A political and economic system not satisfied with *subjugating* the poor, working class, and darker skinned people within its self-imposed borders, but is rapidly moving to consolidate its occupation of Iraq—its land and resources. It is a period of history when the loyal *corporate media* proudly displays images of American soldiers greeted by an Iraqi people bearing flowers, instead of truthfully discussing the *perils* and *consequences* of war and conquest. Where, "every day the airwaves are filled with warning, veiled and unveiled threats, spewed invective and hatred directed at any voice of dissent" (Robbins, 2003, p. 1). The occupation of Iraq and subsequent *politic* in this nation have created an educational *context* where the terms of "patriot" and "good teacher" are characterized by teachers who are obedient, *compliant,* and silent; those teachers who dutifully *implement* a *hegemonic* curriculum. As the United States flexes its political muscle internationally, here at home the terms "teaching for social justice" have become the *elusive quest* of *progressive critical educators* who challenge not only repressive educational policies, but who also struggle with the majority of parents and colleagues bamboozled into thinking the "war is over." An oil-thirsty administration that *simultaneously* occupies a foreign country, controls the media and tightens its rein on education has seemingly convinced much of the American public and its educators that "victory is ours." The federal administration and its educational policy misnamed "No Child Left Behind" holds school districts *hostage* by threatening the loss of federal monies. School districts are *coerced* into accepting and implementing repressive legislation in exchange for badly needed funding. Section 9528 of this legislation, the "No Child Left Unrecruited" bill, requires school districts to allow military recruiters access to the names, addresses, and phone numbers of every high school student. Most parents, especially immigrant parents, do not know they can insist that such information be withheld. Civil liberties groups and civil rights organizations have tried to inform many parents of this right; however, the failure to publicize this information in Spanish-speaking communities has denied many parents the opportunity to protect the anonymity of their children.

Listening to political *pundits* who justify the invasion of an *impoverished* nation and portray the killing of innocent civilians as democracy in action and who talk about how we were engaged in war of liberation, sicken me. I cannot help but experience feelings of *déjà vu*. I made my decision to become a teacher on the heels of the Chicano/a movement and during another war, the Vietnam War. The decision to teach was undeniably a political act. The opportunity to serve my community as a teacher was a personal response to the demands of students, parents, and community members who insisted that schools recruit teachers who looked like me. I, like so many others, answered the call for Chicana/o teachers. Teachers who would serve as role models for our students, teachers who would understand the language and culture of a *marginalized people,* teachers who could *infiltrate* our schools and teach a history and culture that has been repressed and silenced for centuries. "For the Chicano movement, access to education meant not only the literal access of bodies into the classroom, but also to a curriculum where Chicana/o history, culture, politics, and identity were also central" (Elenes, 2003, p. 192). As social movement activists, adopting a Chicana identity was not simply a label of ethnic identification, it was an *ideological decision*. Many of us entered the university and majored in Chicano Studies, because we believed that the *strategic* political role of Chicano Studies was to "generate and to organize a social consciousness of cultural solidarity" (Contreras, 1999, p. 102), and *infuse* into the community a "historical consciousness of a Chicano cultural identity" (Contreras, 1999, p. 105). This newfound consciousness led to a political *undercurrent* in the field of Chicano/a Studies that became explicitly anti-racist and anti-*imperialist*. As the movement progressed, many students began to realize that only through radical *reconstruction* could we transform an educational system that had lied to us about our history, dishonored our people, disrespected our language, and devalued our culture. A political and economic system that *endeavored* to *confine* our population at the lower end of the economic scale, while *systematically* exploited our labor for profit and greed. As our movement grew in political sophistication, we became a part of a new student movement, one that waged campaigns against war and actively promoted social justice.

As a Chicana activist and educator, I hope that by sharing my insights and experiences in this act of teaching for social justice might encourage critical educators to continue the "struggle for an educational *praxis* and a way of life that could support the democratic forms of economic and social existence" (Darder, 2003, p. 499), for our community. At the very least, I hope to engage my compañeros/as in a dialogue about what it will take to build a broad-base social movement that would establish a space for *progressive* Chicano/a teachers to raise not only issues of global justice, but the struggle for economic, political, and social justice in the United States. I hope to begin the discussion of how, as Chicana/os, we can engage in a dialogue with our progressive colleagues in schools and classrooms throughout this nation about what it means to "teach for social justice" in revolutionary terms.

Déjà vu

As Chicano/as who grew up with the movement, we have a different understanding of American history, of civil liberties and educational justice. As activists we tasted victory, however short-lived those victories were. As Chicano/a movement activists we benefited from affirmative action, ethnic studies, and bilingual education—all gone. All eradicated by a bankrupt judicial system and racist political initiatives. As activists we were a part of a larger, broader political movement and this *legacy* that we can pass on to our youth. We can teach young activists that while it is important to oppose the war, we cannot build a movement if we cannot provide a *viable* alternative to the existing social order. For once the war is declared over, the movement for peace and social justice continues. The idea of social and economic justice must be more than a vision statement; it must be a real and attainable goal. For those scores of Black and Latino activists who sacrificed their lives for the meager victories that we presently enjoy, the terms "social justice" were not simply political slogans or religious *mantras*. Social justice was a revolutionary *clarion call* and those who responded were revolutionaries who were engaged in building a social and political movement against oppression. As Chicano/a movement activists we organized against domestic violence directed at our young people in the barrios, for the right to decent wages and working conditions for campesinos, and for cultural and educational justice in our schools. The struggles ablaze were not limited to the barrios of Aztlan. Chicano/as are part of "third world movement," comprised of African-American, Asian and Pacific Islanders—"third world people," who collectively incited political struggles throughout the United States. As our movement advanced we became members of an international struggle; we challenged the global hegemonic agenda throughout the world.

During the height of the Vietnam War, there was an increasing awareness of the overrepresentation of Chicanos on the frontlines and the underrepresenation of Chicano/as in the universities. In the 1970s, Chicanos represented 10% of the general population and 19.4% of the causalities. A visit to the Vietnam Memorial in Washington, D.C., will verify this atrocity; one in four names on the wall are Latino surnames (Furumoto, 2003). During the Chicano Moratorium against the war, Rosalio Muñoz criticized the national draft board for sending Chicanos to Vietnam in higher numbers than white youth (Muñoz, 1999). In this nation people of color were nothing more than cheap labor and *cannon fodder*.

The sad reality is that little has changed. The intentional recruitment of Latino youth into the military continues today. The *deplorable* social conditions our people face have not changed significantly, while our population has grown significantly. In 2003 we represent 13% of the U.S. population, but we are still the highest percentage of those who drop out of school and we *comprise* 17% of military combat positions (Mariscal, 2003). As Chicano movement activists we recognize the connection between war, the economy, and race, and as activists it is our responsibility to present this truth. Whether a person believes that this most recent war was one of *aggression* or one seeking to end the rule of a despot, it is difficult to deny that "military action" has had a devastating effect on the lives of Black and Brown youth. The military targets low-income youth of color. In the United States, our children are trapped by a form of *economic conscription,* referred to as the "push-pull phenomenon." A *phenomenon* that forces Black and Brown youth into the military, pushed by poverty and economics of racism and pulled by the military benefits (Berlowitz & Long, 2003). At Roosevelt High School in the heart of Chicano/a East Los Angeles, there are five military recruiters for every one college counselor (Sanchez, 2003). This does not reflect a nation interested in an educated Chicano. On the contrary, the hegemonic curriculum in our schools brainwashes our youth by creating a false hope of easy access to the American dream, machismo in a uniform—all yours, if only you are willing to die for the lie.

The *JROTC* plays a significant role in convincing our young people that the military is a viable alternative to low-income jobs, a life of poverty, or imprisonment. Ill-prepared by our nation's schools, our sons and daughters cannot enter colleges and universities. Instead, by promises of developing job skills, a post military college education, and the fast track to U.S. citizenship, many are *enticed* to enroll into JROTC programs. This is an inviting *proposition* for those who do not wish to face the vast bureaucracy of the U.S. Immigration Service alone. Today, as our nation moves to implement tougher immigration regulations, 37,000 of the American troops are Mexican and Central American immigrants. Many of these young people were recruited into the military straight out of JROTC programs. In the Los Angeles Unified School District, the overwhelming majority of JROTC students are immigrant students who seek an opportunity to attend college, learn a job skill, and travel. What they are not told is that students "are locked in by JROTC requirements, which are so time consuming that they *preclude* most college preparatory courses" (Berlowitz & Long, 2003, p. 102). It was never this nation's intent to educate our people, but to recruit our young men and women so that they would die for oil. I wonder how many of our young people clearly understand the consequences of joining the JROTC, of facing *depleted uranium,* of finding chemical weapons, of killing and dying. As aptly stated by Sonia Nieto (2003), "This is a war waged by the children of the powerless, for the powerful" and inner-city schools are the profitable sites for recruitment.

Clearly a major component of the educational *agenda* is to provide a steady supply of disciplined and obedient soldiers and low-level officers to carry out imperialistic policies (Furumoto, 2003). The current focus on standardized test scores, scripted curriculum, threats of school takeovers, funding cuts are all part and parcel of an educational plan directed at the *militarization* and *corporatization* of schools. This country has spent 75 billion dollars at the start of this war and is planning to spend another 150 billion dollars on the occupation. School funding, on the other hand, is a mere 8 billion dollars. The present educational and political climate is one that attempts to *de-professionalize* teaching using *blatant* union busting and corporatization tactics. The capitalists intend to use the same tactics that were used to *deconstruct* the craft unions. Let us not forget how the introduction of assembly lines led to the *demise* of specialized crafts. The assembly line with its intensive division of labor created a workforce that was not paid to think, but follow routine. A workforce that would produce the product in the most *expedient* and "efficient" way, in the same way the imperial powers wish for teachers to create an assimilated *deculturalized,* non-critical student. It is easier to convince the world's people about the *despot* in Iraq than speak about the profit to be made by a U.S. elite using *slash* and burn tactics in oil-rich *devastated* Iraq. It is our government's belief that it is more profitable to engage the rebuilding, reconstructing and *reorienting* of a nation worn and defeated, than to spend those funds rebuilding our inner cities. In fact, after this nation's leaders starved that country's populace, disarmed its military, and convinced 42% of America that Saddam and Al Queda were *first cousins,* this nation has the *audacity* to talk about liberation. Lest we be fooled, as the wealthy "reconstruct" Iraq, the social and economic conditions in our barrios and inner cities will continue to decline. As educators we should never forget that we are teaching in a system where *"neo-liberal and neo-conservative discourses* in education have been *theoretically and ideologically* fueled by the corporatist logic of the free market" (McLaren & Fischman, 1998, p. 126). It is corporate greed that fuels our political and economic system. "The project of corporate *mobilization* has cracked the code. Free elections, a free press, an independent judiciary mean little when the free market has reduced them to commodities on sale to the highest bidder" (Roy, 2003). Do we as educators, think that we will not be affected by this nation's move to silence voices of opposition at home?

Teaching in Unjust Times

As an educator, I recognize that teachers and professors are currently teaching in a *jingoistic* climate of blind *patriotism* when the exposure of the imperialistic nature of U.S. foreign policy in a Social Studies class is considered "anti-American." McCarthyism once again *invades* our classrooms and teachers are told that they must follow district policies that *affirm* the established social order and are told not to discuss the war or its consequences. In many school districts and universities, "academic freedom" is nothing more than an intellectual buzzword. Recently, a classroom in Vermont was violated when a uniformed police officer, in the middle of the night, snapped photographs of student work and bulletin boards "trying to document what was going on in the classroom of a pacifist history teacher" ("Democracy Now"). The police officer then passed the photos along to conservative talk show host, Rush Limbaugh, who publicly displayed them on his website. A young Chicana teacher told me recently that anti-war activists at her middle schools were receiving threatening phone calls. A district memo had been circulated forbidding teacher activists from wearing union t-shirts proudly displaying the peace sign, and another was told that as a social studies teacher she could not mention the war unless a student asked a question.

What are our responsibilities as social justice teacher activists when our basic fundamental rights of free speech are threatened, when a script replaces teacher inquiry, and the expression of political thought is suppressed? Paolo Freire (1998) said that there is no *alternative* for educators but to defend their rights: the right to freedom in teaching, the right to speak, the right to better conditions for *pedagogical* work, and the right to criticize authorities. As Hutchison (2003) pointed out, a teacher must examine traditional and new ideas, using any number of methods, draw conclusions, share information and knowledge with students, raise questions, and at times offer answers about issues. We must bring our *expertise* to the problem, using inquiry to aid in the development of solutions. We must also recognize that doing so will give rise to the complex and challenging notion of academic freedom.

The Role of Chicano/a Activists

As Chicana/o educators it becomes increasingly important for us to take a step back from the *right wing* political rhetoric, rid ourselves of our political and historical *amnesia,* embrace our *racialized positionality* and remember that we too, are oppressed. In the final analysis, as Chicano/a activists, we must: (a) reflect on our historical experiences, our collective and *vibrant* history of struggle and resistance against the *imperial power* of the United States and at every opportunity challenge those among our people who have bought into the lie; (b) challenge progressive activists who when they talk about injustice in the United States see only one color, who *demean, devalue* and deny our existence as a oppressed people in this nation; and, (c) challenge the ugliness of a national politic that is intent on ruling the world and build a broad multicultural movement for universal human rights. "This is a critical and decisive hour and we are not without voices or tools" (Hartman, 2003). We need to find our voice and use it.

We must refer to our history of resistance and teach our people, many of them new Americans, that ours is an American experience of 500 years of oppression: a history of survival in a country that has done to our people what it is currently doing to Iraq. It is important to be cognizant of the fact that for Chicano/as and Puerto Riqueños the occupation has never ended. As Chicano/a educators we must reacquaint ourselves with this history, educate our youth about what this nation has repressed and teach non-Chicano/as that our history against an imperial power continues in the present. Joel Spring (2003) using a quote by Ulysses S. Grant recently compared the conquest of Mexico to the war in Iraq. It is most appropriate when he said, "The war in Iraq is the second most cowardly American war. The most cowardly war was the Mexican American War." Our children and youth are not taught this history and they are not taught to critically compare this conquest with what is happening in Iraq. It is our responsibility to teach our people that the American occupation in Iraq is an extension of American cultural and economic imperialism, the very same invasion that took place in Puerto Rico, Nicaragua, Cuba, Mexico, and countless others. Capitalist control of the oil in Iraq, the destruction of Iraqi history, art, and culture mirror the *atrocities* committed for imperial resource control of Latin America, Africa, and Asia. Only this time, many soldiers looked like us. Only this time, our sons and daughters were duped into participating in the securing of the resources for an elite who do not care if they live or die. It was our sons and daughters who were ordered to look the other way as history and art were destroyed and oil was protected. It is this reality that should bring this country great shame, not glory. We should not salute the flag of a country that continues to use the power of God and Christianity to conquer and *pillage,* in much the same way that it used the words "Manifest Destiny" to steal our land.

As critical Chicano educators we should take up progressive and revolutionary pedagogies, such as Chicano/a Studies and *critical pedagogy,* and use these theoretical frameworks as the foundation of our curriculum and praxis. As a Chicana educator, teaching in the borderlands, our discourse and our story is one where the struggle for education is a part of "an *oppositional discourse* for Chicana/os (and Mexicanos) constructed from the condition of living in the *margins* of a U.S. society and culture" (Elenes, 2003, p. 194). Chicano/a educators must enact a critical pedagogy that "explicitly works to *transform* these *dimensions* of schooling so that schools become sites for the development of a critical *decolonizing consciousness* and activity that works to *ameliorate* and ultimately end the *mutually constitutive forms* of violence that characterize our internal *neocolonial condition*" (Tejeda, Espinoza, & Gutierrez, 2003, p. 20). For Chicano/a educators that decolonizing pedagogy includes Chicano/a Studies, border pedagogies, feminist theory, and critical pedagogy; all pedagogical models that are *inherently* anti-capitalist, anti-racist, and anti-imperialist. We must use these radical theories and pedagogies to build a broader movement for peace and social justice.

Finally, as Chicano/a educators we need to learn from the thousands of young Chicano/a educators who are actively engaged in the struggle to teach for social justice, and who view this struggle as an essential part of a social movement for educational, political, and economic justice. We must listen to our youth as they share their perspectives and analysis of the Xicano/a movement. We should work alongside young Chicanos as they build a growing, *cross-generational*, multicultural, multi-class political movement. As veteran activists, our mission is not just to lead and teach, but also to follow and learn. All of us, *novice* and seasoned activists, should *reclaim* our history of resistance and activism, adopt a democratic vision for peace and social justice, and breathe new life into the present movement for peace and social justice.

References

Berlowitz & Long. (2003). The proliferation of JROTC: Educational reform or militarization. In K. J. Saltman & D. A. Gabbard (Eds.) *Education as enforcement: The militarization and corporatization of schools* (pp. 163–174). New York: RoutledgeFalmer.

Contreras, R. (1999). Chicano Studies: A political strategy of the Chicano movement. In M. Antonia Beltrán-Vocal, M. de Jesús Hernandez-Gutiérrez, & S. Fuentes (Eds.), *Mapping strategies: NACCS and the challenge of multiple (re)oppressions* (pp. 95–112). Phoenix, AZ: Editorial Orbis Press.

Darder, A. (2003). Teaching as an act of love: Reflections on Paulo Freire and his contributions to our lives and work. In A. Darder, M. Baltodano, & R. Torres (Eds.), *The critical pedagogy reader* (pp. 497–510). New York: RoutledgeFalmer.

Democracy Now. (2003, May 9). *Cop takes midnight photos of pacifist teacher's classroom.* Retrieved May 9, 2003, from *www.democracynow.org*

Elenes, C. A. (2003). Reclaiming the borderlands: Chicana/o identity difference and critical pedagogy. In A. Darder, M. Baltodano, & R. Torres (Eds.), *The critical pedagogy reader* (pp. 191–208). New York: RoutledgeFalmer.

Freire P. (1998). *Teachers as cultural workers: Letters to those who dare to teach.* Boulder, CO: Westview Press.

Furumoto, R. (2003, March 19). *Education, empire and militarism.* Presentation at Student Symposium Against the War, Northridge, CA.

Hartman, T. (2003, April 18). *The real war—on American democracy.* Retrieved April 20, 2003, from *www.alternet.org*

Hutcheson, Philo. (2003, April 22). *The enemy within: A post September 11 conversation about academic freedom in historical and contemporary perspectives.* A presidential invited session at the annual meeting of the American Educational Research Association, Chicago, Ill.

Mariscal, J. (2003, March 22). *The militarization of everyday life Latinos on the frontlines, again.* Retrieved March 23, 2003, from *www.counterpunch/mariscal04012003.html*

McLaren, P., & Fischman. G. (1998, Fall). Reclaiming hope: Teacher education and social justice in the age of globalization. *Teacher Education Quarterly,* 125–132.

Muñoz, R. (1999). Speech refusing induction. In J. Mariscal (Ed.), *Aztlán and Viet Nam: Chicana and Chicano experiences of the war* (pp. 217–218). Berkeley, CA: University of California Press.

Nieto, S. (2003, April 23). *The impact of the war in Iraq on education and educational research.* Special Session on Iraq presented at the annual meeting of the American Educational Research Association, Chicago, Ill.

Robbins, T. (2003, April 16). *A chill wind is blowin' in this nation.* Retrieved April 17, 2003, from *www.commondreams.org*

Roy, A. (2003, May 18). *Instant-mix imperial democracy (Buy one, get one free).* Retrieved May 19, 2003, from *www.commondreams.org*

Sanchez, L. (2003). Chicano youth face war in LA. [Electronic version] *War Times* 9, 1. Retrieved May 19, 2003, from *www.war-times.org/current/art9*

Spring, J. (2003, April 23). *The impact of the war in Iraq on education and educational research.* Special Session on Iraq presented at the annual meeting of the American Educational Research Association, Chicago, Ill.

Tejeda, C., Espinoza, M., & Gutierrez, K. (2003). Toward a decolonizing pedagogy: Social justice reconsidered. In P. P. Trifonas (Ed.), *Pedagogies of difference: Rethinking education for social change* (pp. 10–40). New York: RoutledgeFalmer.

Writing Prompts

1. Describe the author's "tone" in this essay. Tone refers to a writer's *attitude* toward (in this case) *her* subject. Give examples by writing some of her phrases or sentences that express tone.

2. What challenge does Montaño present to classroom teachers? Is she talking about high school, college, or both?

3. Explain why Montaño decided to become a teacher. What was her goal or "mission"?

4. What parallel does the author draw between the Vietnam War and the conflict that led to war between the United States and Iraq (2003)?

5. Montaño is critical of the JROTC on college campuses. Give a brief explanation why she opposes this military presence on campuses.

6. The author suggests that teachers should not only "lead and teach" students, but they should follow and learn. Discuss what she means by this recommendation.

Chicana Resistance: Fostering College Aspirations

Valerie Talavera-Bustillos

This paper will present partial findings of dissertation research on the educational experiences of first-generation Chicana college students (Talavera-Bustillos, 1998). The current debate on affirmative action and legislation such as the 1997 California proposition 209 sparked the *impetus* for this research project. The objective of the project was to analyze how Chicana students successfully made their way into institutions of higher education. In order to accomplish this task, two groups of students were analyzed, one enrolled at a community college, the other at a university. Research participants were recent graduates from a variety of high schools in the Los Angeles area. All thirty women were from working-class, low-income, Mexican-American backgrounds. Personal narratives of the research participants were examined and *strategies* employed by the students were identified. From the data, a relationship between *progressive resistance* and college *aspirations* emerged.

Resistance theory is incorporated in the analysis to understand how the students are able to develop their college aspirations. Based on a few *salient* studies of progressive resistance from Anyon (1981), Delgado Bernal (1997), Fordham (1988), Orhn (1993), and Solorzano and Bernal (2001), the experiences of thirty women were examined to identify their expressions of progressive resistance. Through the research one can better understand how Chicana students express progressive resistance.

Theoretical Constructs

Habitus

For this study, an important research question to consider is What shapes a student's college aspirations? First, one needs to investigate their habitus (Bourdieu, 1984). According to Horvat (1996), habitus is "a fluid and constantly *reformulated* set of *dispositions* which are created through personal and social history and thus influence how the world is constructed around us" (p. 57). Thus, habitus guides an individual's *perceptions* and responses. Given this information, habitus is the foundation that shapes how the world is viewed by an individual. Bourdieu (1984) explains, ". . . habitus is necessity internalized . . . it is a general, *transposable* disposition which carries out a systematic, universal application . . ." (p. 170). Habitus is the blueprint to what and how individuals think. It provides a set of standards for thought and behavior. Habitus is the understanding of life, society, and the role of individuals in it. More specifically, habitus serves as an important concept because it plays a role in the *maintenance* and control of the social hierarchy and thus, social inequality. According to

Lamont and Lareau (1988), "The capacity of a class to make its particular *preferences* and practices seem natural and *authoritative* is the key to its control" (p.159). Habitus *constructs* individual thoughts and perceptions that also guides individuals into thinking the perceptions and actions of their socioeconomic class are normal and natural. Habitus illustrates how and why an individual thinks and acts and makes sense of the world around them and their place in it. Habitus influences how individuals think and feel about their status within society. One's immediate physical environment is important but what makes habitus crucial is how it shapes norms, values, and expectations.

The habitus or mentality of individuals within three critical social structures : general society, family, social networks (friends/neighbors) were important in understanding Chicana experiences. Based on their personal narratives, this research will focus on how these research participants: (a) reflected on their habitus, (b) expressed resistance, and (c) developed college aspirations.

Resistance Theory

For the purposes of this study, understanding Chicana educational experiences within the *context* of progressive resistance is necessary. According to Giroux (1983), "The concept of resistance must have a revealing function that contains a *critique of domination* and provides *theoretical opportunities* for self-reflection and struggle in the interest of social and self-emancipation" (p. 282). An analysis was conducted on the personal narratives using three key criteria: (a) critique of domination, (b) struggle, and (c) interests of social and self-*emancipation*. In order to authentically identify progressive resistance included are only situations and behaviors that strictly fit Giroux's theoretical concepts. An analysis of the personal narratives of the *research participants* exposed behaviors that fit the criteria, resulting in the documentation of progressive resistance. The women in this study reflected on the habitus from society, family, or friends and resist these thoughts, norms, values, and expectations.

It is necessary to examine how and why progressive resistance occurs. From the data, the important relationship between the expression of resistance and the events that *"triggered"*[1] or initiated them emerged. Before progressive resistance occurs, it needs to be triggered by an action or event. A trigger initiates progressive resistance; it can be a statement, question, or doubt regarding an individual's desire to move away from their habitus, established ways of thinking and behaviors that are shaped by the norms. Usually, the individuals who present the trigger attempt to maintain habitus and the resulting inequalities. The triggers identified from the personal narratives of the research participants were key in uncovering the reasons and nature of progressive resistance. Figure 2-1 illustrates the important manifestations of the triggers of progressive resistance that *emerged* from the data and they are: (a) family status, (b) racism, (c) sexism, and (d) neighborhood environments. The following section will describe the trigger of progressive resistance and provide examples for each expression of resistance.

Chicana Resistance

Family Status

Family status was responsible for the majority of resistance students expressed in the study and was related to a student's parent or family education, occupation, or lifestyle. Eva, a community college student, shared her thoughts:

> My best friend [said], "It would be nice to be home all day," [instead of going to college] . . . [To that I say] I've lived on welfare and I don't want that now that I have my family, I won't depend on that. My mom depends on that and I don't want to. I want to be able to do something. If something would happen to my husband [he dies], I want to be able to take care of myself and take care of my baby and not just cook and clean. I want to have some experience . . . She's

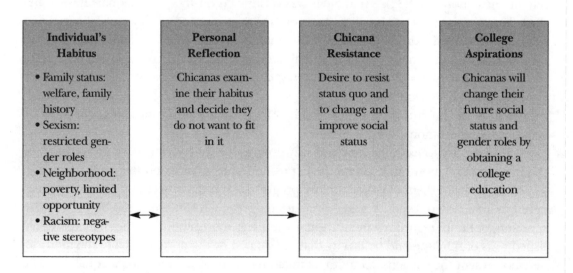

Figure 2-1. Habitus and Chicana Resistance in the Formation of College Aspirations.

[her mom] dependent on welfare and I don't want that; I want to support my family (Interview, August 4, 1997).

Eva resisted her family's pattern of welfare dependency. To prevent that for herself, she wanted to work to support her family and be self-sufficient. Another example came from Margarita, a university student:

Some of my relatives, they discouraged me [from going to college]. So, they keep on saying, "Well, Margarita, she's going to be just like her mother, like mother, like daughter. She's just going to get married, get pregnant, she's never going to make it." So I used to hear a lot of that from them. I tried not to listen, I never made any comments about it, I just stayed quiet, and left it at that. I had to prove them wrong. I told my mom . . . "Why do they keep saying that? I know, I am not like you, I'm not like my other sister . . ." (Interview, September 8, 1997).

Margarita resisted her family's pattern of early pregnancy, which was expected by her relatives, and was determined to obtain a college degree. These students were presented with low educational and occupational expectations from some of their family members.

Sexism

Sexism was the second most frequent area of resistance and occurred in *gender-related* situations, such as marriage and motherhood. Esperanza, a university student, remembered,

So I wanted to go to [this university, and thought], I'm going to go, cool, I'm going to be a doctor. My father, he'd say . . . "I was hoping too high, to be a doctor" . . . and [he would] just say I should be a nurse, because I could never be a doctor . . . And I said, I could go . . . I could go to [the university], I could do this. . . . He [said] . . . "it's impossible to be a nurse," because of his machismo. He has the notion that females and school, it [going to college] wasn't it [what women did]. They [women] married, education was not for women (Interview, September 3, 1997).

Esperanza resisted her father's sexist views and low expectations of her because of her gender. Despite his *skepticism,* she remained committed to becoming a doctor. Another example of sexism within the family comes from Rocío, a community college student,

> *I have an uncle that, he made a comment a few months before I graduated. He started saying that "Why am I going to school?" . . . Supposedly saying that if I don't do work at the house, then what am I good for? He made that comment and it got me mad. I go [said], . . . Just because I don't know how to do something in the house, cleaning, doesn't necessarily mean that I'm not good for anything else. I might not be good at this, at being a housewife, [but] I'm going to be good at working and being more independent (Interview, August 11, 1997).*

Rocío resisted her uncle's sexist views and low expectations of her. In this and the other examples, the women in this study confronted expectations of females based on traditional, *restricted* gender roles of staying home, and raising a family. However, it was clear that these students did not view themselves as fitting into these restricted gender roles. These students *defied* the traditional gender roles by defending their high college and career aspirations.

Neighborhood Environment

Another area of resistant behavior was a student's neighborhood environment and lifestyles. In this study, the neighborhood environment included such factors as poverty, teen pregnancy, welfare dependence, minimum-wage employment, and dropping out of high school. These factors helped create the social norms and expectations found within the neighborhood environment. Dora, a university student, explained:

> *Where I live, I didn't want to end up [working] in McDonald's or anything like that, so it was basically no choice . . . . in my neighborhood, there was no choice. . . . the whole environment and the violence . . . you can't go out after certain hours. All of that . . . just made me realize how I don't want to be there anymore. I just had to get out; the only choice was college. I don't want what I see [around the neighborhood], I am not cut out for living that way. You see your parents or other families and you can't get what you want [because of poverty]. Well, I never got what I wanted and I [was] practically limited [to what I could have], but I don't want to live like that forever. It is either work a minimum wage job after high school or [go to] college, I think I'll go to college (Interview, September 3, 1997).*

Dora resisted the environment and norms of her family and *specifically* of her neighborhood. She resisted the expected lifestyle, including obtaining a minimum-wage job. Marisol, a community college student, stated:

> *A friend [questioned her college plans]. [I said] I want to go to college . . . Basically my parents have told me that too . . . "You might as well have a career, you can do something for yourself and your family." . . . I don't want to rely on welfare. It's my friends, all of them are on it [welfare], all of them in my neighborhood. I don't want anyone else to support me. I want to work and be proud of the work I do. I am not going to be like them [welfare recipients]. My best friend would say I should stay home, not me (Interview, August 13, 1997).*

Marisol *resisted* the environment of her neighborhood, including dependence on welfare. The students like Marisol and Dora who *encountered* their neighborhood environment as a trigger were determined to live their lives differently than those individuals they grew up with.

Racism

Racism was the final area of resistance and included situations involving racial stereotypes, *stigmas* of affirmative action or lowered expectations. One example of resistance triggered by racism was from Lupe:

> *I don't have a 4.0 and a lot of people think about affirmative action and they say, "If you want to get this, you have a good chance, a better chance of getting in [to college]." That has undermined my pride in being accepted into a nice college. . . . I don't want to be here because I'm Hispanic, that's not something I would be proud of . . . but I am not going to say, "I'm not going to go there [to college], let someone go instead of me!" . . . Some people see affirmative action as a free ticket [into college], it's an* assumption *that you are unqualified if you are Mexican . . . . It goes to a deep prejudice . . . (Interview, September 13, 1997).*

Lupe realized her college plans were indirectly challenged by assumptions that she, as a person of Mexican descent, was unqualified to be accepted into a university. She resisted these lowered expectations, and remained committed to her college aspirations. Students like Lupe were presented either directly or indirectly with racism that was related to their college aspirations and attendance. These students were determined to stay focused on their goal of college attendance, despite the racial statements questioning their academic ability.

Combinations of Triggers

Data analysis revealed a combination of triggers for some expressions of resistance. Below are some examples of how a combination of triggers initiated resistance. Family status and sexism were both triggers in the following experience. Virginia, a community college student stated,

> *No, I think I let them [family] know that my kids are going to grow up hav-ing two parents who work hard at something, not like my mom . . . she's never been out there [in the work force]. I can't say she's ignorant in a bad way, but ignorant as in no information of what's out there, and anyone could just come up to her and [say], "Sign this and she's like, "That's fine [and she'd sign it]." . . . My mom never worked [and] made life seem easy, to be sup-ported by a husband. I want to show my son . . . to struggle, to realize life isn't easy. I think [I want] to go [to college] to make a difference. It's a fam-ily thing. All of my family is on AFDC [Aid to Families With Dependent Children], and that's not what I want (Interview, August 14, 1997).*

Virginia resisted the pattern of welfare dependence and the limited role females were given in her family. To break free of this cycle, she wanted to pursue a college education and be employed. The next example illustrates a combination of triggers that include family, neighborhood, and sexism. Esperanza, a university student, explained:

> *I guess seeing everything with my neighbors, you see everything and you just want to get out. It's [college] like the only way out. I just thought, like, what am I going to do? I had to get out . . . the poverty, moms on welfare, single parents and violence. It's like parents just prepare you for marriage. Some of my mom's friends . . . they talk about their husbands' cheating, or who got beaten, and they say, "At least you don't get hit in the face!" like it's Okay, better! Education is the way out (Interview, September 3, 1997).*

Esperanza resisted the role of females and their lifestyles in her family and neighbor-hood and wanted to pursue a college education.

Chicana resistance was in response to the habitus in four major areas: (a) family status, (b) sexism, (c) racism, and (d) neighborhood environment. Based on this research, one can understand that Chicana resistance to habitus and the perpetuation of social inequality can influence them to develop college aspirations.

Conclusion

During most of the interviews and focus groups, the students expressed the desire to improve their *social status*, either through education or employment. Their personal narratives indicated that these research participants viewed themselves as being on a journey to improve their social status by *pursuing* a college degree, as they provided *insights* and critical thoughts from their working-class habitus. Therefore, the women in this study realized a connection between a college education and advanced social and economic positions in society. The resistance to their habitus fostered their college aspirations.

The majority of the students in the study made conscious decisions to change their social status by deciding to pursue a college education. The research participants, at one point or another, reflected on their economic hardships, limited gender roles, negative stereotypes based on their working class, minority backgrounds. The narratives illustrated how the students' college aspirations were challenged by the expectations of individuals in those three structures: family, social networks, and school environments found in their habitus. This research examines how Chicana students develop and maintain their college aspirations. By understanding the challenges and responses to them, one can understand the relationship between progressive resistance and college aspirations in the lives of these first-generation Chicana college students. The findings of this research help to better understand what students have to contend with and how they cope with the pressures of social inequality. In addition, this research expands on the theoretical concepts of habitus (Bourdieu, 1984), and *tenants of resistance theory* (Giroux, 1983) and allows for new directions in understanding the *dynamics* of Chicana progressive resistance in education.

Notes

1. Triggers is a theoretical concept that will be elaborated on in a paper that focuses on the triggers of Chicana progressive resistance. (V. Talavera-Bustillo, forthcoming)

References

Bourdieu, P. (1977). Cultural reproduction and social reproduction. In J. Karable and H. Halsey (Eds.), *Power and ideology in education* (pp. 487–511). New York: Oxford University Press.

Bourdieu, P., & Passeron, J. (1979). *The inheritors: French students and their relation to culture.* (R.Nice, Trans.). Cambridge, MA: Harvard University Press.

Delgado Bernal, D. (1997). *Chicana school resistance and grassroots leadership: Providing alternative history of the 1968 East Los Angeles blowouts.* UCLA dissertation.

Giroux, H. (1983). Theories of reproduction and resistance in the new sociology of education: A critical analysis. *Harvard Educational Review, 53* (3).

Horvat E. (1996). *African-American students and college choice decision making in social context.* Unpublished doctoral dissertation, University of California, Los Angeles.

Lamont, M., & Lareau, A. (1988). Cultural capital: Allusions, gaps and glissandos in recent theoretical developments. *Sociological Theory, 6,* 153–168.

McDonough, P. (1997). *Choosing colleges: How social class and schools structure opportunity.* State University of New York Press.

MacLeod, J. (1995). *Ain't no makin' it. Aspirations and attainment in a low income neighborhood* (2nd ed.). Boulder-Westview Press.

Ohrn, E. (1993). Gender influences and resistance in school. *British Journal of Sociology of Education 2* (14), 147–158.

Solorzano, D. G. (1992). Chicano mobility aspirations: A theoretical and empirical note. *Latino Studies Journal, 3* (1).

Solorzano, D., & Bernal, D. D. (2001). Examining transformational resistance through a critical race and Lat Crit Theory Framework: Chicana and Chicano students in an urban context. *Urban Education 36,* 300–342.

Talavera-Bustillos, V. (1998). *Chicana college choice and resistance: An exploratory study of first generation college students.* Doctoral dissertation, University of California, Los Angeles.

Urahn, S. K. (1989). *Student and parent attitudes about financing education: Effects on postsecondary attendance and choice for Blacks, Whites and Hispanics.* Dissertation.

Writing Prompts

1. Talavera-Bustillos introduces the concept of "habitus" at the beginning of her essay. Why is it necessary for her to provide this background? Start by defining her theory of habitus.

2. In your own words, write an explanation of "resistance theory."

3. Name the four obstacles that threaten to keep Chicano/a students from attending college. Write a brief explanation of each and how they counter college aspirations.

4. How does the author use the term "trigger(s)" in the context of "resistance theory"?

5. Consider the three concepts above: (a) habitus, (b) resistance theory, and (c) triggers. Write a brief summary of this essay by bringing together how (a), (b), and (c) interconnect one with the other.

Words to Learn

"Message from the Borderlands to Chicana/o Educators: Seeking Peace, Social Justice, and Quality Schools in Unjust Times"

conform—to go along with things, not challenge the status quo, obey rules and regulations

indignation—to become very upset, but not to be sad; to become angry

subjugating (subjugate)—to conquer, to subdue, to dominate

corporate media—television, newspapers, telecommunications are owned and controlled by rich companies; i.e., AOL Time Warner, Disney, etc.

peril and consequences—the idea that there is danger in making a decision to do something risky and that one will pay a penalty

spewed (spew)—to discharge, to eject something

dissent—to oppose, to disagree

politic—when something is politic; it usually has to do with a political message or agenda; diplomacy

context—the situation or surroundings

compliant—to go along with the status quo without challenging the situation or to obey willingly without protest

implement—to take action on a program, law, or policy; to make certain that an idea becomes real *hegemonic* (hegemony)—to control, to dominate, to try to control the hearts and minds of people

elusive quest—a vision or goal that is hard to attain; a dream that seems impossible to get

progressive critical educators—teachers and other educators who are willing to take on injustice and inequity, to challenge the status quo; teachers who are change agents

simultaneously—at the same time

hostage—to take someone prisoner

coerced (coerce)—force to do something against your will

anonymity—to do something in secrecy; withhold your name or identity

pundits (pundit)—someone who is or thinks that he/she is an authority or an expert on an issue

impoverished (impoverish)—poor

marginalized people—someone who is not equal; people who are not allowed to be part of the mainstream of society

infiltrate—break into a place or become a member of an organization in order to spy

ideological decision—to make a decision due to your political or philosophical beliefs or ideas

Strategic (strategy)—plan

infuse—to fill, to integrate

undercurrent—something that is beneath the surface, unseen

imperialist—an empire builder

reconstruction—rebuild something

endeavored (endeavor)—to try to reach a goal

confine—to isolate or contain something; to shut something in

systematically (systematic)—to approach something in an organized and orderly fashion

praxis—the connection between the theory (idea) and practice (action)

progressive—people who are committed to changing society and/or political systems

legacy—your historical contribution to society; what you want to be remembered for

viable—something valid or true; something practical

mantra—a saying, a motto, or a hymn

clarion call—a call to action

cannon fodder—attracting bullets, weapon fire, a decoy for the military *deplorable*—terrible

comprised (comprise)—made-up, consist of

aggression—hostile action

economic conscription—when soldiers are recruited into the military, because they are poor; a poverty draft

phenomenon—a rare fact or occurrence

JROTC (Junior Reserve Officer's Training Corps)—a training ground for future soldiers in school grades 9 through 12

enticed (entice)—attract, invite, or tempt

proposition—a proposal, an idea, a plan or suggestion

preclude—to stop something from happening

depleted uranium—wasted uranium, left to rot after the war

agenda—a program, schedule of events, or plan

militarization—to turn something into an arm or servant of the military

corporatization—to turn something into the arm or servant of rich companies or corporations

de-professionalize—to take someone with a professional degree and devalue to demean their competency; to ignore the professionalism of an educated person

blatant—obvious, done without secrecy

deconstruct—to take down, to break down into smaller parts, to take apart

demise—the downfall, the end, the failure

expedient—the most practical, the easiest way of accomplishing a task

deculturalize—to take away someone's culture

despot—a tyrant, a dictator

slash—to cut or slice

devastated (devastate)—destroyed, left without anything valuable or meaningful

reorienting (reorient)—to familiarize someone with his/her new surroundings

audacity—the nerve; a person who is so bold as if to do something risky

neo-liberal or neo-conservative discourse—new liberals or new conservatives talk; left wing or right wing talk

theoretically (theory) *and ideologically* (ideology) *fueled*—an action taken by someone because of his or her thoughts/thinking or idea/beliefs *mobilization*—to organize large numbers of people to do something, a large political action

jingoistic—blind patriotism

patriotism—a strong loyalty to a nation

invades (invade)—to enter a country or territory by force

affirm—to support, encourage, or agree with

alternative—another choice or action, a different path

pedagogical—to do with the art of teaching

expertise—an area of specialization, to be an expert in something

right wing—to hold ultraconservative political views; to oppose change

amnesia—forgetfulness, not to remember

racialized positionality—your position or status in society according to your race; where you fall in the societal construct according to your race

vibrant—exciting

imperial power—extreme authority and control of a country or a body of people

demean—to reduce somebody to a much lower status in a humiliating way

devalue—to become reduced in value or importance

atrocities—a shockingly cruel act, especially an act of violence against a population

pillage—to rob a place using force

critical pedagogy—the act of teaching that is anti-status quo striving to change conventional teaching

oppositional discourse—a study or discussion resistant to traditional approaches

margins—least integrated with its center, least often considered, least typical, or most vulnerable

transform—to change completely for the better

dimensions—a feature or distinctive part of something

decolonizing consciousness —to enable free thinking; to challenge colonial thought

ameliorate—to improve something or make it better

mutually conservative forms—in favor of preserving the status quo and traditional values and structure

neocolonial condition—the domination by a powerful structure of regulations that is politically independent but has an economy that is greatly dependent on the weaker segment of its population

inherently—naturally

cross-generational—a diversity of people who were born at different times or eras, and not having shared interests and attitudes

novice—somebody who has just started learning or doing something new and has no previous experience in the skill or activity

reclaim—claim back something that has been taken away

"Chicana Resistance: Fostering College Aspirations"

impetus—something that provides energy or motivation to accomplish something

strategies—carefully devised plan of action to achieve a goal, or the art of developing or carrying out such a plan

progressive resistance—opposition to political structure

aspirations—a desire or ambition to achieve something

resistance theory—oppositional rules and principles based on a set of facts, propositions, or principles

salient—particularly noticeable, striking, or relevant

theoretical constructs—something that has been systematically put together, usually in the mind, especially a complex theory or concept

reformulated—to alter the appearance or the thought of something

dispositions—usual mood or temperament

perceptions—the process of using the senses to acquire information about the surrounding environment or situation

transposable—to make two things change places or reverse their normal order

maintenance—the continuation or preservation of something

preferences—the right or opportunity to a course of action that is considered more desirable than another

authoritative—convincing, reliable, backed by evidence, and showing deep knowledge

constructs—something that has been systematically put together, usually in the mind, especially a complex theory or concept

context—the circumstances or events that form the environment within which something exists or takes place *critique of domination*—the discussion or comment on something while giving an assessment of power

theoretical opportunities—inclined to or skilled in speculative contemplation or theorizing

emancipation—the act or process of setting somebody free or of freeing somebody from restrictions

research participants—people who participate in methodical investigation into a subject in order to discover facts, to establish or revise a theory, or to develop a plan of action based on the facts discovered

triggered—stimulus that sets off an action, process, or series of event

emerged—to come out of an experience, condition, or situation, especially a difficult one

inequalities—unequal opportunity or treatment based on social or economic disparity

gender-related —connected to the characterization of masculine and feminine

machismo—an exaggerated sense or display of masculinity, emphasizing characteristics that are conventionally regarded as typically male, usually physical strength and courage, aggressiveness, and lack of emotional response

skepticism—an attitude marked by a tendency to doubt what others accept to be true

restricted—subject to controls or limits

defied—to challenge openly somebody's or something's authority or power by refusing to obey a command or regulation

specifically—more than usual or more than in other cases

resisted—to oppose and stand firm against somebody or something

encountered—to meet somebody or something, usually unexpectedly

stigmas—shame or disgrace attached to something regarded as socially unacceptable

assumptions—something that is believed to be true without proof

data analysis—information, often in the form of facts or figures obtained from experiments or surveys, used as a basis for making calculations or drawing conclusions

social status—relating to human society and how it is organized

pursuing—working at something or carrying it out

insights—the ability to see clearly into the nature of a complex person, situation, or subject

tenants of resistance theory—occupier of a thought that opposes rules and principles based on a set of facts, propositions, or principles

dynamics—the forces that tend to produce activity and change in any situation

9/11: Its Impact on the Chicano/a Community

Chapter 3—Anticipation Guide

Directions: Rate each statement below according to the following:

4—*Strongly Agree*   3—*Agree*   2—*Disagree*   1—*Strongly Disagree*

1. The United States (March 2003) war in Iraq was justified.

2. The United States needs oil to maintain its standard of living.

3. It is alright for the United States to declare war on other countries in order to control a country's oil fields.

4. The United States went to war with Iraq to free that country from the rule of Saddam Hussein.

5. The Iraqi people are likely to have a free and democratic society because of the March 2003 U.S.–Iraq war.

6. It is important for the U.S. president and the president from Mexico to maintain a fraternal relationship because it helps immigrants in the United States.

7. The United States depends on the labor pool provided by undocumented immigrants.

8. Undocumented immigrants take jobs from U.S. citizens.

9. The president of Mexico (Fox) did not support the U.S. war with Iraq (2003); therefore, President Bush is unlikely to work with the president of Mexico to improve and change conditions undocumented Mexicans face in the United States.

10. Any individual running for public office will need to pay more attention to Chicano/a and Latino communities because their population(s) increased in the United States.

on my father's grave, i swear

Victor Carrillo

the dream says now is not the time for silence
Mother Earth is in pain
the dream says too many soldiers are prepared to kill
the dream says too many civilians are sure to die
the dream says too many loyal P.A.T.R.I.O.T.s
are willing to play along and pretend that war is a moral path to peace
the dream says get a life: war is a curse
the dream says real bombs
destroy real land,
kill real people,
erase real hopes
the dream says tranquility is so much more than waking up late on the weekend
and has nothing at all to do with CHRISTIANITY overpowering ISLAM into submission
the dream says family communion with *pan dulce* and *Chocolate Abuelita*
is fine on any given Sunday,
but life-affirming comfort food does not
fall from the heavens in yellow plastic wrapping
trailed by all-american cluster bombs dropped on Afghanistan
in our christian names
the dream says you're in a fog
the dream says you're in a deeper fog than you know
the dream says don't abuse 911 calls
system overloads affect us all
the dream says the fog is the perfect host for the banished father and the unholy son
the dream says the ghost be to ashes as the ghost be to bloody dust
the dream says everywhere there is pain
the dream says a personal war is still a war
the dream says the grass is not greener over your father's grave
after nearly ten years of neglect
the dream says let it go, just let him be
the dream says the mud on your hands belongs on his grave
the dream says *sácale el machete,* let time heal the wounds
the dream says *tequila* was your father's family doctor,
but no one ever understood

the dream says your mother's *té de canela* is better medicine
than your father's *tequila:*
just consider who remains alive
the dream says either remedy will do in a time of need:
blend them both with some honey and lemon juice
and you have the perfect cure
for a nagging sleep-depriving cough
the dream says natural time has nothing to do at all
with little hands for hours and big hands for minutes
the dream says productive time is not a paycheck
cashed at a favorite bar
the dream says time on this planet is precious,
settle all scores and enjoy what little you have left
the dream says don't confuse your desire for healing music
with your desire for a resurrected father
the dream says just replace the broken strings on your father's guitar:
he still will not be here to play it for you,
but, when you embrace it, your fingers will feel the passion he knew
the dream says remember forgiveness if you want peace in your heart
the dream says mystical music grows in places you have not seen
the dream says your mother is alive
and living creatures need tending to: yes, food, water and sunshine are fine,
but she will live happier if you sing to her each day
the dream says visit her garden, praise her flowers,
celebrate her fruitful life on earth
the dream says nurture the living
the dream says play with the living
the dream says work with the living
the dream says laugh with the living
the dream says cry with the living
the dream says eat with the living
the dream says dance with the living
the dream says chant with the living
the dream says pray with the living
the dream says dream with the living
the dream says honor the dead, but live for the living
and defend all life as yours

the dream says CELEBRATE LOUD with the living
because NOW is NOT a good time for SILENCE,
Mother Earth is in TOO MUCH PAIN

Los Angeles, California
November 3, 2001

Suggested Writing Activities

1. Listen carefully and take notes as the professor reads the poem. Next, write about any ideas that come to mind. Students have seven minutes to complete the writing activity. Afterward, take turns reading aloud.

2. Each of three students takes a turn reading the poem in front of the class.

3. Students can also read silently, and ask questions later.

September 11, 2001: The death of a promise?

Lawrence Littwin

"We are welcoming a new day in the relationship between America and Mexico" (Gomez). These were the optimistic words of George W. Bush, newly minted president of the United States as he stood next to his friend Presidente Vicente Fox of Mexico. The date was February 17, 2001, and this was President Bush's inaugural foreign trip. The meeting took place at Fox's Rancho San Cristobal in his home state of Guanajuato. He had just won a historic election, defeating the "Official Party," the PRI, ending 71 years of that party's rule. This was to be a new day, both for Mexico and for its relationship to its powerful northern neighbor. To some in Mexico, Fox, in these heady days of his new presidency, revived memories of Lazaro Cardenas, the revered revolutionary general who brought reform to Mexico's agriculture and had stood up to the United States in nationalizing Mexico's oil. The optimism preceding this meeting between the two new presidents was *palpable*. Both had ambitious agendas. Migration appeared to be among the most important.

President Bush went on to reflect on the potential outcome of this fresh relationship. "Each nation has a new president and a new perspective. Geography has made us neighbors; cooperation and respect will make us partners. And the promise of the partnership was renewed and *invigorated* today" (Gomez).

Addressing the issue of migration, President Fox greeted the new partnership with these words, "certainly there is a new attitude, there is a new way of approaching things, a much more positive approach to things on this issue" (Gomez).

During this trip to Mexico, Bush also visited the home of President Fox's mother, Mercedes Queseda de Fox, and met with other members of the Mexican president's family. Bush *amplifying* the importance of Mexico to the United States emphasized that Mexico was the first foreign nation that he had visited as president. "Our nations are bound together by ties of history, family, values, commerce and culture. Today we have a chance to build a partnership that will improve the lives of citizens in both countries" (Gomez).

At the press conference that ended this meeting, a certain *portentous* set of questions posed by reporters seemed to momentarily *override* the issues addressed by the two presidents. For this moment, Iraq suddenly became more important than migration, drugs, and trade. While the presidents discussed these issues, U.S. and British planes had been attacking Iraqi radar installations in the "No Fly Zone" of Southern Iraq. Suddenly President Fox was in the background along with all of the promise of this new relationship. The focus was now on Bush and what the United States and its other ally, Great Britain, were doing in the Middle East.

Nevertheless, this important meeting had taken place, significant issues had been addressed, and the future of Mexican-American relations appeared to be launched in new and promising directions. Fox, having hosted the American president, had *underscored* the importance of his electoral victory. Bush appeared to be on his way to establishing his credentials with the large Mexican population of the United States. If this were truly to be a new relationship and the problems that had *beset* our two nations were on the way to being solved by a Republican president, perhaps the apparent *stranglehold* of the Democrats on the Mexican-American vote might be over. Who knew, maybe California and the rest of the American Southwest might be deliverable to the Republican Party? After all, George Bush appeared very authentic in his approach to Mexico. He was known to have visited Mexico many times as governor of Texas. He spoke some Spanish, even delivered some of his remarks in Mexico in that language. His brother Jeb, governor of Florida, is married to a Mexican woman, making the American president's focus on family ties between the two countries more substantial by being personal. And given his welcoming approach to Mexico as governor of Texas, this appeared to be the right moment and the right president to establish a new, friendly, and dynamic relationship between the two nations.

By the fateful month of September, not much progress had been made on the ambitious February Guanajuato agenda. President Bush was preoccupied with establishing his *fledging* administration. President Fox was enduring his own multiple problems at home trying to confirm his *legitimacy* in the face of a hostile congress. His own party, The National Action Party (PAN), was in the minority and even so, not all of PAN's members were sure that they stood behind the president. In order to win the election he had had to assemble a coalition going beyond the *confines* of his own political party and its members.

Nevertheless, the new Mexican president had been invited to come to Washington, to meet with Bush, and to address the United States Congress. By extending this invitation, President Bush had reemphasized the importance of our relationship with Mexico and also hoped to raise Fox's stock at home. Mexican immigration and the status of Mexicans in the United States were major topics of the Fox visit. Fox had hoped to move toward controlled migration and "regularization," if not legalization of undocumented Mexicans who live in the United States. Fox said of his mission that he hoped "to advance the countries' partnership one step, two steps, three steps forward" (Smith). In other words, he recognized that there was a lot of work to do on both sides of the border for a new relationship to be truly solidified. In a short five days after the Fox visit, Washington and New York were to be the targets of the terrorist attacks that changed history and made all of these hopes for renewed *amity* between our two nations seem an impossibly distant goal.

This is an essay about migration, that from Mexico to the United States shortly before and after the *tumultuous* events of September 11, 2001. It should be understood that migration is not a new phenomenon. It is certainly not exclusive to the two thousand mile border between our two nations. Migration is as old as human history. The fact that humanity is distributed around the globe the way it is is very much the product of human movements from our earliest beginnings in the valleys and plains of Africa to the wholesale movement of populations caused by today's *cataclysms* of war and *famine*. In short, people have always moved and resettled. The reasons why are *manifold*. They range from the need to follow herds of food-providing animals to violent conflicts forcing one group out and installing another group so it can temporarily dominate an area. At times, drought, earthquake, and all of the naturally destructive elements that beset the fragility of the human condition force people to move and resettle. Basically, it has been the need for survival, to work and gain *sustenance* and security.

Consider the two countries that are the subject of this essay: Mexico and the United States. The great Aztec civilization that emerged in the Valley of Mexico was built by the Mejicas, a nomadic hunting people, who conquered their way south to Lake Texcoco and there established the heart of their empire, the city of Tenochtitlan. As history tells us, the Spaniard Cortes, motivated by gold and personal power, arrived with his conquering forces in 1519. The current Mexican story is a result of the *intermingling* of people, descendants of the conquered and the conquerors. All moved from somewhere else, warred against each other, and finally built the nation we now know as Mexico. Likewise, the country we call our own resulted from *myriad* migration and conquest; we conquered and absorbed half of Mexico in what we call "The Mexican-American War" and the Mexicans call "The War of the Northern Invasion." This conquest, which took place from 1846–48 and ended with the Treaty of Guadalupe, added the American Southwest, including California, to our nation. The border established by the treaty was two thousand miles long, cutting a *swath* from the Pacific Ocean and the Gulf of Mexico. In part, between the two Californias, the line that separates us is a thin one over which is planted the imposing arches under which U.S. and Mexican officials guard the frontier. Further east, between El Paso and Ciudad Juarez the narrow ribbon of the river called the Rio Grande north of the border, and El Rio Bravo by the Mexicans, stands between the two countries.

In the words of one observer of the border region, "The 2000-mile-long international boundary between the United States and Mexico gives shape to a unique economic, social and cultural entity" (Lorey). It has "the distinction of being the only place in the world where a highly developed country and a developing nation meet and interact" (Lorey). This fact has not always had the significance it has today. Until the early part of the last century, the border was not much more than a line in the sand. Migration took place as it always had, and sometimes, such as during the Mexican Revolution of 1910, with a greater flow of people than others. But no one seemed to mind or pay attention. Between 1848 and 1900, the border was not even patrolled. The populations of northern Mexico and the border areas of California, Arizona, Texas, and New Mexico were *sparse*. Their economies were based on mining, ranching, and farming. Those who moved north from Mexico blended with the Mexicanos who already lived in those areas. Movement of people within Mexico itself was fairly infrequent. Until 1929, the concept of "illegal" immigration from Mexico did not exist. Only after that year was it a crime to enter the United States from Mexico without papers.

The big *surge* in the movement of Mexicans into the United States came in the 1940s. The United States was at war. Someone had to harvest the crops while Americans were in the armed forces or working in defense factories. For that purpose, Mexican farmworkers were recruited to harvest the fields of this country through a program called "The Bracero Agreement." The impact of that program was more profound than originally thought. Its impact is very much with us today as the battle about immigration continues to be fought. The Bracero program contributed to the establishment of networks of labor migration reaching into the southern reaches of Mexico and today extending as far north as New York and Alaska and including states like the Carolinas and up through the American heartland. In other words, all of the United States is linked to all of Mexico as Mexicans migrate, stay, and establish their lives north of the border, while maintaining their links to the "Patria." They send millions of dollars home and visit when they can. One interesting example of Mexicans living here while linked to their hometowns and villages is the Zacatecan community in California. The government of the state of Zacatecas supplements funds sent home from the United States by Zacatecan clubs in the United States for public projects like roads, dams, and schools back home.

One might think that this is all benign. It has been pointed out that Mexican immigration to the United States is more a function of the employment needs north of the border than of unemployment in Mexico. All well and good; the United States needs labor. Mexicans provide the labor and Mexico itself receives the *remittances* that fund badly needed public projects. But, of course, the total picture is much more complex and intensely more *conflicted*.

Although the flow of Mexican immigration was initiated and encouraged during World War II, the industrialization of the American Southwest and the postwar intensification of that process made migration ever more attractive. However, the complexities and certainly the conflicts emerging from the ever-increasing tide of Mexican immigration brought our two presidents to Guanajuato in February of 2001.

Adding to and encouraging immigration to the United States was the 1960s Border Industrialization Act. With this act, international corporations were encouraged to build factories in cities all along the border. As a result, what had been small towns, such as Tijuana,

Mexicali, and Juarez, became huge sprawling urban centers. Tijuana, which had a population of 242 in 1900, exemplifies this population explosion. At midpoint in the last century, Tijuana's population had grown to 60,000.

Because of the industrialization of the border with the establishment of numerous internationally owned factories, called "maquiladoras," about one million and a half people now populate greater Tijuana. They come from all over Mexico and live in extremely diverse conditions. They inhabit the luxury suburb of Playas de Tijuana and they dwell on the *vulnerable* unstable hillsides surrounding the city. They survive in tin and cardboard shacks without electricity, freshwater, or public services. Many have and will attempt to better their lives by crossing the border over and around the fence and into the desert areas of eastern San Diego and Riverside counties. Some are caught by the Border Patrol. Some die of thirst in the desert. Those who are lucky survive and follow the vast immigration networks to join their compatriots in all parts of the United States.

Statistics vary widely as to the number of Mexican immigrants living in the United States. The INS indicates that of that population, whatever the actual count, 4.8 million are undocumented. (The job of accurately depicting the undocumented population is extremely problematic. Many illegal immigrants are counted multiple times as they come, go, get caught, are deported, and return.) All that can be said is that the immigrant population is very large and growing.

The policies of the 1980s and '90s only added to the size of the permanent immigration population. In 1986, The Immigration Reform and Control Act *amnestied* a large number of undocumented migrants and gave them a chance for permanent residency and citizenship. Going in the other direction, in 1994 the United States implemented two border security programs, "Operation Gatekeeper" at the San Ysidro border and "Hold the Line" in Texas. These operations made it much more difficult to cross over, and as a result, many more undocumented migrants chose to stay in the United States and not take the risks of returning home and attempting to cross again. The situation has been complicated by policies implemented through NAFTA and *globalization* in general. Agribusiness and its need for size and *efficiency* has undermined small-scale farming, and therefore, livelihood for thousands of agricultural workers in rural Mexico. Many have protested in the Mexican capital, others have been challenged to cross the border and try their luck "al Norte." For many who make it and stay in the United States, life is often better, at least economically. Although surveys show mixed reviews, Mexican migrants are pleased that their children have an opportunity for a better education and a more open future. Again, this is all to the good from the migrants' point of view. However, this picture is clouded by the negative attitudes of Americans. Some are paranoid about being surrounded by a people and a language differing from their own. Furthermore, they fear that Mexicans are taking jobs from American workers. These attitudes prompted the passage of anti-immigrant initiatives such as California's Proposition 187. Some border residents have demonstrated their displeasure by forming anti-immigrant *vigilante* groups focused on aiding the Border Patrol in hunting down undocumented Mexicans trying to find their way through the desert areas of southern California and Arizona. And as stated before, migrants forced into these deserts by ever stricter and strengthened border control have often died of thirst and exposure. In addition, these poor people have all too often been victimized by unscrupulous "coyotes," people paid large sums to guide migrants to freedom. Coyotes have been known to rob, rape, and abandon their *"pollitos."*

All of these issues constitute a complex political brew. It was one that both Vicente Fox and George W. Bush were promising to address and sort out when they met in Guananjuato. As indicated above, expectations were high and the promise of solutions was just over the horizon. On September 11, 2001, 19 Al Queda terrorists commandeering four jet airliners appear to have demolished more than buildings and murdered thousands of innocent people. At least for the time being, they appear to have destroyed the promise of Guananjuato. Instead of more open borders and the regularization of millions of undocumented Mexicans, we are confronted by a greater fear of foreigners and an intensified border militancy. Everyone coming across is suspect. Anyone without the proper documents is liable to arrest and deportation. Shortly after September 11, the Immigration and Naturalization Service conducted an investigation of all workers at the Los Angeles Airport, *ostensibly* to root out potential terrorists. They succeeded in discovering fifty undocumented Mexican baggage handlers. These unfortunate people quickly became victims of the new "War on Terrorism." They were arrested, charged with felonies for misstating their legal status, and placed in detention pending deportation. Headlines like the following have become ever more frequent: "2 Killed, 13 Injured as Pickup Flips Over During Border Patrol Chase" (Garrison and Silver). In this instance, the Border Patrol used a spike strip to disable the "coyote's" pickup truck. The Mexican consulate protested.

Today, President Bush appears *enmeshed* in the war with Iraq. President Fox has been badly weakened by political *squabbling* at home. For the United States, questions of Mexican migration and the status of the Mexicans among us seem to have been *immolated* in the flames of war. One can only hope that peace, when it comes, will revive the focus on this issue. In the meantime, as in all of history, the migrants will continue to arrive. The need for a better life and sheer survival always triumphs, no matter how the politicians play.

Works Cited

Garrison, Jessica, and Beth Silver. "Border Pursuit Crash Kills 2, Hurts 13." *The Los Angeles Times* 10 Jan. 2003: B1.

Gomez, Berta. "Presidents Bush and Fox Meet in Mexico to Shape Agenda." *Washington File* 16 Feb. 2001. 23 June 2003. <*http://usinfo.state.gov/regional*>.

Lorey, David. *The U.S.-Mexican Border in the Twentieth Century.* Wilmington Delaware: SR Books, 1999.

Smith, Elliot Blair. "Mexican Leader Lowers Ambitions for Summit." *USA TODAY* 05 Sept. 2001. 23 June 2003 <*http:www.usatoday.com/news*>.

Writing Prompts

1. What was the most significant issue for President Fox in his discussion with President George W. Bush, when the two met in Guanajuato on February 17, 2001?

2. Bush hoped to advance his position with which U. S. community, as a result of his visit with President Fox, according to the author? Explain, using examples from the essay.

3. The author suggests that Bush's relationship with President Fox would release "the stranglehold (of) the Democrats (have) on the Mexican-American vote." Given the tone (attitude) of the writer, do you think Littwin favors or frowns on this? Explain.

4. Littwin indicates that the history of migration from Mexico to the United States occurred infrequently before 1929. Explain what happened after 1929?

5. Describe the purpose of the Border Industrialization Act. How did it change border towns? How does immigration from Mexico to the United States affect Mexican immigrants and Chicano/a families in this country?

The "War on Terrorism": Thinking Critically in the Chicana/o Community

David Rodríguez

President Bush engaged in *fallacious reasoning* when he claimed that Iraq possessed weapons of mass destruction that threatened the United States and required action now, or our nation would pay a price later. This reasoning led to the war with Iraq. This type of fallacious reasoning is called a false dilemma. "A false dilemma is a dilemma that can be shown to be false [and] one way to do this is to demonstrate that the premise . . . is false by showing that there is at least one other viable possibility" (Kahane & Cavender, 2002, p. 60). The one "other viable possibility" was that Iraq did not have weapons of mass destruction and thus was not an *imminent* threat to the United States. Bush's claim that inaction would be disastrous ignored the fact that United Nations weapons inspectors were making progress in Iraq and required more inspection time. Moreover, the U.N. weapons team had not found any weapons of mass destruction when Bush announced on March 17, 2003, that Saddam Hussein and his sons had forty-eight hours to leave Iraq or our government would use military force.

Most Americans accepted Bush's fallacious reasoning despite earlier concerns. A Time/CNN poll conducted in August 2002 found that 68 percent of Americans believed that Bush should use military force only with congressional authorization (Time, 2002). Chicanas/os were among the Americans who initially expressed concerns about a war but eventually accepted Bush's fallacious argument. However, a California survey conducted during the summer of 2002 found that Chicanas/os believed that their general quality of life after 9/11 had worsened (Institute for Justice and Journalism, 2002). In addition, studies continued to show that Chicanas/os constituted one of the most economically disadvantaged groups in the United States and that *wage gaps* between Chicanas/os and whites had not changed (Grogger & Trejo, 2002; Reed & Cheng, 2003).

Bush's false dilemma masked a reason the administration went to war in Iraq (Vidal, 2002). It also *obfuscated* the aftermath of 9/11 and its effect on the Chicana/o community. The following essay argues that the reason we went to war with Iraq was oil and not weapons of mass destruction and that the Chicana/o community needs to be more critical of the "war on terrorism."

The question of "Where are the weapons of mass destruction?" is extremely significant, since the United States claimed victory in Iraq on May 1, 2003, and no weapons of mass destruction have been found to date. Chief U.N. weapons inspector Hans Blix said in a farewell appearance before the Security Council, "Iraq's failure to account for its alleged biological, chemical or nuclear weapons did not mean that it possessed them—or posed an imminent threat" (Farley, 2003, p. A11). Deputy Defense Secretary Paul Wolfowitz revealed in a *Vanity Fair* interview: The truth is that for reasons that have a lot to do with the U.S. government bureaucracy, we settled on the one issue that everyone could agree on which was weapons of mass destruction as the core reason (as cited in *USA Today*, 2003). In addition, Secretary of State Donald Rumsfeld admitted, "Iraq's weapons of mass destruction may have been destroyed before the war" (USA Today, 2003). Remarkably, President Bush now is saying that "Iraq had a weapons program" with the emphasis on the word "program" (Miller, 2003b, p. A1).

The above statements made since the Bush *proclamation* of victory are quite extraordinary. It is unlikely that weapons of mass destruction will ever be discovered that have *operational capability*. Why then war? Why was the Bush administration quick to "pull the trigger" and impatient in the *diplomatic process*? Let us critically review the events and issues that led us to our current *dilemma*.

On September 11, 2001, the World Trade Center in New York and the Pentagon in Washington, D.C., were attacked. As a result, nearly 3,000 people died. That evening President Bush told the nation, "the search is under way for those who are behind these evil acts" and "we will make no distinction between the terrorists who committed these acts and those who harbor them" (Bush, 2001a). The next day, Bush announced that "the deliberate and deadly attacks which were carried out yesterday against our country were more than acts of terror. They were acts of war" (Bush, 2001b). Thus, the "war on terrorism" came into being and the Bush administration hastily and recklessly set into motion a dangerous turn in U.S. foreign policy and *global political hegemony*.

The day after Bush's declaration on the "war on terrorism," the administration began organizing an *international coalition* against terrorism. British Prime Minister Tony Blair offered total support for the war and Pakistani President Pervez Musharraf pledged support for the United States. *The North Atlantic Treaty Organization (NATO)* was called into action and the U.N. Security Council passed Resolution 1368, which condemned the attacks and recognized national self-defense. No serious discussion or debate was made over the vagueness of the notion "war on terrorism," especially since "terrorism" has been a problem in human history.

On September 14, the U.S. Congress passed a resolution that authorized the president "to use all necessary and appropriate force against those nations, organizations, or persons he determines planned, authorized, committed, or aided the terrorist attacks that occurred on September 11, 2001, or harbored such organizations or persons" (Congressional Record, 2001). Bush's National Security team began planning for war and Paul Wolfowitz, Deputy Secretary of Defense, argued to fight against other sponsors of terrorism including Iraq's Saddam Hussein. However, Bush decided that the primary focus of the war on terrorism would be on Afghanistan because of the administration's belief that the 9/11 attacks came from the Al Qaeda terrorist organization that was led by Osama bin Laden. Iraq was put on the back burner for the time being.

In early October, the United States and Britain began air strikes against Taliban government targets and Al Qaeda training camps in Afghanistan. But, the terrorist camps had already been largely abandoned and much of the Taliban *infrastructure* had already been destroyed by years of war. By October 19, the United States began a ground war that *culminated* with the final collapse of the Taliban leadership and the eventual election of pro-American Hamid Karzi as president of Afghanistan. However, many Al Qaeda and Taliban leaders were able to flee and Osama bin Laden remained on the loose. The United States turned to the Iraqi regime.

The United States had been attempting to change Iraq's regime since the 1991 Persian Gulf War but it was not until 1998 that regime change in Iraq became an official U.S. policy when Congress passed and President Bill Clinton signed into law the Iraq Liberation Act (Disarming Iraq, 2002, p. 293). "The Act gave the President authority to provide funds to opposition groups in Iraq, and stated that the United States should support efforts to remove Saddam Hussein's regime" (Disarming Iraq, 2002, p. 299). The Bush administration "emphasized regime change as the *cornerstone* of U.S. policy toward Iraq" (Disarming Iraq, 2002, p. 293). Bush's State of the Union speech in January 2002 threatened to take action against Iraq and named Iraq as part of an *"axis of evil"* that included Iran and North Korea. Eight months later at the U.N. Bush emphasized Iraq's efforts to develop weapons of mass destruction and urged enforcement of Security Council resolutions against Iraq, or the United States would take action against Iraq.

On September 20, 2002, the Bush administration released its first national security strategy document (National Security Strategy of the United States of America). The document focused on topics that could be grouped under the following themes: (a) promoting human dignity through political and economic freedom; (b) providing security against terrorism and weapons of mass destruction; and (c) engaging conflict areas and *allies* (Corbin, 2002). The most controversial part of the document was a new emphasis on *preemptive* attacks against adversaries. "The strategy proposed expanding the concept of true preemption—striking first against an imminent, specific, near certain attack—to the far broader concept of striking first to prevent the possibility of a longer term threat even developing, which might better be labeled preventive war" (Corbin, 2002). Todd Gitlin argued:

> *The United States has many times sent armed forces to take over foreign countries for weeks, years, even decades. But the Bush doctrine is the first to elevate such wars of offense to the status of official policy, and to call "preemptive"*

(referring to imminent peril) what is actually preventive (referring to longer-term, hypothetical, avoidable peril). This semantic shift is crucial. When prevention of a remote possibility is called preemption, anything goes. C.I.A. caution can be overridden, Al Qaeda connections fabricated, dangers exaggerated—and the United States will have a doctrine to substitute for international law (Gitlin, 2003).

On October 7, Bush spoke in Cincinnati and presented several "immediate requirements" that he insisted be in a new U.N. Security Council resolution (Disarming Iraq, 2002, p. 299). They included demands that Iraq destroy all weapons of mass destruction and provide unlimited access to U.N. weapons inspectors. He also stated that if Iraq failed to comply, the United States would act with the full power of its military. By October 11, Bush was able to get from Congress a war resolution that allowed him to attack Iraq if Saddam Hussein refused to surrender weapons of mass destruction. Finally, through a great deal of pressure from the United States, the U.N. Security *unanimously* passed Resolution 1441 on November 8, deciding that "Iraq has been and remains in material breach of its obligations" and warning Iraq "that it will face serious consequences as a result of its continued violations of its obligations" (Text of UN Resolution on Iraq, 2002).

In his State of the Union address in January 2003 Bush stated that "Saddam Hussein aids and protects terrorists, including members of al Qaeda . . . [and] . . . could provide one of his hidden weapons to terrorists, or help them develop their own" (Bush, 2003a). On February 5, Secretary of Defense Collin Powell spoke to the U.N. and offered more details. On March 17, Bush delivered a fifteen-minute televised speech to the American people that *reiterated* his views on Iraq and declared in a "Dodge City" fashion that Saddam Hussein and his sons had 48 hours to leave town. Included in his speech was a plea to the Iraqi people to "not destroy oil wells, a source of wealth that belongs to the Iraqi people" (Bush, 2003b). It was very clear that Bush was going to invade and occupy Iraq, regardless of any opposition. On March 19, 2003, the United States started bombing Iraq and the predicted war became a reality and nightmare.

Many critics of the Iraq war were not accepting the weapons of mass destruction argument. Millions throughout the world *mobilized* anti-war demonstrations and chanted "no blood for oil." A more *plausible* explanation for why we went to war with Iraq is offered by Robert Dreyfuss shortly before the war (Dreyfuss, 2003). Dreyfuss explains,

If you were to spin the globe and look for real estate critical to building an American empire, your first stop would have to be the Persian Gulf. The desert sands of this region hold two of every three barrels of oil in the world—Iraq's

reserves alone are equal, by some estimates, to those of Russia, the United States, China, and Mexico combined. For the past thirty years, the Gulf has been in the crosshairs of an influential group of Washington foreign-policy strategists, who believe that in order to ensure its global dominance, the United States must seize control of the region and its oil. Born during the energy crisis of the 1970s, and refined since then by a generation of policymakers, this approach is finding its boldest expression yet in the Bush administration—which, with its plan to invade Iraq and install a regime beholden to Washington, has moved closer than any of its predecessors to transforming the Gulf into an American protectorate (Dreyfuss, 2003, p. 41).

Dreyfuss argued that the Persian Gulf "region is crucial not simply for its share of the U.S. oil supply . . . but because it would allow the United States to maintain a lock on the world's energy lifeline and potentially deny access to its global competitors" (Dreyfuss, 2003, p. 41). Iraq is a "strategic prize of unparalleled importance" (Dreyfuss, 2003, p. 41). Iraqi oil is very "accessible and, at less than $1.50 a barrel, some of the cheapest in the world to produce" (Dreyfuss, 2003, p. 41).

Although oil is profitable in the region, the administration is after much more. According to Michael Klare, "controlling Iraq is about oil as power, rather than oil as fuel" (Dreyfuss, 2003, p. 41). Furthermore, Klare states, "control over the Persian Gulf translates into control over Europe, Japan, and China. It's having our hand on the *spigot*" (Dreyfuss, 2003, p. 41). Thus, global hegemony becomes a key to U.S. national security, allows U.S. maintenance of the world's energy lifeline, and potentially denies access to U.S. global competitors (Dreyfuss, 2003).

Dreyfuss explained how the Bush administration has been building on various steps taken by military and policy planners over the years. The establishment of a Rapid Deployment Force, the development of a Central Command, the Persian Gulf War, and the war in Afghanistan boosted America's strength in the region. The removal of Saddam Hussein in Iraq "could be the final piece of the puzzle, cementing an *American imperial presence*" (Dreyfuss, 2003, p. 43). Some individuals who have contributed to the process included neoconservatives such as Robert Kagan, William Kristol, and former C.I.A. director James Woolsey. Among the group's *affiliates* in the Bush administration were Dick Cheney, Donald Rumsfeld, Paul Wolfowitz, and others.

Dreyfuss's claims are further *bolstered* by an investigative report by Jim Vallette, Steve Kretzmann, and Daphne Wysham (2003). The authors reported that "regime change is simply the latest and most aggressive posture the U.S. has assumed in an effort to ensure the long-term availability of Iraqi oil for U.S. industry and consumers—an effort that dates back

40 years to a CIA-aided *coup*" (Vallette, Kretzmann, & Wysham, 2003). The study demonstrated that the Bechtel Corporation and the Reagan administration were involved in an attempt to secure Iraqi oil exports and establishing an oil pipeline from Iraq to Jordan. Moreover, the Reagan administration ignored the gassing of Iranians by Saddam Hussein's regime while they pursued Iraqi oil. The claim from the Bush administration that oil was not the issue, but instead weapons of mass destruction, is *disputed* in this brief that examined never-before-published government and corporate memoranda, letters, and telegrams.

Some of the key findings of the study showed that under President Reagan's administration, Secretary of State George Shultz, on behalf of his former company, Bechtel, "orchestrated initial discussions with Iraq" (Vallette, Kretzmann, & Wysham, 2003), over the opening of an oil pipeline from Iraq to Jordan. Second, on December 1983, Donald Rumsfeld, as a special Middle East envoy appointed by President Reagan, met with Saddam Hussein to talk about the oil pipeline and help Iraq to increase its oil exports and later met with Iraqi Deputy Prime Minister Tariq Aziz on March 26, 1984, on "the same day that a U.N. panel unanimously concluded that Iraq used chemical weapons on Iranian troops" (Vallette et al., 2003). Third, the U.S. State Department desk officer for Iraq "pressured U.S. Export-Import Bank to initiate short-term loans for the Iraq" (Vallette et al., 2003) pipeline project. Fourth, "the U.S. Export-Import Bank and U.S. Overseas Private Investment Corporation . . . was pressured by the Reagan administration" (Vallette et al., 2003), and Bechtel lobbyists to provide "over $500 million" to the pipeline project. Fifth, two years after Donald Rumsfeld pitched the plan, Saddam Hussein issued a "*terse* rejection" on the grounds that the proposal did "not meet the specific requirements of the project," and did not satisfy their objectives. Last, "many of the same officials . . . involved in the pipeline project have orchestrated the Bush/Cheney initiative against Iraq" (Vallette et al., 2003).

The study pointed out that Bechtel's failed pipeline *spawned* an independent council investigation that led to Attorney General Edwin Meese's resignation. "Most importantly, Iraq's refusal to approve the *lucrative* project for Bechtel signaled a turn in U.S.-Iraqi relations. Many of the project's promoters became architects of the present Bush-Cheney campaign against Iraq" (Vallette et al., 2003). Key players who were identified in the study included Donald Rumsfeld, Edwin Meese, George Shultz, James Schlesinger, Robert McFarlane, Lawrence Eagleburger, and Judge William Clark.

Another major U.S. corporation involved in Iraq is Halliburton, which is a Fortune 500 construction corporation that works primarily for the oil industry (Chatterjee, 2003b). Vice President Dick Cheney, a former CEO of the corporation with *deferred compensation* of $1 million a year, has been accused of conflict of interest charges because Halliburton "has a key position as a Pentagon contractor to assess Iraq's oil infrastructure in the war's aftermath" (Fineman, 2003, p. A3). Halliburton already has profited from the Iraq war when thousands of its employees worked alongside U.S. troops in Kuwait and Turkey under a package deal worth close to a billion dollars (Chatterjee, 2003a). When the Bush administration revealed that it was preparing to award contracts valued around $900,000 to rebuild a postwar Iraq, Halliburton was listed among five domestic construction companies to bid on the main contract (King, 2003, pp. A3, A6). Other corporations invited to bid were Bechtel, Flour, Louis Berger, and Parsons (King, 2003, p. A6). Only American corporations were invited to bid.

The first major contract to rebuild Iraq was awarded to the Stevedoring Service of America, which "will develop plans to reopen and operate Umm al Qasr, Iraq's only deepwater port and a critical entry point" (Fineman, 2003, p. A3). The U.S. government announced on April 17, 2003, that it selected Bechtel to receive a $680 million contract to oversee the rebuilding of Iraq (Streitfeld & Fineman, 2003, p. A1). However, government officials said that the total would be "far higher" (Streitfeld & Fineman, 2003, p. A1).

With oil as an essential reason for war, Bush's public declarations that a new government in Iraq would serve as an inspiring example of freedom and democracy for other nations in the region cannot be taken seriously. A classified State Department report, leaked to the *Los Angeles Times* before the war, expressed doubt that installing a new government in Iraq would spread democracy to the rest of the region (Miller, 2003a). This so-called "domino theory" of democracy was not considered credible in the report that was produced by the State Department's Bureau of Intelligence and Research (Miller, 2003a). The report said, "economic and social problems are likely to undermine basic stability in the region for years, let alone prospects for democratic reform" (Miller, 2003a, p. A1). The United States has had a very poor record of spreading democracy in the world (Palast, 2002).

Recent behavior of the Bush administration in Iraq does not *resonate* with democracy. Iraqis will be turning on their television sets and see "Dan Rather, Tom Brokaw, Peter Jennings, Jim Leher, and Brit Hume" delivering their evening news (Getlin, 2003, p. A3). It is part of an "ambitious effort that White House officials say will show Iraq what a free press looks like in a democracy" (Getlin, 2003, p. A3). With funding by the U.S. government it will feature "CBS, NBC, ABC, PBS, and Fox News" with a goal of providing 24-hours-a-day broadcasts (Getlin, 2003, p. A3).

"The U.S. government is structuring Iraq's vast oil industry much like a corporation, with a chief executive and a management team *vetted* by American officials who would answer to a multinational board of advisers . . . The chief executive would be performing virtually the same role as the former oil minister" (Warren, Cummins, & Bahree, 2003, p. A3). Phillip J. Carroll, former chief executive of Shell Oil Co., will be the chairman of the board, and with other officials would be counted on to "run the nuts and bolts of the oil operations" (Warren, Cummins, & Bahree, 2003, p. A3).

In addition, the Bush administration hired a company to develop new curriculum in the Iraq school system. Creative Associates received a $2 million contract to remake Iraq's primary and secondary schools and to get more than 4 million students back in class by the fall of 2003 (Trounson & Fineman, 2003). "The total amount of the award is expected to reach as high as $62.6 million for the first year alone" (Trounson & Fineman, 2003, p. A10). The contract does not include the production and delivery of new textbooks, which will be awarded in a later contract, and a separate award will be made for the reconstruction of damaged schools since the 1991 war with the United States (Trounson & Fineman, 2003).

These recent developments in Iraq do not include the participation of the "liberated" Iraqi masses. A lack of basic services and security is creating Iraqi *disillusionment* with the U.S. occupation. Hunger, crime, diseases, contaminated water, and a rise of *religious fundamentalism* has contributed to discontent. Since the declaration of U.S. victory, well over forty Americans have died as a result of Iraqi resistance. The departure of some American troops in Iraq is being delayed. Congressional investigations are being held on the weapons of mass destruction claim of the Bush administration. Amnesty International in its 2003 report said, "Governments have spent billions to strengthen national security and the 'war on terror.' Yet for millions of people, the real sources of insecurity are corruption, repression, discrimination, extreme poverty and preventable diseases" (Amnesty International, 2003).

Bush's "war on terrorism" must be viewed more critically in the Chicana/o community. Although Bush's reaction to the attacks on the United States and his wars in Afghanistan and Iraq created a majority of American support, which included the Chicana/o community, the "war on terrorism" has been problematic from the beginning to the present. Using the fear of weapons of mass destruction, the Bush administration successfully masked an essential reason we went to war. Oil is a more *plausible* reason for going to war as outlined in this essay.

Chicanas/os historically and contemporarily have struggled for liberation in the United States (Acuña, 2000). Despite years of racial, gender, class, and sexual orientation discrimination, Chicanas/os have served their country well in times of war. They have been the largest group of ethnic minorities to receive the Congressional Medal of Honor. In the war in Iraq, they have also served and sacrificed. Unfortunately, the "war on terrorism" puts the Chicana/o community again in a position of demonstrating blind loyalty and patriotism to the American flag. Thinking critically in the Chicana/o community about the "war on terrorism" should be a virtue, not a vice.

References

Acuña, R. (2000). *Occupied America: A history of Chicanos* (4th ed.). New York: Longman.

Amnesty International. (2003). *Amnesty International Report* 2003. March 28, 2003. Retrieved June 19, 2003, from *http://web.amnesty.org/web/web.nsf/print/index-eng*

Bush, W. (2001a). The White House. 11 September 2001. Retrieved July 27, 2003, from *http://www.whitehouse.gov/news/releases/2001/109/20010911-16.html*

———. (2001b). The White House. 12 September 2001. Retrieved July 27, 2003, from *http://www.whitehouse.gov/news/releases/2001/09/20010912-4.html*

———. (2003a). The White House. 28 January 2003. Retrieved June 15, 2003, from *http://www.whitehouse.gov/news/releases/2003/01/20030128/19.html*

———. (2003b). The White House. 17 March 2003. Retrieved March 18, 2003, from *http://www.whitehouse.gov/news/releases/2003/03/20030317-7.html*

Chatterjee, P. (2003a). Cheney's former company profits from supporting troops. *CorpWatch.* 20 March 2003. Retrieved March 27, 2003, from *http://www.corpwatch.org/issues/PID.jsp?articleid=6008*

———. (2003b). "Cheney's close ties to brown and root." *CorpWatch.* 20 March 2003. Retrieved March 27, 2003, from *http://www.corpwatch.org/issues/PID.jsp?articleid=6028*

"Congressional Record: September 14, 2001 (House) p. H 5638." Federation of American Scientists. 14 September 2001. Retrieved June 19, 2003, from *http://www.fas.org/irp/threat/useofforce.htm*

Corbin, M. (2002). The Bush National Security Strategy: A first step. Center for Defense Information. 26 September 2002. Retrieved October 7, 2002, from *http:www.cdi.org/national-security-strategy/washington.cfm*

Disarming Iraq: The case against Saddam Hussein. (2002). *Congressional Digest, 81*(10).

Dreyfuss, R. (2003, April). The thirty-year itch. *Mother Jones,* pp. 40–45.

Farley, M. (2003, June 6). Blix's final words to Security Council on Iraq are of Caution. *Los Angeles Times,* p. A11.

Fineman, M. (2003, March 25). First major contract to rebuild Iraq awarded. *Los Angeles Times,* p. A3.

Getlin, J. (2003, April 15). U.S. nightly news shows to make their Iraqi television debut. *Los Angeles Times,* p. A3.

Gitlin, T. (2003). America's age of empire: The Bush doctrine." *Mother Jones.* February 2003. Retrieved February 18, 2003, from *http:bsd.mojones.com/commentary/columns/2003/02/ma_205_01.html*

Grogger, J., & Trejo, S. J. (2002). *Fall behind or moving up? The intergenerational progress of Mexican Americans.* San Francisco: Public Policy Institute of California.

King, Jr., N. (2003, March 10). U.S. prepares for rebuilding of Iraq. *Wall Street Journal,* pp. A3, A6.

Miller, G. (2003a, March 14). Democracy domino theory "not credible." *Los Angeles Times,* pp. A1, A12.

———. (2003b, June 10). Bush tempers talk of weapons. *Los Angeles Times,* pp. A1, A4.

Palast, G. (2002). *The best democracy money can buy: An investigative reporter exposes the truth about globalization, corporate cons, and high finance.* London: Pluto Press.

Post–9/11 Survey. (2000). Institute for Justice and Journalism. 5 September 2002. Retrieved September 9, 2002, from *http://.ascweb.usc.edu/news.php?storyID=9*

Reed, D., & Cheng, J. (2003). *Racial and ethnic wage aps in the California labor market.* San Francisco: Public Policy Institute of California.

Streitfeld, D., & Fineman, M. (2003, April 18). Bechtel Lands Iraq Contract. *Los Angeles Times,* pp. A1, A17.

Text of U.N. Resolution on Iraq. (2002). CNN. 8 November 2002. Retrieved November 8, 2002, from *http://www.CNN.com/2002/US/11/08resolution.text/index.html*

Trounson, R., & Fineman, M. (2003, April 15). Politically Neutral School Plans. *Los Angeles Times,* p. A10.

Vallette, J., Kretzmann, S., & Wysham, D. (2003). Crude vision: How oil interests obscured U.S. government focus on chemical weapons use by Saddam Hussein. Institute for Policy Studies. 24 March 2003. Retrieved June 11, 2003, from *http://www.ips-dc.org/*

Vidal, Gore. (2002). *Dreaming war: Blood for oil and the Cheney-Bush junta.* New York: Thunder's Mouth Press.

Warren, S., Cummins, C., & Bahree, B. (2003, April 25). For Iraqi oil, a U.S. corporate mold. *Wall Street Journal,* pp. A3, A6.

What We Think. CNN/TIME Poll. (2002, September 9). *Time,* p. 18.

Wolfowitz comments revive doubts over Iraq's WMD. (2003, May 30). *USA Today.* Retrieved June 11, 2003, from *http://www.usatoday.com/news/world/iraq/2003-05-30-wolfowitz-iraq_x.htm*

Writing Prompts

1. Explain in one or two sentences the author's premise (thesis) in this essay.

2. Rodríguez states that Bush and members of his administration began to build a case against Iraq through media outlets. Was this propaganda or fact? Explain your answer(s).

3. Why does the author lay out a series of public statements made by President Bush and other officials at the beginning of the essay? What is the writer's intention?

4. Define the Iraq Liberation Act? How did President Bush use this?

5. What is the difference between "preemptive" attacks and preventive ones?

6. Rodríguez introduces another argument for war with Iraq suggested by writer Robert Dreyfuss. Re-read that section and explain the rational Dreyfuss offers.

7. According to a study by Jim Vallette and others, large U.S. corporations like Bechtel and Halliburton were companies that had "special interests" in Iraq. Give one or two examples of Vallette's report.

8. According to Rodríguez, Bush's claim that he wanted to establish "a free and democratic Iraq" "cannot be taken seriously." Following the writer's line of thinking, why is Bush's statement hard to believe?

9. The Bush administration gave a U.S. company (Creative Associates), a contract to introduce new courses in the Iraqi school system. What are the implications of classes being planned and introduced by Creative Associates?

10. Rodríguez wrote his article because he wanted the Chicano/a community to critically examine "the big picture" in Iraq so that the people do not accept U.S. government policies with "blind" loyalty. Briefly summarize your reaction to the essay (pro or con).

Words to Learn

"September 11, 2001: The Death of a Promise"

palpable—obvious (in this case, if you were there, you could feel the possibilities)

invigorated—given new strength

amplifying—emphasizing

portentous—indicating the possibility of future danger

override—give less importance to the issues of the conference

underscored—made even more important

beset—troubled

stranglehold—absolute control by the Democrats

fledgling—new

legitimacy—accepted as lawful or having the right to govern

confines—the limits of his own party

amity—friendship

tumultuous—violent

cataclysms—terrible events

famine—extreme lack of food

manifold—many

sustenance—enough nourishment to survive

intermingling—mixing of people

myriad—countless

swath—a line

sparse—not crowded, populations settled with wide spaces between them

surge—sudden growth

remittances—money sent home to Mexico by immigrants

conflicted—indicating a troubling lack of agreement

vulnerable—weak (in this case, hills that break away in landslides in heavy rain)

amnestied—forgiven for being undocumented and given the chance to be a legal immigrant

globalization—the new worldwide economic system of trade and investment among nations

efficiency—to produce with a minimum of waste and effort

vigilante—in this case unlawful armed groups

pollitos—The Mexican term for the immigrants under the protection of the border crossing guides called "coyotes"

ostensibly—the stated reason (in this case, the excuse given)

enmeshed—tangled up

squabbling—arguing

immolated—burned up

"The Aftermath of 911 and Its Impact on the Chicana/o Community"

fallacious reasoning—bad reasoning that suppresses relevant evidence, contains a questionable premise, or is invalid

imminent—likely to occur at any moment

wage gaps—differences in money paid or received for work or services

obfuscated—to confuse or to darken as if to make difficult to understand

proclamation—to announce officially or formally

operational capability—the ability to exert force or influence

diplomatic process—a systematic series of actions employing tact and conciliation especially in situation of stress

dilemma—situation requiring a choice between equally undesirable alternatives

global political hegemony—leadership or domination of one nation over others in a world context

international coalition—a political alliance among nations

North Atlantic Treaty Organization (NATO)—organization established under the North Atlantic Treaty of 1949 to create a single unified defense force to safeguard the security of the North Atlantic area

perpetrators—to carry out; to commit

infrastructure—basic framework of a system or organization

culminated—to reach the highest point or climatic stage

cornerstone—something that is essential or basic

"axis of evil"—President Bush's characterization of Iraq, Iran, and North Korea as a political threat to the United States and the world

allies—having or being in close association with nations in a united manner

preemptive—seizing of an initiative such as attacking first to prevent the possibility of a future threat or attack

peril—grave risk; jeopardy

unanimously—being in or showing complete agreement

reiterated—to say or do again or repeatedly

mobilized—to assemble and organize for action or use, such as war or anti-war

plausible—credible; believable

crosshairs—one of the fine wire or threads in the focus of the eyepiece of an optical instrument used as a reference line in the field or for marking the instrumental axis

protectorate—a weak state or territory that is protected and controlled by a stronger state

spigot—a plug for stopping the vent of a cask; a faucet

American imperial presence—American extension of rule or authority over other nations

affiliates—to bring into close association or connection

bolstered—to support with

coup—a successful, unexpected act, or as in coup d'etat, a sudden overthrow of a government by force

disputed—to argue against

terse—curt; brusque

spawned—to bring forth; produce

lucrative—profitable; moneymaking

deferred compensation—delayed monetary payment

resonate—to relate harmoniously

vetted—to subject to expert appraisal or correction

disillusionment—to free from or deprive of illusion, idealism

religious fundamentalism—movement or point of view characterized by a return to fundamental principles, by rigid adherence to those principles, and by intolerance of other views and opposition to secularism

plausible—credible; believable

Addiction: Fiction, Fact, and Recovery

Chapter 4—Anticipation Guide

Directions: Rate each statement below according to the following:

4—Strongly Agree   *3—Agree*   *2—Disagree*   *1—Strongly Disagree*

1. Chicanos/as have more problems with alcohol and drugs than other people.

2. Weak people are alcoholics.

3. Alcoholism is a disease.

4. If people "party" with alcohol and drugs every weekend, they have an addiction problem.

5. Belief in a higher power will save people from addiction.

6. Drug and alcohol abuse is genetic.

7. If one parent is an alcoholic, more than likely one or more of the children will be alcoholics.

8. Alcoholism is an individual dilemma and not a family problem.

9. Psychological abuse leads to addiction.

10. A person who has had more than two drinks can safely drive home from a party.

The Playboy Lounge

Diana Marie Delgado

Outside the bar's back door,
a dead boy is found in Friday's dumpster
of trash. He's buried in a sea of moss
green bottles of beer, cigarette butts,
wilted napkins kissed with lipstick
and grease. When the police find him,
one of his arms is poking through
the garbage, a palm turned towards the sky,
his fingers unfurled the way dahlias do,
when they open their petals
and try and cup the light.

Writing Activities

1. Write a poem about someone you know who takes drugs or drinks. Consider that you would like to send the poem to this person. Be creative, candid, and helpful.

2. Write a poem about something the title of the poem suggests.

Myths and Facts about Alcohol Abuse:
A Latino Cultural Perspective

Juana Mora

Myth 1

If my father can "handle" his beer, drinking more than anyone else at family pachangas, and can still function, it means he is a "real strong, macho" man.

Fact

It probably means he is biologically predisposed to developing a physical and psychological dependence on alcohol and later as his dependence increases, he will not be able to have as much control over his drinking.

Myth 2

If someone in my family is an alcoholic, I should not tell anyone because that would hurt my mother, mi abuelita, and all the extended family. Mi abuelita tells me that all that person needs from me is love, patience and that I should pray to the virgin.

Fact

The longer you keep this a secret, the sicker (more alcohol dependent) the person will get. Share your concerns with someone as soon as possible.

Myth 3

If I drink and then have sex with my boyfriend, it is not my responsibility because I was too high to know what I was doing.

Fact

If you are not ready to have sex, don't drink and place yourself in a situation where it is likely that you will have sex. You are responsible for your choice to drink or to have sex.

Myth 4

If my husband or boyfriend gets a little aggressive with me from time to time, it is because he has been drinking. It wasn't him; it was the alcohol.

Fact

If your partner exhibits any signs of violence towards you, your children, or even pets, you need to seek help immediately. Alcohol abuse is associated with most incidences of domestic violence, but it is not an excuse for violent behavior.

Myth 5

If a young Chicano male gets stopped for drinking and driving, it is an example of "racial profiling" and police brutality against our community.

Fact

If a young Chicano male gets stopped for drinking and driving, it is because he was probably drinking and driving. An arrest for drinking and driving is a signal that this person is becoming alcohol dependent.

Targeting Hispanics

Bruce Maxwell and Michael Jacobson

For years, alcohol and tobacco companies have targeted Hispanics with major advertising campaigns. "They are some of the bigger players in this area," said Ed Fitch, a managing editor at *Advertising Age* who specializes in reporting about Hispanic marketing.

"They're smart marketers, and they're always quick to spot an opportunity," Fitch said. "Regardless of what you think of them, they sure know how to sell products."[1]

Indeed they do. Today, the Hispanic community is paying the price for the marketing *savvy* of the alcohol and tobacco companies with increased levels of drinking and smoking. The increases are particularly apparent among Hispanic women, who have been specially targeted by the alcohol and tobacco companies because of their traditionally low rates of drinking and smoking, and young people.

Officials of the alcohol and tobacco industries *vehemently* deny they've targeted Hispanics. "Anti-smoking groups make this allegation (about targeting) as one of the rounds of ammunition they try to come up with in terms of looking for ad-ban legislation or ad-restriction legislation," said Gary Miller, assistant to the president of the Tobacco Institute, the industry lobbying group. "Their allegation is that (companies are) trying to recruit smokers among these ranks. Now, really what it is is that through just typical marketing research, just as with any particular product, cigarette companies have found that these people, Blacks and Hispanics, enjoy smoking. There's a large percentage of smokers in these groups, so let's get our message to them."[2]

As we shall see, the connection between the targeting of Hispanics by tobacco and alcohol companies and increased smoking and drinking seems too clear to dispute. The alcohol and tobacco companies like to claim there's no connection, that they advertise not to hook new drinkers and smokers but only to preserve their market share and to steal market share from other brands. But these industries are killing off some of their best customers, and must have new customers to survive.

The targeting of Hispanics by disease-promoting companies, including fast-food and soft-drink firms, is apparent in the annual list compiled by *Hispanic Business* of the top advertisers in Hispanic media (see Table 4-1). In 1988, four of the top six advertisers were disease-promoting companies. These included Philip Morris (cigarettes, coffee, frozen foods, Miller beer, Oscar Mayer hot dogs, Post cereals), Anheuser-Busch (beer), McDonald's (hamburgers, french fries), and Adolph Coors (beer). The soft drink companies PepsiCo and

Table 4-1. Top Advertisers in the Hispanic Market, 1988

Rank	Company	Hispanic ad spending (in millions)
1	Procter & Gamble Co.	$20.8
2	Philip Morris Cos.	13.1
3	Anheuser-Busch Co.	8.6
4	Colgate-Palmolive Co.	7.9
5	McDonald's Corp.	6.6
6	Adolph Coors Co.	5.1
7	Johnson & Johnson	4.9
8	Ford Motor Co.	4.1
9	Kraft, Inc.	3.7
10	Sears, Roebuck & Co.	3.4
15	PepsiCo Inc.	2.9
25	Coca-Cola Co.	1.6

Source: *Hispanic Business*[3]

Coca-Cola placed 15th and 25th, respectively. The biggest advertiser, Procter & Gamble, sells a wide variety of soaps, toothpastes, and such fatty foods and Pringles potato chips, Crisco shortening and oil, and Jif peanut butter.

In this chapter, we examine how the alcohol, tobacco, fast-food, and soft-drink industries have targeted advertising to Hispanics.

Alcohol

The 1960s may have been the decade for Black achievement, but the 1980s are "The Decade of the Hispanic," according to a slogan popular in the community.

One might think such a slogan was coined by a Hispanic organization. It wasn't. Instead, it was created as part of an advertising campaign by the Adolph Coors Co., a beer brewer whose relationship with Hispanics has been rocky at best. The Hispanic magazine *Nuestro* said it was "a sad irony" that the slogan was conceived by Coors "in order to sell more beer."[4]

The Coors example makes it clear that alcohol companies have no shame when it comes to trying to hook Hispanics on their products. That lack of shame is *exemplified* by an advertising campaign for Olde English "800" malt liquor, which is manufactured by the Pabst Brewing Co. Malt liquor is similar to beer, but has 10 to 50 percent more alcohol.

In the billboard version of the ad, a buxom Hispanic woman wearing a string bikini crouches on the beach next to a tiger. Super-imposed on the scene is a picture of a can of Olde English "800" malt liquor and the slogan in Spanish: "It's the Power."

In promotional materials sent to liquor retailers, the brewer says billboards featuring the "Lady and the Tiger" design are "strategically placed in ethnic neighborhoods," and radio and television ads with the same theme are being run "in all major Ethnic markets." Why would Olde English "800" appeal to ethnic people? "More emphasis on taste—its smooth, mellow taste brewed for relatively high alcohol content (important to the Ethnic market!)," according to the promotional materials.

The *cynicism* underlying the campaign is clear, as is the message in the ads relating heavy drinking to sexual conquest. However, other brewers are following Pabst's lead in targeting Hispanics with malt liquor. In March 1989, the G. Heileman Brewing Co. announced it was rolling out a dry malt brew called Colt 45 Dry, which it planned to aim at Hispanic and Black drinkers.[5]

The Olde English "800" ad campaign may be the most offensive effort aimed at Hispanics by an alcohol company, although there are many other alcohol campaigns strongly competing for that *dubious* honor.

A series of huge billboards placed in California Hispanic neighborhoods showed six bottles of Corona beer serving as "pillars" for an ornate building that could easily be a government center. "Pillars of Society," read the inscription underneath.

When one of the billboards appeared in Los Angeles County, Dr. Ebenezer Chambi, Ray Chavira, and a group of people who came primarily from the Seventh Day Adventist Church decided to take action. "We felt it was kind of like a slap in the face," said Chavira, a community activist and board member of the California Council on Alcohol Problems. "Now that they're pushing [Corona beer] a lot all over the place, they have the audacity to tell us that it's a pillar of society. What could be further from the truth?"

To protest the signs, Chambi, Chavira, and the group organized a sidewalk demonstration outside the Los Angeles County Hall of Administration and met with the Board of Supervisors' staff. Television and newspaper reporters from both the general and Spanish-language media covered their protest. The board chairman complained to a top official of Gannett Outdoor Advertising, which owned the billboard, and another supervisor wrote a letter to Gannett protesting the sign. "Within days, the Corona sign was taken down," Chavira said. Identical billboards in other parts of the state also were removed.

Chavira said there's an important lesson to be learned from the experience of his citizen's group: "Big companies and big and powerful politicians do have a conscience and they do listen, because every little bit of bad p.r. and bad publicity hurts their profits."[6]

Most of the time, though, the ads go unchallenged no matter how offensive. A series of billboards and subway posters sponsored by Glenmore Distilleries, a liquor distributor in the Northeast, exploited the use of wine in Catholic ceremony. The Spanish-language ad showed a priest and a monk gazing toward a light shining from above while holding glasses of Felipe II brandy. Translated, the copy read: "To drink it is not a sin."[7]

Marilyn Aguirre-Molina, assistant professor at the University of Medicine and Dentistry of New Jersey, said the Felipe ad was "one of the most appalling ads" she's seen in recent years. It played off the Hispanic culture's respect for the Catholic church, and Aguirre-Molina said many of the alcohol ads focus on aspects of the Hispanic culture.

"The one thing that they have focused on in the Latino market is really understanding the cultural *nuances* of family, friends, and drinking patterns, and they've really managed to capture that dynamic in their advertising," she said. "They know something about drinking patterns among Latinos. They know more about our culture than I think health service providers know."[8]

The use of cultural themes is an attempt to legitimize the use of alcohol, which is already *pervasive* in the Hispanic culture. The targeting of alcohol advertising to Hispanics "simply expands the favorable climate toward alcohol use," said M. Jean Gilbert, scholar in Hispanic alcohol studies at UCLA's Chicano Studies Research Center.[9] Many of the ads are tied into Hispanic celebrations such as Mexican Independence Day and Cinco de Mayo.[10]

Billboards advertising alcohol are *ubiquitous* in most Hispanic neighborhoods across the country. "It's obvious when you drive around the Hispanic areas of San Antonio or Los Angeles that there are more and more billboards advertising alcohol products with Hispanic faces on them," said Dr. Kyriakos Markides, professor of preventive medicine and community health at the University of Texas Medical Branch in Galveston.[11] Merrill Singer, director of research at the Hispanic Health Council in Hartford, Conn., said there are a "noticeable number" of billboards advertising alcohol in the Puerto Rican community he serves.[12]

Since the 1970s, the alcohol industry has been the second leading advertiser on billboards behind the tobacco industry, according to Scenic America, the nation's leading anti-billboard organization. The billboard industry has *saturated* low-income neighborhoods, particularly Hispanic and Black areas, with thousands of new signs advertising tobacco and alcoholic beverages. "A much higher percentage of billboards in ethnic neighborhoods advertise alcohol and liquor products compared to billboards in other areas," according to the coalition.[13]

The beer industry also advertises heavily on Spanish-language radio and television stations. "We are definitely seeing an increase in the number of beer commercials that have dancing Hispanics on TV," said Jane Garcia, executive direction of La Clinica de la Raza in

Oakland, Calif. Garcia said she's troubled by the commercials. "When you have these visions of it being such a fun time and there are no health *ramifications* to it, then it sure makes it attractive," she said.[14]

Many of the beer commercials feature Hispanic sports figures and other personalities as spokesmen. For example, an ad for Miller Lite beer showed former welterweight champ Carlos Palomino sitting in a bar surrounded by friends. "Y'know, one of the best things about coming to America was that I got to try American beers," Palomino said in the ad. "I tried them all. And the one I like best is Lite Beer from Miller."[15] Miller has also used other Hispanics such as ex-Oakland Raider Ben Davidson, an ex-bullfighter, and Paul Rodriguez, star of the ill-fated television series, "a.k.a. Pablo."[16]

One of the most popular advertising vehicles on Spanish-language television is the hit show Sabado Gigante (Giant Saturday), a *raucous* blend of music, skits, talk, and out-and-out huckstering that runs for three and a half hours each Saturday night on the Univision network. "The show is a marketer's dream," says *Business Week*. "Brands such as Coca-Cola and Coors are openly pitched during the program, their names repeated dozens of times."[17]

The show's host, don Francisco, even leads the audience in singing advertising jingles for products that sponsor the program. And the viewership numbers are unbelievable: Some 47 percent of all U.S. Hispanic households watched the show in February 1988. The Cosby Show, by comparison, was only watched by a comparatively *paltry* 27.8 percent of all U.S. households during an average week of the 1987–88 season.[18]

Until 1987, hard liquor was advertised regularly on Spanish-language television. English-language radio and television stations rarely accept ads for distilled spirits, under a longstanding voluntary agreement among broadcasters and liquor companies. However, the Spanish-language stations accepted the ads until a coalition of public health and Hispanic organizations pressured the two Spanish-language television networks to stop the practice.

Univision, the largest Spanish-language television network, stopped accepting ads for hard liquor in late 1987, and Telemundo dropped most of its ads as of January 1, 1989 (it said it had a commitment to run Bailey's Irish Cream ads in 1989).[19] Organizations involved in the campaign to get the liquor ads pulled included the Center for Science in the Public Interest, California state PTA leaders, National Council on Alcoholism, Doctors Ought to Care (DOC), Latino Caucus of the American Public Health Association, LULAC Foundation, Community Service Organization of California, El Congreso Nacional de Asuntos Colegiales, and National Coalition o f Hispanic Health and Human Services Organizations (COSSMHO).

The Spanish-language television stations have been able to do without the modest amount of lost advertising, but some observers believe that some Hispanic newspapers and magazines would shrink in size, or even fold, without advertising from the alcohol and tobacco industries. "Without these two core advertising groups, their margin of profit would be cut pretty slim, and I think you would probably see some of these publication go out of business," said Ed Fitch, the *Advertising Age* editor who specializes in Hispanic marketing.[20]

Jerry Apodaca, the former publisher of *Hispanic* magazine, agreed with Fitch. "If we had done away with the tobacco and beer ads, we'd have been in serious trouble," he said.[21]

In 1988, the National Association of Hispanic Publications gave Philip Morris (Marlboro cigarettes, Miller beer) its company-of-the-year award, showing once again the close link between Hispanic publications and the alcohol and tobacco industries.

That link is apparent in reading most Hispanic publications. For example, the March 1989 issues of *Hispanic*—one of the leading magazines for Hispanics—featured a full-page article on the creation of a world-record, 119,000-person conga line at Miami's Calle Ocho Festival in March 1988. The article, while a year out of date, prominently featured comments from Scott Fortini, identified as "a representative of Guinness Stout." He apparently was quoted because the conga line was going to be listed in *The Guinness Book of World Records*. But a major section of the article was devoted to helping Fortini push Guinness Stout:

> *The Hispanic community treasures a long relationship with foreign beers, said Fortini. "Guinness has a very loyal Latin following," he said. "The Cuban and Latin market has traditionally very loyal Guinness drinkers (sic)." Foreign beers such as Guiness have always been widely available in the homelands of many Hispanics. Thus, they still drink it in the United States, because their parents drank it, and they like "prestigious" brands, Fortini said. "They're very image-conscious."[22]*

Within less than 30 pages, readers came across a full-page ad for Guinness Stout to reinforce the article's message. The sensual ad featured a bare-chested Hispanic man being stroked by a Hispanic woman whose lacy nightgown had fallen from her shoulder, exposing much of her right breast. The man faced the camera directly, while the woman's face was hidden by his head. This *subservience* plays on the cultural dominance of Hispanic males.

According to Juana Mora, research analyst at the Los Angeles County Office of Alcohol Programs, "In the case of alcohol advertising to Latinos, there is a deliberate practice of influencing beliefs and behaviors by appealing to 'cultural nostalgia'—traditions, images, and norms that many of us grew up with."

In the same issue, a four-page article previewed a Latin American art show that was about to begin a national tour. The tour sponsor was Philip Morris, the nation's top tobacco company and number two brewer. According to the article, Philip Morris supported the exhibition with a $350,000 grant, "as well as with marketing and public relations assistance to reach out to the Hispanic community." Part of that "marketing" included a full color, two-page ad in the center of the magazine which prominently listed all the Philip Morris *sub-sidiaries* sponsoring the tour.

Readers found yet another positive plug for Philip Morris on the magazine's last page. In a full-page article titled "Our Mother Tongue," Frank Gomez, director of public affairs programs for Philip Morris, *decried* the impact of Anglicisms on the Spanish language. "If indeed, Spanish is so valuable, let us defend it, cherish it, nurture it, treat it as we would our mother," Gomez concluded. "As we prepare to commemorate the *Quincentenary* in 1992, we must protect our Spanish language, to use it as best we can and to encourage others to use it correctly." Not exactly controversial stuff, but a great piece of free public relations for Philip Morris.

Summing up health experts' concerns, Juana Mora said, "The problem with alcohol advertising is that it distorts the true impact of excessive and high-risk consumption on health. These powerful advertising campaigns totally undermine the educational efforts of families, school, and non-profit organizations."

Notes

1. Telephone interview, March 13, 1989.

2. Telephone interview, March 14, 1989.

3. D. Carlos Balkan, "The Hispanic Market's Leading Indicators," *Hispanic Business,* December 1988, p. 26.

4. "Alcoholism—Severe Health Problem for Latinos," *Nuestro,* March 1982, p. 35.

5. "Heileman Unveils a Dry Malt Brew, Called Colt 45 Dry," *The Wall Street Journal,* March 29, 1989, p. B6.

6. Telephone interview, Feb. 27, 1989.

7. Bruce Nash and Allan Zullo, *The Mis-Fortune 500* (Pocket), p. 88.

8. Telephone interview, March 12, 1989.

9. Telephone interview, Feb. 28, 1989.

10. "Alcohol Promotions Target Hispanics," *Prevention File*, Winter 1989, p. 11.

11. Telephone interview, March 8, 1989.

12. Telephone interview, March 15, 1989.

13. Coalition for Scenic Beauty (now Scenic America), "Fact Sheet: Alcohol and Tobacco Advertising on Billboards," undated (Washington, D.C.).

14. Telephone interview, March 1, 1989.

15. Marc Kornblatt, "Targeting the Hispanic Market," *Liquor Store*, June 1985, p. 22.

16. Ibid., p. 25.

17. Pete Engardio, "Fast Times on Avenida Madison," *Business Week*, June 6, 1988.

18. "Spanish-Language TV Blooms," *The Miami Herald*, July 11, 1988.

19. Letter from Donald G. Raider, chief operating officer, Telemundo Group Inc., June 2, 1989.

20. (to come)

21. (to come)

22. "Can You Conga?" *Hispanic*, March 1989, p. 20.

Writing Prompts

1. Look up the definition of the word "subliminal." How does it apply to the message in the article?

2. Imagine a woman wearing a bikini and standing holding a can of beer in a liquor advertisement. Explain the intention the image conveys in this ad.

3. The article argues that alcohol companies specifically target "Hispanics" in their ad campaigns. Describe what attracts this group to purchase alcohol based on the influence of the ads, according to Maxwell and Jacobson.

4. Create two slogans for alcohol advertising that suggest moderate drinking.

5. Take notice of three alcohol ads in your neighborhood or in a magazine. Write a brief description of each. Then analyze and explain any subliminal and overt messages "hidden" in the ad.

An Interview with Elena Contreras

Interviewer*: To begin with, can you tell me how you define substance abuse?

Elena: Abuse is measured by the quantity and frequency of alcohol use. For example, some-one who drinks more than five drinks per sitting, more than twice a week, is considered to be a heavy drinker. Addiction or physical dependence versus "abuse" is measured or diagnosed through physical symptoms such as withdrawal symptoms, physical tolerance, and other physical measures.

Interviewer: Would you say that alcohol addiction and abuse are different?

Elena: Some people feel that they are similar psychological processes. They are different in terms of how quickly individuals experience physical dependence symptoms and psy-chological symptoms. For example, some people can abuse alcohol or drugs for periods of their lives and then change their lives with no lasting effects of the abuse. However, when someone is addicted (physically and psychologically), there is a need for medical and therapeutic intervention to help the person with the addiction.

Interviewer: Are you opposed to drinking entirely?

Elena: No, of course not. There are people who can drink recreationally and responsibly; then there are people who because of circumstances in their lives or family history, will move from that to become irresponsible and ultimately physically and psychologically addicted.

Interviewer: I've always wanted to understand the role of the spouse who is married to an alcoholic. Do you think the spouse is a victim?

Elena: The spouse is an enabler. But it's a family problem also. If a spouse is not ready to confront his or her partner's alcohol problem, and keeps it a secret, then the one who is the nondrinker is the enabler. Now once the nonalcoholic goes outside the family sys-tem for help, then he or she is no longer an enabler.

Interviewer: One of the reasons I was interested in talking with you was because you too were an enabler at one time, right?

Elena: For a long time I was a terrible enabler. I made excuses for him.

Interviewer: Was this your husband?

---

*Interviewer: R. Orona-Cordova

Elena: He was my boyfriend for many years, and then we got married.

Interviewer: Did you know he was an alcoholic from the beginning?

Elena: I didn't for a long time. I met him when I was young and just starting college. He was my first really serious, long-term relationship. It was really hard to realize, to admit that he had a problem with alcohol because it was during those college years when everyone was drinking and smoking pot. Now that I look back at it, I remember he would wake up and smoke weed. He was older than I and a leader on campus. People looked up to him, and I did too. I didn't see that his alcohol and weed smoking, at the time, was a problem. I mean, everyone was doing it. I remember when we went out on dates he was always high on something. I realize now he was a real awful danger and risk. I was in the car with him many times when he drove in an intoxicated state.

Interviewer: At what point did you recognize he had a problem?

Elena: Not until we got married six years after we started going together. Before that I was still making excuses for him; for example, I think the first year or second year we were together he got arrested for drinking. I just made excuses, and I'd say, "Poor guy. He has to spend time in jail." At the time, I didn't feel his drinking affected me negatively. He was never mean to me, nor did he hurt me physically or anything like that.

Interviewer: How long were you married?

Elena: Just two years. We lived together for all those early years. The marriage was an attempt to save the relationship.

Interviewer: Sometimes people get married to get a divorce.

Elena: I know. I often ask myself why I married an alcoholic, since my father's not an alcoholic. I didn't grow up with alcoholism in my family, but there were a lot of dependency issues I had to face. I come from a large, traditional family, and I was living far away from home. My father was upset I went away to school, and I needed someone to help me with that process, and my husband did. He was dependable when he wasn't drinking and he took care of me really well. For many years I was dependent on him; then after we got married, I started to become more liberated.

Interviewer: Can you give me an example?

Elena: We were living in married student housing when we were graduate students. It was a two-bedroom apartment and he was the only one who had an office in the house. That was symbolic. I finally put my foot down and told him that I needed an office too, and that I couldn't progress in my graduate work unless I had an office. What I decided to do was move us into the living room where we had a sleeper couch. I turned our bedroom into my office.

Interviewer: Was this the first time you started taking care of yourself?

Elena: It was frightening for him that I was becoming independent. He was dependent on alcohol and I was dependent on him. But this dynamic started to change slowly. The worst part is that before we got married I became very isolated from my women friends; that's another part of the alcoholic or abusive relationship. Then he and I, as a couple, became isolated from other people.

Interviewer: He was never physically abusive?

Elena: It got to the point where he could've been. He was starting to have a lot of mood swings because of his many years of drinking. I was not happy anymore, and I started thinking about leaving. I wasn't strong enough at the time, and he sensed that I wanted to leave.

Interviewer: How did you manage to finally break away from him and end the relationship?

Elena: Since I was already questioning the relationship and the fact that he had these mood swings I was ready because of how unhappy I was; and then something happened. We went to a friend's wedding and he got very drunk. We never had arguments. That evening he got very jealous. He took his shoe off and threw it at me. I realized that night I had to leave the relationship. It could have hurt. It could have physically hurt me. I knew then that that was the beginning of a potentially violent relationship and I decided that night I had to leave. It took me another year after that to actually leave the relationship because I had to deal with my own dependency fears of being alone, and starting my life all over again. That night was a big night—I saw a big problem.

Interviewer: Did anyone see him throw the shoe at you?

Elena: No, but everyone else saw how drunk he was. After that night, I started talking to him about getting help through Alcoholics Anonymous (AA), but he refused to go to a meeting. We tried marriage counseling on campus, but he was so smart he outsmarted the therapist.

Interviewer: Did you continue to see a therapist on your own?

Elena: I went to an Al-Anon meeting. I walked in and there were only wealthy, white women in tennis outfits; I felt out of place. I thought to myself, "What do other Mexicanas do?"

Interviewer: How long did you attend these meetings?

Elena: I kept going for about a couple of months. I picked up some skills and it helped. I started reconnecting with my friends, my women friends, and that was really helpful in making the decision to leave the relationship. I was missing my family, also. I wanted to get back home.

Interviewer: When did you finally leave?

Elena: I had an opportunity to do research at another university in my hometown. I got a fellowship, so I had a legitimate reason to leave my husband. He had to stay behind and finish his graduate work. We didn't talk about it as a separation, and I didn't tell my family that we were separated. Then when I moved away, I saw myself more as a single person than a married one. I started counseling after I left.

Interviewer: Would you say you were naïve, and then as you educated yourself, you grew-up and, therefore, away from this dependent relationship?

Elena: Absolutely, absolutely. It gave me a lot of strength and empowerment, for example, once I got my office it was very symbolic. I started doing very well. I actually finished my dissertation before he did. That did not make him happy. The feminist movement was strong at the time, and I didn't really see him being supportive of my self-empowerment and advancement.

Interviewer: So all those years you were the enabler?

Elena: Yes, for the first eight years of our relationship.

Interviewer: Let me shift the focus here. What are some "markers" to look for to determine if a person has an alcohol or drug problem?

Elena: Drinking and driving arrests are "markers." Studies tell you this. Also, drinking or smoking weed early in the morning is a marker, a sign that there is a problem; also, drinking and driving arrests, and relationship problems. These are definitely symptoms.

Interviewer: What about anger and rage?

Elena: Not all alcoholics have anger and rage. Some are passive drinkers. So that's not really a symptom. Blackouts. My husband would blackout at parties. That's a symptom. There were so many clues, but I was in denial. It was that wedding reception. That was it. When he threw that shoe at me, it woke me up. It could have turned out worse. I feared that could be the beginning of physical abuse, and I wasn't going to stand for that.

Writing Prompts

1. Why did Elena remain in this relationship so long?

2. How do you define abuse? How does Elena define it?

3. What symptoms or "markers" indicate and "announce" a person has a problem with alcohol or drugs?

4. Did Elena give up her role as an enabler as she became more educated; or did her decision to end the marriage depend on her "natural instincts"? Explain.

5. What symbolic statement did Elena make when she set up her own office in the bedroom she shared with her husband?

Second Chance: An Interview with Dora Daniels

Interviewer*: Can you tell me why you started using drugs?

Dora: There is only one reason I started drinking alcohol and taking drugs and that was because I wanted to escape reality, and because life was "mean." People were mean and I turned to alcohol and drugs to run away from the pressures of life. People never protected me. I always felt like I was alone, by myself.

Interviewer: Where were your parents?

Dora: My mother worked a lot and spent time with her boyfriends. She put her boyfriends first. My father lived in another state because my parents were divorced. I remember I used to cry for a father. My dad was nice to me when I was a child and before my parents were divorced, so I missed him. My mother also didn't have a father or mother to protect her when she was young. That's probably why she didn't protect me.

Interviewer: What do you mean when you say your mother didn't protect you? Didn't you live with her?

Dora: I lived with her but she was never there for me; when I told her things she never believed me, or never did anything about it. For instance, my brother was mean to me. He would beat me up—one time because I accidentally dropped a TV on his toe. I lived with a lot of criticism. My brother always told me I was stupid. When I turned to my mother, she would always take his side.

Interviewer: Are you saying he was favored over you?

Dora: Oh, yes. I felt like he had power over me and I was at his mercy. She always believed him. He had a way of manipulating everyone. One time my brother did something to me, and when I told the babysitter, he denied it. The babysitter took his side and for some reason gave him a dog leash and he whipped me with it.

Interviewer: It sounds like you lived a pattern of abuse within your own family.

Dora: Definitely, but I don't want to get into too much of that.

Interviewer: Do you think this abuse led you to alcohol and drugs?

Dora: Yes, after so much of this I hated my brother and in my mind I planned to kill him. It just wasn't in me though because I loved my brother.

---

*Interviewer: R. Orona-Cordova

Interviewer: Do you blame your brother for your addiction?

Dora: No, not all of it. I don't blame him, but yet I later got into an abusive relationship with my boyfriend who beat me up. I can't really blame anybody, though.

Interviewer: Do you have any other brothers or sisters?

Dora: Yes, an older sister who would protect me once in awhile when she was with us. There was a time when she went to live with my mother's girlfriend in another state. It was then my brother and I were alone and he picked on me all the time.

Interviewer: Changing the subject a bit: What kind of student were you in school?

Dora: I wasn't good. I use to cut school in first grade, and go home to watch cartoons. No one knew, and sometimes my brother would cut school with me. I was always in the "slow-learner's" group. No one ever said anything to me about cutting.

Interviewer: Didn't school officials notify your mother?

Dora: Not that I know of; she never said anything to me about it.

Interviewer: Did you graduate from high school?

Dora: No. I got exempt from school when I was in the 8th grade because I would go to school drunk; I would write all over the walls things like "Chicano Power," "Viva la Raza," and all that stuff. My friends and I would come to the school drunk. One time I even got in a fistfight with the principal. Oh, one time I even gave KJ (animal tranquilizer that you smoke) to the cheerleaders. That's probably why I got kicked out, and they called it exempt. Then I started getting involved with guys at 13 and 14.

Interviewer: Tell me about that.

Dora: At 15, I started going with an alcoholic and heroin user who was 30 and was a well-known drug user; he had a police record.

Interviewer: What did your mom say about this?

Dora: She tried to break up the relationship but it was too late. She should have tried to protect me a long time before, when I was a kid. I'd run away to be with him, and I started having sex with him. I thought having sex with him was love. Then at 17, I got pregnant and, during all this time I drank. This guy was abusive and would beat me up.

Interviewer: Why did you stay with him or allow it?

Dora: Because he did show love and attention toward me, yet I was afraid of him too. It's funny because I didn't even like the kind of person he was, but he was nice to me at times, so I stayed with him. When this guy got busted and went to jail, I started hanging around with other girls that did heroine. Through them I met an older man who was 60 and who was a big drug dealer, a big dealer, and he gave me money. I wasn't sleeping with him, but his drug-dealing friends thought we were. I made him look good in front of his friends because I was a young girl. He's the one that introduced me to snorting heroin in my nose. I didn't like snorting, so I stopped doing it right away. I wasn't addicted to anything yet. I didn't get addicted to drugs until after I had my son.

Interviewer: When did you start your addiction?

Dora: I started when my son was a year old. Then I started sleeping with guys for money, to support my habit. This started my life in and out of jail for a period of 20 years.

Interviewer: How did you turn your life around?

Dora: One day I was in a pasture reading a romance novel and I was loaded. By this time, I was 25. I called out to Jesus; but before that, I always wanted to know Him because I knew that He was the Son of God, and He was the one who was going to get me out of this and help me turn my life around. I got up from that pasture and went to a church called Victory Outreach, which is an Assembly of God Church. It was a church where low-riders and gang members went. I had only been in a Catholic Church before, and all I remember from that is sitting next to my mom getting pinched and telling me to be quiet. I could never understand anything the priest would say. Don't get me wrong, I'm not putting down the Catholic Church because they too believe that Jesus is the Son of God who bore our sins in his body, and paid the price for us and rose from the dead. As a little girl, I had a strong desire to know Jesus, and so I even said to my mom one time, "I want to know Jesus." She told me I was too young. If she had let me know Jesus, none of this would ever have happened. I had an aunt who was/is close to God, and she used to pray on beads. As a little girl, it didn't seem right to me. I asked her, "Why are you praying on a necklace?" I tried to pray on it, and it didn't seem right so I stopped, and I didn't pursue Jesus like my little heart wanted.

Interviewer: How did you find Jesus then?

Dora: One day I ended up back in jail. Christians came to the jail to minister the Word of God to the inmates. One of the girls named Kathy, a Christian, came to minister to us, and I knew she could lead me to Jesus.

Interviewer: All this time during your drug-addicted life, you wanted to get out of this addiction?

Dora: Deep inside I knew Jesus was the way out, but every time I got out of jail I started using drugs again. One day, I went to look for Kathy at Victory Outreach to help me learn how to get to know Jesus. Kathy took me to a woman's home in San Francisco for ex-drug addicts and gang members who Jesus had delivered from a life of drugs and gangs. I left the place because they were mean. I went looking for love and instead I felt like I was being used. They made me do all the dirty, cleaning work that no one wanted to do. One time, when we went on a camping trip and while everyone was having fun at the lake, I had to stay behind and do the dishes. These people were mean, so I left and went back to drugs.

Interviewer: So you went back to drugs again?

Dora: Yes, I went back to drugs and sleeping with men for money for several more years.

Interviewer: What happened, or was there something specific you can point to that made you get help again, and finally go straight?

Dora: At this point, after 20 years of this life, I just wanted to die. I remember I was walking down these railroad tracks in Oakland, with a crack pipe in my hand, and a half gram of heroin in my bra, and I cried out to Jesus to help me. I called my mom. She picked me up and took me to this Christian home I knew about. I thought I could de-tox myself by snorting the heroin I had in my bra little by little. Twenty-four hours went by, and I was going through withdrawals. I thought I couldn't take it anymore. I got up to leave the home and to inject the heroin in my vein. As I was about to walk out the door there was a Christian lady talking to another girl about the blood of Jesus. The Christian lady said she read in the *Los Angeles Times* about a woman who daily prayed "I plead the blood of Jesus over my spirit soul and body and over my house." The lady who said this prayer daily was in one of the big Los Angeles earthquakes, and all the houses around her got damaged, except hers. I asked the Christian lady to tell me more about this. She had her Bible with her, and she opened it to Exodus Chapter12, Revelation 12:11, and read it to me. Immediately after I left that home, I went and sold my body to buy drugs. I was then standing on a street corner loaded, and was ready to sell my body for more money and for drugs. As I stood on the corner, I started praying "I plead the blood of Jesus over my spirit soul and body." As I was praying, I felt in my heart, "I'm going to die and I'm going to heaven now." I didn't know Jesus was going to give me a new life. A week later, I was sitting at a school watching these kids gamble. Somebody called the police on the kids, and since I was with these kids I got arrested also. They found a crack pipe and needle on me and so I went back to jail. This time when I went to jail I went to get my "kick package" (pills and stuff), but the nurse wouldn't give me anything because I had no withdrawal symptoms. When I got out of jail, I had no desire for drugs. I had never been clean in my life. I've been free of drugs for four years.

Interviewer: What happened? Why did your desire, your need for drugs stop?

Dora: Because the blood of Jesus delivered me.

Writing Prompts

1. What in Dora's personal history influenced her to turn to drugs?

2. Dora admits she alone accepts the blame for her addiction. What does this suggest about her attitude and understanding of her former problem?

3. Dora believes a higher power rescued her. Briefly describe how this happened and comment if you agree or disagree.

4. She reveals her boyfriend physically abused her. Consider this situation, then explain why Dora, or any woman (or man), accepts physical abuse.

5. Analyze and discuss Dora's explanation for changing her life.

Lost and Found

Maria Victoria

One day, four and a half years ago, I realized I had a serious and deadly problem. I self-diagnosed my disease of addiction. Alcohol and drugs had taken complete control of my life. I was powerless over them and also powerless over how I behaved under the influence. The outcome of drinking and using became more and more unpredictable. I was lost and stuck between being miserable and not being able to quit. My drug use was out of control, and no more fun. The unexpected car accidents and unexpected ugly, raging outbursts were frightening. Death was not out of reach. It almost happened a few times.

The biggest indication the highs were no longer working was how sad and lonely I felt. Nobody knew how important getting high was to me. It had become my whole purpose in life. An addict like me lives to use. To any normal person this sounds crazy. For me this was a way of life. I had the sickest empty feeling, and hope to never feel that way again.

Professionals say addiction is a genetic phenomenon. In my case this is true. My father's side passed it down. He has been a heroine junky for over forty-eight years. Dad lives imprisoned in his own house in his own madness. You could say he is a slave to smack. He has depended on it to survive his whole life. Driving by to visit him once a year is not easy. Approaching his house is eerie. The beat up, broken-windowed house is behind a 10-foot chain link fence. The gate always remains locked with a pad lock. When I visit him he comes to the fence, opens it, and we stand just outside the fence. After 15 minutes he says he has to go inside. Dad is not comfortable with visitors lurking outside. He also worries a drug deal may go down while I'm there. Or, worse yet, a bust may go down. He never invites me in because he doesn't feel proud of what I might see. I assume he's ashamed of his lifestyle. I can't say I blame him; he's not much of a role model. Having this in one of my parents isn't so bad. It takes getting used to; there was no choice. I understand his deal, and I have compassion for his story. This doesn't keep me from caring about him. Lately, when we talk on the phone, we've been more open and honest. It's nice to know it's never too late to get to know a parent better. I love him regardless.

The most important point I want to mention is I do not blame either one of my parents for my problems with drugs and alcohol. No one is to blame but me. Doctors have proven that addiction is a mental obsession of the mind and an allergy in the body. Therefore, addiction is classified as a disease, which is good news because this means it can be contained. I take full responsibility for my participation in nurturing my disease. I fed it with all kinds of horrible, self-destructive behavior.

Let me back track for a minute and give some examples of how it all began. At eight years old my cousin and I broke into the family bar. We dipped into the vodka until we were both passing out on the bathroom floor. I vaguely remember, but she and I did touch each other sexually. She initiated it and then she backed off when I tried to take charge. I had a few ideas about sex, but she wasn't willing to take it as far as I wanted. In this half black-out state, I retreated and backed off with shame. Remembering this incident fills me with embarrassment. Many of the naughty behaviors disgust me when I look back. Drinking brought out the worst in me. Drinking and using always leads to sex. That's just how it is.

The same relative also introduced me to smoking pot when I was twelve years old. Bonding with her gave me a sense of connecting with another family member. Why did it have to be her? The immediate answer is because I am a drug addict, alcoholic. I only blame myself. It's hard to believe that at such an early age I was captivated by how drugs and alcohol helped me bond with people. It made me feel a connection with whomever I would get high with. It didn't matter if I liked the person or not. We bonded through drugs. This relative and I never mentioned any of this to each other.

Looking back, I now recognize that there was a correlation between my fears around relationships, and how drugs helped me interact with people. Life was scary, so I had to be high and drunk. I couldn't live without being high.

My first sexual experiences were with women. I felt safe with girls; fooling around with them taught me everything I needed to know about sex. When I started having sex with men, I had to use drugs and alcohol. When I was young, sex scared me, so when I fooled around, I had to do it stoned. I realize now that I was always afraid to be open and vulnerable with anyone. I was never aware of any of this until I finally got clean and sober.

Smoking pot was my favorite drug. I remember buying one-dollar pinner joints from this guy named Sammy. It seems like yesterday as I recall how proud I was to have my very own joint stash. Walking around the high school stoned was a trip. The high is as clear to see and feel as it was then. I felt so good. It felt like walking on clouds. My body tingled with freedom and excitement. The part I particularly remember is the sensation that I liked being alone stoned. It was liberating to not need anyone else to feel this good. I had found something I could enjoy all by myself. No one else needed to participate to help me feel secure. It made me okay with myself.

At fifteen, I met an older man in a head shop in San Francisco where I stopped to pick up some rolling papers. This crazy nut started joking around with me. He was buying a proto pipe. Proto pipes are these brass contraptions which you smoke out of and it has a chamber where you stash the weed. The bowl itself is made out of brass and you have to keep the bowl clean with this brass pin that is attached to the pipe. I loved proto pipes. Whoever had a proto pipe was a veteran pothead.

Flirtation and attention always won my heart. This man invited me to join him in the back of his black Lincoln Continental to smoke out. This was the first time I smoked Moroccan hash. We were cracking up so hard. He knew how to party and the party was on.

I did not hesitate to stay in touch with him. It didn't matter to me that he was twice my age. This was the first time I ever had my own private stash of hash. He broke off a piece and gave it to me. He also taught me his special joint rolling techniques. I was very proud of this. I showed off to my friends how well I could roll a joint. My technique was always better than anyone else's. This was the type of activity I was proud of during my days as a drug user.

We became boyfriend and girlfriend. My mother was not happy with this at all. She didn't want to accept it, but eventually she did. I don't think she knew he was a big time drug dealer. What was so strange is he lived right down the street from me. Where we met was way across town. In a way this was meant to be. It was working for me. All that mattered was I could have all the weed I wanted. I would weigh out the bags of pot and bindles of cocaine. I did this to earn my own supply of drugs. How insane is this? I had to work for my supply. I wasn't the only one. He had a whole entourage of people helping him.

When I was sixteen years old he bought me a gorgeous Fiat Spider convertible. My mother approved for a hot minute. She must have thought I was crazy. She didn't approve for long. She insisted I get rid of the car after he gave me $3500 to run away to Hawaii. My mother threatened to put him in jail if he didn't help get me back from over seas. So he gave her money to fly out to get me. When we returned from Maui she put me in juvenile hall. After being locked up for a week, I was never to see him again. She would lock him up if he continued to see me.

Looking back on this I can see how pathetic I was. He actually bought the car back from me for $3500 after I insisted I would sell it to someone else if he didn't. I put this money in the bank and later used it to go to Europe for three months. I did wild shit like this all the time. I am not proud of these things, but it does make me laugh a little. I was ruthless.

Keep in mind I wasn't eighteen yet. When I think about it, I feel sad. I realize I was so lost. I now see that what I did was destructive. My poor mother kicked and screamed putting up with all this insanity.

Throughout my twenties my life with men, sex, alcohol, and drugs continued. Cash was always there as well. In fact, cash became a big part of the high. There was nothing better than the power of having drugs, sex, and cash. Not too many people admit this. A little cash along with great sex and killer drugs ruled my life for too long. Eighteen years of it burned me out.

The partying, the sex, and the lack of friendships finally made me feel empty, and spiritually bankrupt. There were a series of very painful events that made it possible for me to let go: my boyfriend of three years died driving his car over 100 miles an hour on Pacific Coast Highway. Another boyfriend put me in the hospital after trying to strangle me. After all this suffering, I wanted to stop using. I was desperate. Something deep inside me, my spirit was ready to surrender to change. A voice within, told me to put it all down. I remember marking that date. It was September 21, 1998. This came about blindly and unexpectedly.

One week after I stopped using, a girlfriend of mine called and told me Gordon's photo was all over the news. He was the last man I was seeing before I quit. He went to prison for nine counts of rape. I found this out by seeing his photo plastered all over the news. He was spiking girl's drinks with rape drugs. Some other girls turned him in. What was I thinking? My head was so toxic from all the drugs, I couldn't take care of myself anymore. It's a miracle I survived. There is so much to be grateful for; thank God I was willing and ready to change.

I live my life today as though everything depends on sobriety. It is a serious matter I don't take lightly. My every free moment is put to working with others in recovery. Helping others who are suffering the way I did helps me.

Today, I have three and a half years without a drink or a drug. I would like to say I stayed clean and sober from September 21, 1998; but I can't. I had put one year of clean time under my belt and I slipped. My new sober date is January 1, 2000. It was the perfect way to start off the new millennium.

Cleaning up the wreckage of my past is taking a long time, and has taken a lot of hard work and dedication. There are many lost years, but luckily there is a chance to make it right, and now I can work toward all the goals I have as a sober woman. I was able to accomplish what I have today with the help of a twelve-step program and other amazing people in recovery. My fiancée is one of them. We have a special relationship and we are living together helping each other continue living our lives in sobriety. The most beautiful part of our bond is we are living a clean, honest life. Neither of us are in the clutches or bondage of our disease. He will be ten years sober at the end of this year.

There is nothing better than to have someone I can share my truth with; someone who understands, someone who is not judgmental, and who has compassion for my former crazy life. Where I have been and where I have walked could have kept me from having this sweet way of life.

Writing Prompts

1. Analyze and explain what Maria means by the title "Lost and Found."

2. Examine Dora's decision and Maria Victoria's need to change their lives. Discuss similarities and differences using examples.

3. What were the self-destructive "markers" or symptoms Maria describes?

4. Respond to Maria by writing a letter to her. Give her advice and/or applaud her.

5. Write a story about someone you know who has a similar problem.

Words to Learn

"Targeting Hispanics"

savvy—to understand something, especially what somebody has said

vehemently—expressed with, or showing conviction or intense feeling

exemplified—to give an example or examples in order to make something clearer or more convincing

cynicism—doubting or contemptuous of human nature or of the motives, goodness, or sincerity of others

dubious—uncertain about an outcome or conclusion

nuances—the use or awareness of subtle shades of meaning or feeling, especially in artistic expression or performance

pervasive—spreading widely and occupying a great area

ubiquitous—present everywhere at once, or seeming to be

saturated—completely packed or full so that no more can be added

ramifications—a usually unintended consequence of an action, decision, or judgment that may complicate the situation or make the intended result more difficult to achieve

raucous—loud and hoarse or unpleasant-sounding, or characterized by loud noise, shouting, and ribald laughter

paltry—insignificant or unimportant

prestigious—having a distinguished reputation or bringing prestige to the person who has it

subservience—in a position of secondary importance

subsidiaries—the principle that political power should be exercised by the smallest possible unit

decry—to express strong disapproval of or openly criticize somebody or something

Quincentenary—a 500th anniversary

Chicana/o Queers Speak Their Minds

Chapter 5—Anticipation Guide

Directions: Rate each statement below according to the following:

4—Strongly Agree   *3—Agree*   *2—Disagree*   *1—Strongly Disagree*

1. Gays and lesbians will never be accepted.

2. People are born homosexuals.

3. Children raised by a homosexual parent will also be gay or lesbian.

4. Gays should be allowed in the military.

5. Homosexual couples have a right to adopt children.

6. Discrimination against gays and lesbians is the same as racial discrimination against Chicanos/as.

7. Gays should not wear clothing advertising their sexual preferences.

8. Heterosexuals who socialize with gay and (or) lesbians are really closet homosexuals.

9. More and more people are "turning" into homosexuals.

10. Gays and lesbians should be allowed to marry.

Authentic

Barbara Morales-Rossi

My mother did not expect a girl.
I spent my childhood praying—
God
make me a boy by morning.
It took three decades to create
the authentic woman I am—
one who loves women.

Suggested Writing Activities

1. Write a poem or story that reflects conflict: gay or lesbian versus society.

2. Pretend you are gay or lesbian. Using the first person singular "I," write a poem or story about being a homosexual.

A Divided Nation: A Chicana Lésbica Critique

Cherríe Moraga

> *We are free and* sovereign *to determine those tasks which are justly called for by our house, our land, the sweat of our brows, and by our hearts. Aztlán belongs to those who plant the seeds, water the fields, and gather the crops and not to the foreign Europeans. We do not recognize* capricious *frontiers on the bronze continent.*

—From "El Plan Espiritual de Aztlán"

When *"El Plan Espiritual de Aztlán"* was conceived a generation ago, lesbians and gay men were not envisioned as members of the "house"; we were not recognized as the sister planting the seeds, the brother gathering the crops. We were not counted as members of the "bronze continent."

In the last decade, through the efforts of Chicana feministas, Chicanismo has undergone a serious critique. Feminist critics are committed to the preservation of Chicano culture, but we know that our culture will not survive marital rape, battering, incest, drug and alcohol abuse, AIDS, and the *marginalization* of lesbian daughters and gay sons. Some of the most outspoken criticism of the Chicano Movement's sexism and some of the most impassioned activism in the area of Chicana liberation (including work on sexual abuse, domestic violence, immigrant rights, Indigenous women's issues, health care, etc.) have been advanced by lesbians.

Since lesbians and gay men have often been forced out of our blood families, and since our love and sexual desire are not housed within the traditional family, we are in a critical position to address those areas within our cultural family that need to change. Further, in order to understand and defend our lovers and our same-sex loving, lesbians and gay men must come to terms with how *homophobia*, gender roles, and sexuality are learned and expressed in Chicano culture. As Ricardo Bracho writes: "To speak of my desire, to find voice in my brown flesh, I needed to confront my male mirror." As a lesbian, I don't pretend to understand the intricacies or intimacies of Chicano gay desire, but we do share the fact that our "homosexuality"—our feelings about sex, sexual power and *domination*, femininity and masculinity, family, loyalty, and morality—has been shaped by heterosexist culture and society. As such, we have plenty to tell heterosexuals about themselves.

When we are moved sexually toward someone, there is a profound opportunity to observe the *microcosm* of all human relations, to understand power dynamics both obvious and subtle, and to *mediate* on the core creative impulse of all desire. Desire is never politically correct. In sex, gender roles, race relations, and our collective histories of oppression and human connection are enacted. Since the early 1980s, Chicana lesbian feminists have explored these traditionally "dangerous" topics in both critical and creative writings. Chicana lesbian-identified writers such as Ana Castillo, Gloria Anzaldúa, and Naomi Littlebear Moreno were among the first to articulate a Chicana feminism, which included a racial woman-centered critique of sexism *and sexuality* from which both lesbian and heterosexual women benefited.

In the last few years, Chicano gay men have also begun to openly examine Chicano sexuality. I suspect heterosexual Chicanos will have the world to learn from their gay brothers about their shared masculinity, but they will have the most to learn from the "queens," the *"maricones."* Because they are deemed "inferior" for no fulfilling the traditional role of men, they are more marginalized from mainstream heterosexual society than other gay men, they are more marginalized from mainstream heterosexual society than other gay men and are especially vulnerable to male violence. Over the years, I have been shocked to discover how many femme gay men have grown up regularly experiencing rape and sexual abuse. The rapist is always heterosexual and usually Chicano like themselves. What has the Gay Movement done for these brothers? What has the Chicano Movement done? What do these young and once-again men have to tell us about *misogyny* and male violence? Like women, they see the macho's desire to dominate the feminine, but even more intimately because they both desire men and share manhood with their oppressors. They may be *jotos,* but they are still men, and are bound by their racial and sexual identification to men (Bracho's "male mirror").

Until recently, Chicano gay men have been silent over the Chicano Movement's male heterosexual hegemony. As much as I see a potential alliance with gay men in our shared experience of homophobia, the majority of gay men still cling to what privileges they can. I have often been severely disappointed and hurt by the misogyny of gay Chicanos. Separation from one's brothers is a painful thing. Being gay does not preclude gay men from harboring the same sexism evident in heterosexual men. It's like white people and racism, sexism goes with the (male) territory.

On some level our brothers—gay and straight—have got to give up being "men." I don't mean give up their genitals, their unique expression of desire, or the rich and intimate manner in which men can bond together. Men have to give up their *subscription* to male superiority. I remember during the Civil Rights Movement seeing newsreel footage of young Black men carrying protest signs reading, "I AM A MAN." It was a powerful statement, publicly declaring their humanness in a society that daily told them otherwise. But they didn't write "I AM HUMAN," they wrote "MAN." Conceiving of their liberation in male terms, they were *unwittingly* demanding the right to share the whiteman's position of male dominance. This demand would become consciously articulated with the emergence of the male-dominated Black Nationalist Movement. The liberation of Black women per se was not part of the program, except to the extent that better conditions for the race in general might benefit Black women as well. How differently Sojourner Truth's "Ain't I a Woman" speech *resonates* for me. Unable to choose between suffrage and abolition, between her womanhood and her Blackness, Truth's 19th-century call for a free Black womanhood in a Black- and woman-hating society required the freedom of all enslaved land *disenfranchised* peoples. As the Black feminist Combahee River Collective stated in 1977, "If Black women were free, it would mean that everyone else would have to be free since our freedom would necessitate the destruction of all the systems of oppression." No progressive movement can succeed while any member of the population remains in submission.

Chicano gay men have been reluctant to recognize and acknowledge that their freedom is intricately connected to the freedom of women. As long as they insist on remaining "men" in the socially and culturally *constructed* sense of the word, they will never achieve the full liberation they desire. There will always be jotos getting raped and beaten. Within people of color communities, violence against women, gay bashing, sterilization abuse, AIDS and AIDS discrimination, gay substance abuse, and gay teen suicide emerge from the same source—a racist and misogynist social and economic system that dominates, punishes, and abuses all things colored, female, or perceived as female-like. By openly confronting Chicano sexuality and sexism, gay men can do their own part to unravel how both men *and* women have been formed and deformed by racist Amerika and our *misogynist*/catholic/colonized *mechicanidad;* and we can come that much closer to healing those *fissures* that have divided us as a people.

The AIDS epidemic has seriously shaken the foundation of the Chicano gay community, and gay men seem more willing than ever to explore those areas of political change that will ensure their survival. In their fight against AIDS, they have been rejected and neglected by both the white gay male establishment and the Latino heterosexual health-care community. They also have witnessed direct support by Latina lesbians.[1] Unlike the "queens" who have always been open about their sexuality, "passing" gay men have learned in a *visceral* way that being in "the closet" and preserving their "manly" image will not protect them, it will only make their dying more secret. I remember my friend Arturo Islas, the novelist. I think of how his writing begged to boldly announce his gayness. Instead, we learned it through vague references about "sinners" and tortured alcoholic characters who wanted nothing more than to "die dancing" beneath a lightning-charged sky just before a thunderstorm. Islas died of AIDS-related illness in 1990, having barely begun to examine the complexity of Chicano sexuality in his writing. I also think of essayist Richard Rodríguez, who, with so much death surrounding him, has recently begun to publicly address the subject of homosexuality; and yet, even ten years ago we all knew "Mr. Secrets" was gay from his assimilationist *Hunger of Memory*.[2] He he "come out" in 1982, the white establishment would have been far less willing to promote him as the "Hispanic" anti-affirmative action spokesperson. He would have lost a lot of validity . . . and opportunity. But how many lives are lost each time we cling to privileges that make other people's live more vulnerable to violence?

At this point in history, lesbians and gay men can make a significant contribution to the creation of a new Chicano movement, one passionately committed to saving lives. As we are forced to struggle for our right to love free of disease and discrimination, "Aztlán" as our imagined homeland begins to take on renewed importance. Without the dream of a free world, a free world will never be realized. Chicana lesbians and gay men do not merely seek inclusion in the Chicano nation; we seek a nation strong enough to embrace a full range of racial diversities, human sexualities, and expressions of gender. We seek a culture that can allow for the natural expression of our femaleness and maleness and our love without prejudice or punishment. In a "queer" Aztlán, there would be no freaks, no "others" to point one's finger at. My Native American friends tell me that in some Native American tribes, gay men and lesbians were traditionally regarded as "two-spirited" people. Displaying both masculine and feminine aspects, they were highly respected members of their community, and were thought to possess a higher spiritual development.[3] Hearing of such traditions gives historical validation for what Chicana lesbians and gay men have always recognized—that lesbians and gay men play a significant spiritual, cultural, and political role within the Chicano community. Somos *activistas, académicos y artistas, parteras y políticos, curanderas y campesinos.* With or without heterosexual acknowledgement, lesbians and gay men have continued to actively redefine familia, cultura, and comunidad. We have formed circles of support and survival, often drawing from the more egalitarian models of Indigenous communities.

Notes

1. In contrast to the overwhelming response by lesbians to the AIDS crisis, breast cancer, which has disproportionately affected the lesbian community, has received little attention from the gay men's community in particular, and the public at large. And yet, the statistics are devastating. One out of every nine women in the United States will get breast cancer: 44,500 U.S. women will die of breast cancer this year (*Boston Globe*, November 5, 1991).

2. See Rodríguez' essay "Late Victorians" in his most recent collection, *Days of Obligation: An Argument with My Mexican Father.*

3. This was not the case among all tribes nor is homosexuality generally condoned in contemporary Indian societies. See "Must We Deracinate Indians to Find Gay Roots?" by Ramón A. Gutiérrez in *Outlook: National Lesbian and Gay Quarterly,* Winter 1989.

Writing Prompts

1. Imagine one of your family members reveals that he or she is gay or lesbian. Write a response to this person who "comes out of the closet."

2. What does Moraga mean in the opening line of her essay when she reveals that "lesbians and gay men were not envisioned as members of the 'house' in 'El Plan Espiritual de Aztlan'"? What is the metaphor of the "house"?

3. Why, according to Moraga's point of view, do gays and lesbians defend and work on behalf of victims of domestic violence, sexual abuse, and undocumented workers?

4. Analyze and explain Moraga's position on the similarity between white male superiority, Chicano heterosexuals *and* gay men. Conclude by discussing whether or not you agree or disagree.

5. Read Moraga's closing paragraph. She proposes a new Chicano/a movement that includes acceptance of gays and lesbians. She says together they will help the community of Chicanos/as and will save people from violence and abuse referred to in #3. Do you agree or disagree? Explain in detail.

Transgendered Mannerisms: A Chicana Lesbian Story

Maria C. González

When I was a few months old, my parents had a pediatrician pierce my ears. I asked my mother why they did this to me. Her response was because her ears were pierced. Although I immediately challenged any form of heterosexual *gender identification,* beginning with the deliberate loss of my earrings, within the Mexican-American community, baby girls have their ears pierced as part of the cultural pressure to *differentiate* between the genders.

But why would the Latino community be so preoccupied with knowing what a baby's gender is and making sure one can see that difference? That answer is simple for those of us who believe in the *social construction* of identity, appearance equals identity, and gender is a very important *classification* in all societies. In the Mexican-American community, the *signals* of gendered appearance announce those who are female and those who are male, all with the fundamental understanding that everyone is heterosexual. Very few people are *non-gender specific,* and you would be hard pressed to name someone completely *androgynous.* Our society is clear about what male and female genders look like. What you look like is who you are, thus, we have to start dressing and treating children differently immediately, or they may grow up confused about their gender and sexuality. And if that happens, what happens to the society?

Furthermore, within the Latino community, *mannerisms* are also identified as masculine and feminine. If gender differentiation does not occur early enough, a female might *mimic* male mannerisms. If a female mimics the mannerisms of a male, she is *transgendered* in her mannerisms.

Mexican-American culture assumes clear *distinctions* in how each gender should perform their appropriate mannerisms and expects its members to display them appropriately. Those who mix their *designated* mannerisms are transgendered in their response. While we can point to style of dress and physical appearance for the male, short hair and slacks, those clearly differentiated markers are now no longer so carefully *patrolled.* Many women and girls have short hair, and everyone can now wear slacks. However, certain mannerisms are still designated for each gender in the Latino community.

The Mexican-American community I grew up with was far more formal than the mainstream society. A Latino child was taught to respect adults and not to treat them as one would a friend. My parents expected my siblings and me to stand up when someone entered a room, male or female. Appropriate manners for each gender were taught to children, and since I grew up in a household with three brothers, I mimicked the manners my brothers were taught, such as pulling out a chair or opening a door for a woman. Included in the appropriate behavior was machismo. Machismo is a highly coveted masculine behavior trait.

If you are a boy, you are told, "Boys don't cry." That was sad for my three brothers because they were pressured to keep their emotions under control. Because I wanted to play with them, it applied to me as well. My brothers insisted that I needed to be tough if I wanted to participate in their games. I liked playing football, and the rule was, if you got hurt, you did not go to pieces. A certain amount of crying was allowable, but no screaming. They were given a *repressed* emotional model to follow.

I was given an appropriate female model to follow, but I rejected it. My mother would try to get me to mimic her mannerisms, but they were not as obvious to me as my brother's were. She wanted a daughter who played with dolls, wore bright yellow dresses with lots of lace and bows like other little Mexican girls. Unfortunately, for my mother, I preferred toy cars and G I Joe's to dolls, blue slacks to dresses, and "boy's stuff." According to my parents, I had the rough and tough mannerisms of a boy. While I now call this mixing of manners and mannerisms transgendered mannerisms, others simply call it being a "tom-boy."

Girls, however, are supposed to outgrow that "tom-boy" stage, and that magical moment of transition from child to adult is clearly *marked* for females in the Latino community. When girls reach adolescence and discover that their bodies are changing, their parents tell them that they need to start acting more "lady-like." Mothers buy their daughters new clothing and teach them how to dress. Then, within the Latino community, the age of 15 for a girl is an important moment. She has a Quinceañera—a coming-out party to announce that she is now a woman and historically, ready to marry.

I did not want a Quinceañera. My parents were disappointed because a quinceañera was an expected event within the Mexican-American community. However, my parents had already sensed I was different because I was mimicking my brothers' mannerisms. Instead of being a polite young lady, I was a polite gentleman. I stood when someone entered the room, just like my brothers. My handshake was as firm as my brothers and I offered a handshake before the other person offered his hand. This behavior was marked as masculine within the community. Much later, in adulthood, I realized these mannerisms were considered inappropriate for women; however as a girl, I assumed that was the way all children were supposed to respond. Today, I simply embrace transgendered mannerisms.

Once I refused a Quinceañera, I broke a cultural barrier, and I was no longer pressured to perform feminine mannerisms. But also by that point, it was very clear to me that I was a different kind of girl. I liked girls, and I knew this was not a good thing. I had already experienced heterosexist ways of the world. Girls were supposed to like boys, and boys were supposed to like girls. But I wanted to kiss girls, not boys. I knew that was not going to be something my family, my church, and my culture would allow me to experience. I knew that liking girls "that way" was a very, very bad thing.

Today, my mannerisms are considered "butch" within the lesbian *binary* of femme/butch, which have come back into vogue in response to the *overt* feminized lesbian categories of the seventies and early eighties. Within the Latina lesbian community, the femme/butch categories have always been in play. If a person is a Chicana lesbian, what she looks like and what she does to signal her identity is a clear part of her appearance. The butch/femme binary is just as strong a signal within the Chicana lesbian community as is the feminine/masculine binary within the Latino community.

When I went to college (I had to take my younger brother with me), I finally had the opportunity to kiss a girl. I was allowed to go to a Catholic college in a city away from home. Mexican-American families do not encourage their children, male and female, to leave home. The only excuse an unmarried daughter has to move out of her parents' home is to set up a newlywed's household. Going off to college, especially if female, is not encouraged. It is, in fact, downright discouraged. My parents asked me to study at the local university, but I knew I would be trapped if I stayed there. In El Paso everyone knows everyone else: How could I then hang-out in a gay bar in my hometown, where someone might recognize me?

Latino society's judgment of inappropriate appearance and mannerisms was no longer valid for me in San Antonio. I finally discovered lesbian sexuality and identity. I also knew that even within a girl's dorm, certain judgments were made about those of us who were clearly marked as different or inappropriate in our gendered mannerisms. I was more acceptable within the female community at the university because I did not always clearly mark myself as a butch lesbian even though my mannerisms were far more masculine than feminine. I could blend in to a certain degree. While I never put on dresses if I could avoid it, I also never announced which girl I was seeing. Even my closest friends did not know which women I slept with. Most of the girls I dated were also *closeted*. This was the early eighties and the atmosphere was *homophobic*. The two or three women on campus who clearly announced themselves as butch lesbians, both by verbal statements and by appearance were not wholly accepted into the campus community. The "don't ask, don't tell" policy was unwritten, and well patrolled within this good Catholic community.

When I decided to come out of the closet and tell my parents, they asked that I keep it to myself. They did not *disown* me, but they have their own "don't ask, don't tell" policy. Within the Mexican-American community, a polite person never asks about someone's sexuality. However, I now live in a world where I refuse to be invisible as a lesbian. My appearance announces me as a lesbian. I own a wallet with the rainbow symbol on it. My truck has the rainbow sticker on it. And I usually wear the national lesbian uniform: running shoes, a pullover polo shirt, and Dockers.

My appearance and transgendered mannerisms do not necessarily mean I want to be a male. They simply mean I prefer the more "butch" mannerisms associated with a Mexican-

American gentleman than of a Latina lady. When I was asked why I try to mark myself more obviously as lesbian, I explained that if I did not clearly mark myself, I would never date again. As a Chicana lesbian, I embrace the *fluidity* of identity and gender.

Writing Prompts

1. Explain the connection between the personal anecdote, "When I was a few months old, my parents had a pediatrician pierce my ears;" and the theme of González's narrative.

2. Define "transgendered mannerisms," according to the author's explanation. Give an example of how this applies to the author.

3. What rational does González give for gender distinction in Chicano/a families?

4. González preferred boy's clothes and toys when she was quite young. Write your own ideas about whether you think she learned this behavior from her brothers, or whether she was born with an inclination toward "boy's stuff."

5. Analyze and discuss the author's decision to "go away to college." Why did she need to leave home?

No Turning Back: Breaking Down the Closet Door

Javier Ignacio Morelos

Some boys know early on in life that they are different. A few play with dolls and some rummage through mom's closet when no one is home. Others feel a fondness for a close friend of the same sex. Some of these boys grow up to be heterosexual. For others, however, this is the beginning of a life that many people *scorn*. People who think they might be gay should remember that they are what they are, and no one can change that. There will be some who try to hurt those different than them with nastiness and cruel words—this is the nature of people who must compensate for smaller (insert body part of choice here). As an adolescent, I went through many difficulties in order to get to where I am today. To begin with, I had to face the reality I was *unconsciously* in the closet.

The closet I'm referring to is the mental closet buried deep within the brain; the closet with the gigantic steel door that keeps the outside world from seeing into your secrets. Growing up, my closet was large and for a very good reason—my plan was to stay in it indefinitely. There was plenty of space to sit, roam, and to hide. I wanted to hide a part of myself because for the longest time, the world beyond the closet door was unknown and terrifying. I heard gays called a variety of names: homos, perverts, faggots, or queers. Everything I heard about being gay was terrible: gays are social outcasts, made to wear pink, and have careers limited to flower arranging and interior decorating. The last two aren't bad, but they weren't what I had in mind for the future. From early on, everything I heard about gay people was extremely negative. I kept the closet door shut tight for many years.

People often ask me, "When did you know?" or "Why are you gay?" and sometimes even "Do these shoes go with this belt?" One point should be clarified here: knowing all the prejudice and discrimination gays and lesbians face, I don't know who would want to be gay. I did not sign up with a local gay agency; I did not go to gay school; I was not recruited by crazy drag queens and I did not get a toaster; color TV; or any other household appliance for coming out (much to my disappointment). What I like to do when asked why I am gay is to reverse the question: "Why are you straight?" and sometimes, "When did you choose to be straight?" or "Do you really want to wear those shoes with that belt?"

Kids called me a fag in elementary school more than I can remember. And this was Catholic school! Kids can be evil; this is a universal truth. I was mean to others and others were mean to me. I was annoyed mostly because I really didn't know what this and other colorful expressions flung at me meant. Luckily no one ever physically harmed me. All throughout school, however, I wondered why these names were flung at me like monkey poop at the zoo. I didn't know what they were! Was I not seeing something that others did?

It was like speaking in public with your fly down. People see that "you are wide open," but they are too embarrassed to tell you "XYZ!" or "I see London, I see France."

One of those nasty times specifically was in my seventh grade science class. I noticed a group of guys laughing at something on a piece of paper. I wanted to see what the commotion was, so I went over to them. As I got closer, the group got quiet, looked at me and laughed. I grabbed the piece of paper from the desk and before my eyes was a hastily drawn *caricature* of me wearing short shorts, a vest, and a top hat. My right arm extended, my wrist drawn limp ablaze in faggotry. The bubble caption coming from my mouth read "Hi, I'm Javier. Am Fag." Naturally, this infuriated me. I tore the paper up, threw it in the can, and went back to my desk. "You guys don't even know what that word means," I said. The truth was, I didn't know what that word meant either. I didn't want to get angry because it would only *affirm* to the others that I was insecure about my effeminate manners. Becoming fodder for cruel classmate jokes was not what a self-doubting teenager wants to do. What bothered me the most about that portrayal was not that I was drawn like a reject Vegas showgirl or that my wrist was limp. I was most bothered by the *grievous* grammatical error in the phrase "Hi, I'm Javier. Am Fag." I may have been in the closet, but at least I could speak and write properly.

High school was where I admitted to myself that I was gay. I remember the first time I even skirted the gay topic. I was sitting in front of my high school with a friend whose mom was giving me a ride home. I felt that this was the right time to slip something out and take a much thought about chance. The night before, I had a dream that I cannot describe in these pages because it was quintuple X rated. Needless to say, it was an erotic "episode" with a classmate. When I awoke, I was completely confused. Even though I was *mystified,* I remember liking it so much that I tried to go back to sleep for a re-run. It didn't work.

As I sat on the steps, my friend Anthony and I talked about what most teenage boys talk about: sex. As we chatted, I could feel a tense knot form in the pit of my stomach because I was waiting for the right moment to tell him about my dream.

"I had a weird dream last night," I said, finally.

"What was it about?" he inquired.

I could trust Anthony more than anyone. We were both 15, but he was intellectually advanced for his age. He was open-minded and could be trusted completely. For a moment, I had forgotten about all my years of silence, guilt, and fear of the unknown.

"It was weird. I hope you don't think I'm weird." I said.

"I won't think you're weird."

"Are you sure? It's pretty weird."

"What is it then? I'm gonna think you're weird if you don't tell me."

I told him every single detail of my dream. Anthony's reaction surprised me, and it was one I was lucky to get. In my mind, Anthony called me a queer, ran away, and told everyone at school about my revelation. He didn't. He wanted to know more. On those steps we sat like two gossipy neighbors, wondering what the dream meant and how good it was on a scale of one to ten. He was eager to find out more. While I didn't completely come out to him, I did get a good reaction. His understanding helped me realize that coming out was not so bad. It felt good to know that there was at least one person on this earth that knew my secret.

It wasn't until my junior year that I fully realized I was gay. Several months later, and after many more chats about "guys who have dreams about other guys," with Anthony, I decided to face the music. After much thought about my life experiences, my natural feelings for guys that just weren't there for girls, it finally hit me: "I am gay." It was akin to a religious revelation, without the beams of light, choirs of angels, and booming voice of God. It was an inner peace; one that I had come to after many years of denying what was beyond my physical and mental control. This self-affirmation helped me feel comfortable enough to come out to others.

The first person I ever really told about my being gay was my high school guidance counselor. I had visited with her before and respected her advice. She was someone who could help me sort out my feelings and make sense of it all. It was a frightening moment in my life because I knew that it was the start of something new.

My counselor's office was spacious and comfortable. There were a couple of couches, some plants and magazines. It was so quiet that I could hear the silence. Her voice was calming and reassuring, making it easier for me to tell her. The day I told her is still fresh in my mind. I went into her office; my heart raced faster than my thoughts. I sank down onto the couch and let the quiet of the room calm me down.

She asked me in her reassuring voice how I was and why I was there.

I couldn't look at her. My hands trembled with fear. "This was it," I thought. "There's no turning back now." I took a deep breath. I looked around the room and focused on a flower pattern on the couch opposite me.

My tongue suddenly felt like it weighed five tons. I wanted so bad to say what I had to say, but my fear kept the words in a chokehold. I took another deep breath and started again, my eyes still entranced by the flower pattern on the couch.

"I think," I started.

I began to feel dizzy.

"That I might," I continued. At any moment, I felt as if my stomach would pop out of my body like an extraterrestrial newborn in those alien sci-fi movies. "Be gay." My ears began to ring. The silence was deafening, but not menacing. I actually told someone else, someone older than me, someone of authority.

My counselor was extremely supportive. She gave me pamphlets to read and offered me advice that to this day is priceless. She made me feel like I was okay and that I was not alone. She also introduced me to others who I could talk to about being gay.

I gained more confidence and began to come out to more friends. Soon after, I was completely out at high school. I'm sure there were rumors and nasty things about me flung around like chairs on a talk show, but nothing was ever said to my face. I was lucky that way. I know my experience of coming out in a private Catholic high school and not being *ostracized* for it was rare. I was fortunate to have accepting friends, teachers, and counselors who helped me through *agonizing* times.

It was this supportive group of people who helped me during one of the most difficult periods in my life. I was working at a restaurant inside a build-it-yourself furniture mega store when I got a phone call.

"Thank you for calling the build-it-yourself furniture mega store's restaurant. This is Javier. How may I help you?"

It was my brother-in-law and he sounded nervous.

"Hey Jav, your mom knows."

Right away I knew something had happened.

"Knows what?" I said.

"She knows about you and she's crying and freaking out. She just called over here and your sister is crying too."

"Put her on," I said.

Through my sister's muffled voice, in between the sobs and what sounded like an end-of-the-world tone in her voice, I found out that my mom knew I was gay. I could only figure that she found a note I had written to one of my friends in my room. I wasn't very good at hiding notes. I bit my meatball and money smelling nails all the way home. I had never been so scared. When I parked my car, the neighborhood was eerily silent. The cats, stray dogs, and even the night owls seemed to have sensed the anxiety in the air and bolted. I walked up the path to the front door with my apron in hand, shaking nervously. I went to my room as quickly as I could, undressed and got into bed. I shut my eyes so I could escape this reality at least for the night.

The next morning, I got up, showered and dressed and walked out into the living room where my mother was. I could tell she had been crying for sometime. Her watery eyes revealed her pain and disbelief. She asked me:

"Is it true?"

Her voice quivered as she sat on the sofa, surrounded in uncertainty.

"Yes." I said.

She broke into tears, and asked, "Why. Why was I doing this." No one in the family was gay. She was afraid I would get AIDS, get beaten up, and was sure I would start dressing in drag. She cried endlessly. For a while, I felt emotionally wrecked at how this *revelation* caused my mother to act.

For a couple of years afterwards, I came home from work and found her in her bed, crying. She didn't want to go out and she stopped visiting her friends. All her social interactions had come to a complete halt. She finally told my father after months of not telling him why she was crying and depressed all the time. My dad and I have a silent understanding about my being gay. Being Latino and for my own personal reasons, it is hard to talk to my father about this subject. It is something I still struggle with. To this day, my father and I have not talked about it. My mom told him, and he cried and said, "He is our son. He is what God gave us." That is all I have ever heard my father say. In a way, I am content with that until I feel I can talk with him about it. Even though it has been several years since my coming out, the process for some can take many years.

After some time, my mother regained her emotional strength and began to talk to her friends. Since I had come out to my sister way before she found out, she was able to talk to them as well. At 21, I moved in with my boyfriend. I took my boyfriend home for holidays and family celebrations and most everyone in my family accepted him. This calmed my mother a little, once she saw that I was in a stable relationship and that I was surviving on my own, away from home. She became less depressed and soon found an environment where she felt comfortable to talk about issues concerning me.

Anthony's parents head a group for Catholic parents of gay children. A priest *moderates* the group and advises the parents without sounding preachy or overtly biblical. Sodom and Gomorrah is not discussed in this group and its purpose is to help parents accept their children and to learn that having gay children is not the end of the world. This group has helped my mom deal with her feelings and to vent her fears. It has also helped us to form a closer relationship. After going to these meetings, I have seen her change in a way I never imagined. I never imagined her fully accepting me, let alone helping other parents to accept their children, because ultimately, we are still their children.

A poem by Emily Dickinson that helped me through my coming out years still remains with me. It gave me the courage back then, to face my fears, to not give up hope, and to find acceptance with something that was a part of my life. I ended up using it as my senior yearbook quote: "Time does go on-/I tell it gay to those who suffer now-/They shall survive-/There is a sun-/They don't believe it now."

Writing Prompts

1. What aspects of society do you think make it hard for a gay person to come out?

2. Do you think gays and lesbians are more accepted by society than they were 10 years ago, 20 years ago?

3. Do cultural and religious beliefs influence a person's view of homosexuals? How and why?

4. Analyze the reasons the writer states, "I don't know who would want to be gay." Interpret what he means.

5. Identify the main turning point in the author's story.

Words to Learn

"A Divided Nation: A Chicana Lesbica Critique"

sovereign—self-governing and not ruled by any other force

capricious—tending to make sudden and unpredictable changes

El Plan Espiritual de Aztlan—a strategy developed in Denver, Colorado, in 1969 that sets the theme that the Chicanos must use their nationalism as the key or common denominator for mass mobilization and organization

marginalization—to take or keep somebody or something away from the center of attention, influence, or power

homophobia—the fear of homosexuality

domination—the control of others

microcosm—the smaller version of the larger picture

meditate—quiet time for someone to think or pray for solutions to a problem

maricones—Spanish for gay men

misogyny—hatred toward women

jotos—Spanish for homosexuals

subscription—a full agreement with or approval of something

unwittingly—unaware of what is happening in a particular situation

resonates—to have an effect or impact beyond that which is immediately apparent

disenfranchised—to deprive a person or organization of a privilege, immunity, or legal right, especially the right to vote

constructed—something that has been systematically put together, usually in the mind, especially a complex theory or concept

misogynist—someone who hates women

mechicanidad—Chicano students involved in a political organization called MEChA (Moviniento Estudiantil Chicano de Aztlan)

fissures—a division in a group or party

visceral—characterized by or showing basic emotions

"Transgendered Mannerisms: A Chicana Lesbian Story"

transgendered—changing or crossing over from one gender to the other

transgendered mannerisms—the way of changing or crossing over from one gender to another

gender recognition—the way masculinity and femininity is identified

differentiate—to establish a difference between two things or among several things

social construct—the creation of the behaviors, expectations, and organization of a mass group of people

classification—the allocation of items to groups according to type

signals—something that incites somebody to action

non-gender—not relating to masculinity or femininity

specific—particular and detailed

androgynous—neither male nor female in appearance but having both conventionally masculine and feminine traits and giving an impression of ambiguous sexual identity who somebody is or what something is, especially the name somebody or something is known by

mannerisms—a particular gesture, habit, or way of doing something

mimic—to imitate somebody, or copy somebody's voice, gestures, or appearance

distinctions—a difference, or the recognition of a difference, between two or more things or people

designated—to choose something for a particular purpose

patrolled—guarded or protected

repressed—to check or restrain an action that would reveal feelings

marked—very noticeable

drenched—to make somebody or something completely wet

binary—consisting of two parts or two separate elements

overt—done openly and without any attempt at concealment

loathe—to dislike somebody or something intensely

closeted—people who are denying their sexuality

homophobic—a fear of homosexuality

disown me—denied from the family

fluidity—to make a solid move as a fluid

"No Turning Back: Breaking Down the Closet Door"

scorn—open dislike and disrespect or derision often mixed with indignation

unconsciously—not marking by conscious thought, sensation, or feeling

caricature—exaggeration by means of often-ludicrous distortion of parts or characteristics

affirm—to state positively

grievous—serious, grave

mystified—to perplex the mind of

ostracize—to exclude from a group by common consent

agonizing—to struggle with

revelation—an enlightening or astonishing disclosure

moderates—people who are neither in favor or against an issue or a political party

A Fresh Look at Chicano/a-Themed Films

Chapter 6—Anticipation Guide

Directions: Rate each statement below according to the following:

4—Strongly Agree   3—Agree   2—Disagree   1—Strongly Disagree

1. A film is a powerful medium that influences how people think and behave.

2. A movie made from a book tells a better story.

3. Stereotypes in films are not harmful because everyone knows they are not real.

4. American action-adventure films show too much killing and violence.

5. In order for a Chicano/a-themed film to be successful it must have a universal theme.

6. Disney films are important for children to watch because it teaches them about good and evil.

7. Disney's films often portray too many stereotypes.

8. Movie reviewers only understand films that portray white culture.

9. When a Latino-themed book is adapted to film, the cast should be Latino/a.

10. The Chicano/a community should create their own film industry by raising money from wealthy Latinos and Latinas.

Canción Villista

Xocoyotzin Herrera

I will sing to Pancho Villa
An eminent man and famous general,
Who has never given in to the federal government.

La cantaré a Pancho Villa
Hombre eminente
Muy hombre y honrado
Jamás se ha dejada
Del gobierno federal

Listen you, Porfirio Diaz,
So much injustice,
The people are not going to stand for that.
Villa the brave one and all of his
People are ready to fight.

Oye tú Porfirio Díaz
Tanta injusticia
El Pueblo no va soportar.
Que Villa el valiente y toda
su Gente ya están listos pa'
Pelear.

I am present, general,
Ready for the rebellion
That with the Villistas
And the Maderistas,
I will join the revolution.

Presente estoy general
Listo pa' la rebelión
Que con los Villistas
Y los Maderistas
Le entro a la revolución

General Francisco Villa,
His bravery, he proved
To the people.
Doroteo Arango (Villa's real name)
Long live Durango (Mexico)
Which is where he was born.

Que Viva Francisco Villa
Su Valentía
A todo el pueblo demostró
Doroteo Arango
Arriba Durango
Que allí fue donde nació

With his Division of the North
The Centaurus (Villa's nickname)
Could dominate in battle.
Not Pershing
Nor Huerta
With alert forces could defeat him.

Con su División del Norte
En la batalla
Pudo el centauro dominar
Ni Pershing, ni Huerta
Con fuerzas alertas
Lo pudieron derrotar

From Durango to Parral (Chihuahua)	Desde Durango hasta Parral
And passing through Torreon (Coahuila)	Y pasando por Torreón
Presidios, Sandias (towns in Durango)	Presidios Sandías
I sing to Villa	Yo le canto a Villa
Long live the revolution!	Viva la revolución!

(This is an original song composed for an upcoming film, based on the life of Pancho Villa, a Mexican soldier and hero during the Mexican revolution of 1910. The song is performed by Xocoyotzin Herrera, Fermin Herrera, and Ixya Herrera.)

Suggested Writing Activities

1. Find a brief biography of Pancho Villa on the Internet.

2. What does the song say; what does it mean; why does it matter?

3. Pick your own national hero. Write a song or poem about him or her.

4. What can you tell about the character of Pancho Villa based upon the words in the song? Give examples from your research and/or prior knowledge.

Mainstreaming the Dream: *Spy Kids, The Messenger*

Vincent A. Gutiérrez

Archaeologists can be considered the detectives of time because they investigate the mysteries from the past that often bring better understanding of present-day society. In their quest for knowledge they discover elements unearthed from history arranging them in a logical order subjected to the measurement of time. One of the basic measurements of civilization is art. From the Lascaux paintings created 17,000 years ago to works from ancient Mesopotamia to Mayan and Chinese antiquities it is art and its artists that helps the "detectives of time" reveal even the most hidden secrets from a long-ago culture. It can then be said that artists are the translators of the world around them during their lifetime.

Carl Jung proposed the concept of a *Collective Unconscious,* where the ideas of humankind are generated. It would be a place where the knowledge of the world, if not the universe, is kept open to all of humankind at *infinitely divergent* moments. It is from this point in time and space that an artist acts as a receptor from the *Collective Unconscious,* thus becoming a messenger who interprets the present while envisioning the possibilities of the future.

Throughout the ages, artists have labored to master their *medium:* The material used to make art. The art of the 20th century was the medium of the motion picture. This expensive and powerful art form has been manipulated to serve a multitude of issues and causes. *The New York Morning Post* as early as 1923 had already predicted,

> *If the United States abolished its diplomatic and Consular services, kept its ships in harbor and its tourists at home, and retired from the world's marketplace, its citizens, its problems, [. . .] motorcars [. . .] and saloons would still be familiar in the uttermost corners of the world [. . .] The film is to America what the flag was once to Britain. By its means Uncle Sam may hope someday, if he is not checked in time, to Americanize the world. (qtd in Maltby 68)*

Over the years, filmmaking has become an expensive medium (*Matrix Reloaded* cost 150 million dollars to produce), and those few who can control its expression *wield* power over those who do not. Consider Leni Reifenstal's *Triumph of the Will.* This film made in the 1930s shows Adolph Hitler's rise to power in Germany. It is a timeless document of the *exploitation* of imagery and sound, giving Hitler godlike qualities that surely helped him advance his cause, Nazism. Later filmmakers such as directors George Lucas and Ridley Scott were vastly influenced by Reifenstal's work. For example, in Lucas's first *Star Wars,*

> *Shot for shot the ceremonial "great hall" scene that is the most widely seen and noted influence/tribute to Leni Reifenstal [. . .] depict[ing] black booted Rebel Forces [. . .] turning on heel to face the three heroes as they walk up the great hall on the destruction of the Death Star. The* composition *and mood of the sequence is lifted directly from* Triumph of the Will. *("The Art")*

While in his film, *Gladiator,* director Ridley Scott "makes the boldest visual, editing, and soundtrack references to *Triumph of the Will*" ("The Art").

Given the power and the influence of such a medium, where does this leave the Chicano filmmaker? The making of Latino-based stories of quality in the mainstream media continues to be problematic. Decades of negative Latino stereotypical imagery remains the norm especially in television and film that feature Anglo leads while the very minor Latino characters are the usual maids, gardeners, ex-cons, undocumented workers, Latina bombshells, gangsters, drug dealers, and prostitutes. Is this policy or is it ignorance on the part of those in charge of producing movies and television shows for the media? Unquestionably, the media, as a reflection of the people of the United States, fails to depict any *semblance* of reality. According to a UCLA Chicano Studies Research Report,

> *. . . [T]he vast majority of network, prime-time, regular characters were white and only 4% were Latino. . . .*

> *The Latino population is now the largest minority group in the United States, accounting for 13% of the national population. Its* proportion *in the western United States is even more dramatic, nearly one-third of California and the plurality of Los Angeles (45%) yet, while located in Los Angeles Prime-Time Television turns its cameras away from the city's largest ethnic/racial group and presents a world without Latinos. (Hoffman)*

Despite this lack of acceptance by the mainstream media a few Chicanos have managed to break through this wall of resistance.

Indeed, those who live in the shadows of the dominant culture have to learn how to communicate with those who possess the keys to one of the most powerful forces in the world, the film and television image. Emerging from the shadows, a Texas-born Chicano, Robert Rodriguez broke into Hollywood with his legendary film, *Mariachi* (1992). The initial cost of the movie was $7,000.00. At the time he was only 23 years old. He found himself in a town that is notorious for converting artistic energy into corporate greed that can often leave the artist sucked dry of his/her creative integrity. In the next few years Rodriguez *honed* his craft on films *(Desparado, From Dusk Till Dawn, The Faculty)*, that did not compromise his artistic nature. Soon he was given many directorial opportunities but he began to reject them,

> . . . *I turned down a lot of movies . . . that were presold ideas because that's what everything is today. I turned down* Superman Lives, *I turned down even* X-men *early on in 96* . . . Planet of the Apes. *It was only because you go meet with a company and they say, " This is going to be a big corporate film and you're going to have to roll up your sleeves and sell burgers." [. . .] It's going to be a big hit no matter what you do . . . like what's the fun in that? ("Robert Rodriguez Interview")*

Rather than accept the usual path taken by others—selling one's soul to the highest bidder—Rodriguez could not deny the *undercurrents* of his Chicano cultural roots. What emerged was another landmark film for Rodriguez. *Spy Kids* (2001), is a movie that cleverly displays Chicano *sensibilities* in various, crafty and *delectable* ways *culminating* in the defeat of Hollywood's inherent institutional racism. Charles Dutton, a prominent African-American actor agrees:

> *Hollywood [. . .] has been that way for decades. It surprises me when people are surprised that there's racism in Hollywood [. . .] Hollywood's just another American corporation. Just because it's the so-called* bastion *of liberalism doesn't mean an iota that it does not have its own racial and racist policies. (Walker E 1)*

Rather than employing a frontal attack on the motion picture industry's racial policies, Rodriguez chose a *stealthy* process that infused *Spy Kids* with Chicano culture in imagery, casting, and sentiment. "In many ways, *Spy Kids* is a Chicano movie writ large, a sort of Trojan horse that smuggles the goods (ethnic pride, family values), into the multiplex disguised as entertainment" (Rich 37). Undoubtedly, in the hands of the usual Hollywood writer and director, *Spy Kids* would have been just another anglicized version of a reality made up in their own image. The richness of a unique culture would have been whitewashed away, leaving no resemblance to the original intention. Of course, the concept of the film can stand alone on its own merit. The idea of former spies who have married, then retire to raise a family, whose children later themselves become spies has great storytelling appeal. However, in Rodriguez's hands, from the first frames of *Spy Kids*, he wants the audience to celebrate the *vibrant* legacy of being Mexican.

At the beginning of the movie there is the cliff-top Spanish hacienda at the edge of the sea. The musical soundtrack that accompanies the image is filled with Latino soul. Once in the Cortez Hacienda, from the vivid color chosen for the walls to the Mexican colonial furniture, tiles, and pre-Columbian artifacts, Rodriguez *immerses* the viewer in homage to his Chicano heritage. In a flashback, the kids' mother, Ingrid tells them about a couple of spies who meet and marry. In the accompanying filmic images, the wedding cake is adorned with a bride wearing a wedding dress and a groom in a tuxedo who are *calaveras* (skeletons) in honor of *"Dia de los Muertos,"* a Mexican holiday held in respect of the dead. There is also the priest, while marrying the couple, wears a "serape" vestment. In another scene Juni, the Cortez's son, is having problems at school. His father Gregorio reminds him of his legacy, "Remember, you are a Cortez." Juni looks back at his father as he walks away from the car toward school, "What's so special about being a Cortez?" Certainly, Juni's last name is more than just a way to be identified. The name conjures up a historical lineage distinctive to Chicanos, a familial *lineage* that will soon make Juni proud to be a Cortez.

Juni and Carmen (the Cortez's daughter) come upon a safe-house where they need to hide. Remaining true to the spirit of his Mexican heritage Rodriguez makes Carmen repeat her full name in Spanish in order to gain entrance. The minute she says, "Carmen Juanita Acosta Bravo Cortez," the door swings open. In a later scene, a Chicano boy sees the Carmen/Juni look-alike robots fly into the sky powered by their shoes and calls out in Spanish, "I want shoes like that!" Again and again, Rodriguez takes what would otherwise be just another kid's movie and *permeates* it with a Brown people's presence that cannot be denied.

One of the most powerful statements Rodriguez makes in *Spy Kids* is casting Danny Trejo as Machete. Rodriguez turns the usual Hollywood typecasting upside down. Trejo's personal life has been hard from childhood drug addiction, followed by several prisons including San Quentin. He later saved his life on the 12-Step Program; then while helping a friend in the program, he was discovered by the movie industry. What follows is a long career of more than 70 films, most of which he was cast as a villain or a hardened criminal. This is a man with a dramatically scarred face, a thin moustache, strong *Indio* features, and a muscular body etched with tattoos. It is not difficult to assert that without a director like Rodriguez, Trejo would be doomed to always play Cholos, gangbangers, Latino villains, and any other *unsavory* character Hollywood could dream up for him. In the past, when an actor had proved his abilities, even if they appeared *rough-edged,* they would be advanced into better roles. A look into some Hollywood names synonymous with the tough-guy image brings to mind actors like: John Wayne, James Cagney, Humphrey Bogart, Robert Mitchum, and Arnold Schwarzenegger. As a rule, Chicano actors remain typecast and rarely progress further in mainstream media. That is what makes Trejo's Machete such a smart casting move. Rodriguez goes furiously against type, giving Machete the persona of a genius inventor who creates highly sophisticated electronic spy-gear. By the end of the movie he turns out to be heroic. What a concept: a Chicano as a movie hero. Indeed, the entire Cortez family is heroic, and without Rodriguez's *innate* understanding of his culture, Chicano film heroes would still be hard to find, especially for kids.

The battlefield Rodriguez encountered in Hollywood is still unfriendly territory for most minorities. A recent *Los Angeles Times* article agrees:

> *Most have not been in business long enough to advance to the top echelons where decisions on programming and hiring are made. Others have been too busy trying to survive in a brutal industry [. . .] in which Latinos make up only 2% of the producers, directors, and writers guilds—to worry about advancing an ethnic agenda. (Munoz and Braxton F1)*

Perhaps Rodriguez states it best for future Chicano filmmakers in an interview with *Hispanic Magazine:*

> *The problems with Latino filmmakers is that [. . .] they want to make up for all the Latino films that were never made, and their movies turn out to be all this bleeding heart stuff, and nobody goes. You have to be sneakier than that. You have to know how to fool the moneymen. (Rodriguez 34).*

There is a line from a movie, *Witches of Eastwick,* where Jack Nicholson, the Devil, is trying to seduce Cher. He says to her, "Time's the killer." He is pointing out her mortality, that one is only given so much time on earth, and then there's no more. All that will be left behind are the relics from the past. What will those "detectives of time" from some point in the future say about our new millennium? Will they dig up the fallen, decayed fragments that were once the Hollywood sign, dig deeper, and even deeper, revealing bits and pieces of what was once MEDIA; and there, a frame of film is uncovered. More film is unwound until they see that classic Chicano face. It's Danny Trejo as Machete—not the cholo-gangbanger, but the genius inventor, subservient to no one, master of his own fate, all because a filmmaker of vision had to count for something beyond the ordinary. Imagine when that "detective of time" from the vantage point of the future declares that Chicanos/as were an integral part of Hollywood and their society at large.

Works Cited

"The Art of Leni Riefenstahl." *Das Blaue Licht.* 2003. 06 June 2003 <*http://www.dash-blauelicht.net/new*>.

Hoffman, Alison. "Looking for Latino Regulars on Prime-Time Television: The Fall 2002 Season." *UCLA Chicano Studies Research Center.* No 1 Apr 2003. 20 May 2003 <*http://www.sscnet.ucla.edu/csrc*>.

Maltby, Richard. *Hollywood Cinema.* Cambridge: Blackwell Publishers, 1995.

Munoz, Lorena, and Greg Braxton. "An Accent in Progress." *Los Angeles Times.* 6 Jan. 2001, F1.

Rich, B. Ruby. "Mexico at the Multiplex." *Nation.* 14 May 2001: 37.

Rodriguez, Rene. "Latinos Abound in: *Spy Kids.*" *Hispanic.* 30 April 2001: 34.

"Robert Rodriguez Interview—*Spy Kids,* Part 3: Sequels and Zorro." *About.* 12 Apr. 2003. 15 Mar. 2001 <*http:/actionadventure.about.com/2001*>.

Spy Kids. Dir. Robert Rodriguez. Perf. Antonio Banderas, Carla Gugino, Danny Trejo, Alexa Vega, and Daryl Sabara. Dimension Films, 2001.

Walker, Dave. "On the Air." *Times-Picayune.* New Orleans, 20 Oct. 2000. 23 June 2003. Proquest <*http//www.proquest.umi.com*>.

Witches of Eastwick. Dir. George Miller. Perf. Jack Nicholson and Cher. Warner Bros. Pictures, 1987.

Writing Prompts

1. Describe how Robert Rodriguez infuses *Spy Kids* with Chicano/a culture, according to Gutiérrez.

2. Consider the character Machete. Gutiérrez describes Machete's appearance. Compare his real looks to the role he plays in the film. Explain why Rodriguez decided to cast Danny Trejo, according to Gutiérrez.

3. The process of making art is a self-expression of truth. Can corporate-generated art be truthful, according to Gutiérrez?

4. What is the reason Gutiérrez points out that 45% of the population in Los Angeles is Latino? What does this have to do with economic power?

5. The title of this essay reflects the theme. Explain.

No Substitution: The Play vs. the Film
Real Women Have Curves

Fabiola Torres-Reyes

Have you ever had to read a book but did not have time, so you saw the movie instead? If you see the movie *Real Women Have Curves* instead of reading the play, you are wasting your time. However, if you get a chance to see the play, run to the box office.

The play *Real Women Have Curves* is set in a tiny sewing factory with eight sewing machines and a mannequin in the corner. On the surface, this is an outrageously entertaining story of five full-figured Chicanas and Mexicanas racing to meet a nearly impossible deadline to keep their tiny business from going under while they hide from the Immigration Nationalization Service. However, the real story is about Ana's transformation, and how, during the course of the play, she learns to respect women's work, and to appreciate how women come together to support one another.

The story is told from the point of view of Ana, the youngest among them. She just graduated from high school, and dreams of getting out of the barrio, going off to college, and becoming a famous writer. Although she needs money, Ana doesn't like working at the factory, and has little respect for the co-workers who make fun of her ambition and idealistic "feminist ideas." Ana turns her job into an opportunity to write, and chronicles in her journal the daily life of the women working in the garment factory. As the summer unfolds, she slowly gains an understanding and appreciation of the work and the women. Ana eventually writes an essay that wins her a journalism fellowship to study at Columbia University in New York City.

The play presents a desire to find a space between individualism and solidarity with others. The space discovered by Ana and the other female characters is one of emancipation. Emancipation is "the act or process of setting somebody free or of freeing somebody from restrictions" (Riverside Webster's Dictionary). The restrictions presented to the women in the play were *gender* based and connected to the idea of having an ideal woman's body. These are the barriers explained through the voice of Ana. But through this explanation, she learns about resistance and *solidarity*, something that no other activist, philosopher, or feminist could have taught her.

Ana believed that she alone would succeed without the help of anyone. It was clear that the stories of these women provided Ana her access to a fellowship, enabling her to pursue her dream of being a writer. She does *emancipate* herself from minimum wage work, East L.A., and even her family, but the accumulation of every experience she undergoes in the sewing factory, community and in her family contributed to her emancipation.

Josefina Lopez created fully developed characters that change and become self-empowered women. They realize that it does not matter how they look, but how they embrace other women in collective liberation. None of these women, including Ana, could have reached self-confidence and determination if it was not for one other. This message needs to reach all women. Bell Hooks states, "Without knowing what factors have created certain problems in the first place we could not begin to develop meaningful strategies of personal and collective resistance" (14). What other way can this powerful message reach thousands of women? *Real Women Have Curves* was made into a movie in 2002. Finally, Hollywood makes a great film about great women . . . and they happen to be Latinas. Eat your heart out *Steel Magnolias* (1989).

I attended a special screening of *Real Women Have Curves* (2002), at UCLA. I was excited, anticipating an empowering story to unfold before me. Instead, I saw a disturbing film about an angry young woman (Ana), and her irritable, mean-spirited, and "cruel" mother (Carmen). Conflict develops between mother and daughter because she received a scholarship to attend Columbia University. This means Ana will not be able to help her sister and mother in the sewing factory. Plus, Ana will leave the safety of home and family. I asked myself, "What happened? Why was it changed? Did Hollywood think the plot was too radical? Why was the mother so unsupportive? Who is George LaVoo, and why is he the co-writer?" Then I realized that thousands of moviegoers would see a movie about a Mexican mother who did not want her daughter to attend college.

The movie is about Ana (America Ferrera), a first-generation Mexican-American teenager who decides to attend college after her high school teacher (George Lopez) who suggests she apply to Columbia University. However, her mother Carmen (Lupe Ontiveros) rejects Ana's desire to go to college and demands that Ana work for her sister Estela (Ingrid Oliu), in her sewing factory. Ana, who does a lot of exasperated sighing and angry eye-rolling, is bitter about her mother's constant nagging about Ana's weight, the work in the sewing factory, and her family's disapproval of her college *aspirations*. She is drawn to a white classmate named Jimmy because he understands and respects both her dreams in a way her family members cannot. The movie, however, does not allow the audience to see or understand what her goals are, or why she wants to go to college in the first place. This is obvious in Ana's "personal statement" in her college application. After discussing college with her teacher Mr. Guzman, she does not complete the application because she knows her parents will not give her moral support. She finally does take her application to her teacher, without having written the "personal statement." He sends her back home to write one. In a series of (montage) scenes, the visuals show Ana sitting in her nopal-decorated backyard with a notebook. Then she hands the application to her teacher. The audience never knows the contents of the statement that could have been conveyed in voiceover. This was necessary because it would have provided the audience a glimpse of her inner feelings and desires—her personal history, her spirit. The personal statement is significant because this is what gets her into Columbia University.

In the play, Ana uses the restroom as her inner-sanctum. She describes in her journal her daily frustrations and her achievements and reads out-loud for the benefit of the play's audience. Ana reveals her inner-self through journal writing. This does not happen in the film. Director Patricia Cardoso states in the DVD audio commentary that the unspoken is more powerful ("Audio Commentary . . ."). Cardoso also states that Ana's character is believable and real. Real? Ana does not even apply to Columbia University until the summer before the college's fall semester begins. She did not even think a personal statement was necessary. However, when all was said and done, Ana is accepted to Columbia with a full scholarship.

Co-writer George LaVoo explains why the play's immigration plot was omitted from the movie. In the play, immigration status is an important theme. After all, the characters were once undocumented and *persecuted*. But LaVoo states in the DVD audio commentary that immigration plots ". . . are a bit outdated and things have changed." On May 15, 2003, eighteen Latino undocumented immigrants died in a trailer crammed with up to 140 men, women and children in Victoria, Texas (Englingwood and Scott A1). Within the U.S. population, immigration has always been in our stories. "More than 50 percent of immigrants since 1960 have been from Latin America" (Gonzalez XI).

In the audio commentary by Patricia Cardoso, George LaVoo, and Josefina Lopez, Cardoso reveals personal feelings about her own mother. One of her comments stated how **real** it was for Latina mothers to be so "cruel" because her mother was like that. Patricia Cardoso describes the scene when Ana looks at her body the morning after she has sex with Jimmy, an Anglo classmate who has a crush on her. Cardoso says that she wished she could have been strong like Ana. For instance, when Carmen realizes through her motherly *instincts* that Ana is no longer a virgin, Carmen calls her a *puta*. Ana stands up to her mother, and yells back. Cardoso lamented, "I wish I would have stood up and done this to my mother when she called me a *puta*." Moreover, LaVoo backs up Cardoso's comment by saying, "Ana is growing in strength when she yells at her mother." On the other hand, Josefina Lopez responds with, "My mother was understanding." In fact, in the beginning of the audio commentary, Josefina Lopez states that she felt compelled to tell her own mother that Carmen's character was not based on her.

The movie did have an emotional and *empowering* scene when Ana inspires the *voluptuous* women in Estela's sweaty garment shop to strip down to their underwear. It is a scene that one might see in a Nelly video, but with obese women. However, Cardoso's choice not to show Carmen's cesarean scars did the whole scene harm. In the play, Carmen strips down to her underwear to show her aged, scarred body to the other women who have not had children. Carmen's beautiful, curvaceous, aged body demonstrates that women are life's heroines with the scars to prove it. In the movie, after the women strip, Carmen looks at the women in disgust, calling them *desvergonsadas*.

On an upbeat note, the male characters have positive roles in the movie: Ana's grandfather, father, Jimmy, and her cousins. The men support and encourage Ana to pursue her goals. Her grandfather tells her she is "precious as gold"; her father gives her his blessing when Ana decides to go to Columbia University; Jimmy loves her body (especially after having sex); and her cousins hug her and tell her they will visit her in New York. In the end, Patricia Cardoso states in the audio commentary that men came up to her to express their pleasure at seeing positive roles for men. Then she later states that she personally has always had good relationships with her father and other men. This should explain why the male characters were positive in contrast to that of the mother.

According to Cardoso's version of the story's ending, Carmen refuses to say good-bye or give Ana her blessing. To LaVoo, this was a universal moment and a moment of truth. Yet in the play, Carmen never stands in the way of Ana or Estela's dreams. Yes, she does try to convince her two daughters to lose weight so they "can catch a man." "Catching a man" is important to Carmen because her understanding of "womanhood" is connected to motherhood. But as the play develops, Carmen realizes that "womanhood" is about realizing dreams and self-determination. In the end, it is Carmen's idea to contribute to Estela's dream. However, the film ends with no voiceover or explanation of what Carmen or Ana are feeling. The camera only shows Ana walking along a street in New York City.

All in all, Patricia Cardoso's film *Real Women Have Curves* failed to provide an opportunity for women all over America to be *empowered* by Mexican garment workers, bonding in the workplace and encouraging one another's dreams. The film *Real Women Have Curves* presented a story with women working against one another with no reconciliation. It is reconciliation between the "Mexican way" and the "American modern way" that makes the play so valuable. This reconciliation is expressed in the emotional and powerful *monologue* by Ana at the end of the play.

> *I always took their work for granted, to be simple and unimportant. I was not proud to be working there at the beginning. I was only glad to know that because I was educated, I wasn't going to end up like them. I was going to be better than them. And I wanted to show them how much smarter and liberated*

I was. I was going to teach them about the women's liberation movement, about sexual liberation, and all the things a so-called educated American woman knows. But in their subtle ways, they taught me about resistance. About a battle no one was fighting for them except themselves. About the loneliness of being mothers and submissive wives. With their work that seems simple and unimportant, they are fighting . . . Perhaps the greatest thing I learned from them is that women are powerful, especially when working together. (Lopez 69)

The monologue presents reconciliation between submission and resistance, arrogance and humbleness, oppression and liberation, individualism and solidarity.

Both the film and the play present different obstacles toward *self-determination*. The obstacle represented in the play is the inability to *reconcile* between two worlds. It is only when Ana and the other characters realize how the benefits of the "Mexican way" and the "American way" can create a new identity that captures the best of two worlds. On the other hand, the film represented the mother as the obstacle. Patricia Cardoso provided no room for reconciliation between mother and daughter. Cardoso could have used a simple gesture to illustrate a compromise—*la bendición*. Instead, Cardoso portrays a stubborn character unwilling to support her daughter's desire to acquire an education.

Josefina Lopez had to compromise to get this film made, for it is every playwright's dream to see her/his screenplay on the silver screen. Knowing Josefina as I do, she compromised many of her values. She stands firm behind her 11 requirements to becoming a "Chingona": number 9, LOVE YOUR MOTHER; number 8, EMPOWER OTHER HERMANAS (Lopez, "My Low"). These requirements are apparent in the play, but not in the movie. Clearly there is no substitution.

Works Cited

"Audio Commentary by Patricia Cardoso, George LaVoo, and Josefina Lopez." *Real Women Have Curves*. Dir. Patricia Cardoso. 2002. [DVD].

Elingwood, Ken, and Scott Gold. "Headline Title." *Los Angeles Times*. 15 May. 2003: F1.

Gonzalez, Juan. *Harvest of Empire*. New York: Viking, 2000.

Hooks, Bell. *Sisters of the Yam*. Boston: South End Press, 1993.

Lopez, Josefina. *Real Women Have Curves*. London: Dramatic Publishing, 1997.

————. *My Low Self Esteem Days and Other Poetic Thoughts*. Los Angeles: n.p., 1997.

Riverside Webster's II Dictionary. Revised Edition. New York: Berkley Books, 1996.

Writing Prompts

1. What is the conflict between Ana, the main character, and her mother, according to Torres Reyes?

2. How did the women in the factory empower one another?

3. What is the writer's purpose for having the women in the factory take their clothes off in front of one another? Explain.

4. Have you ever had to defend your goals and dreams to your parents?

5. What is the most valuable lesson your mother or father taught you?

Social Imagineering in Disney's *The Lion King:* The Three "C's"

Gabriel Gutiérrez

At the turn of the twenty-first century, democracy in the United Sates is defined by pressures to conform to a *homogenous* national character. To this end British historian E. J. Hobsbawm (1992) writes that attempts at *nationhood* generate "invented traditions," which result from a conglomeration and often *co-optation* of pre-existing belief systems. Such traditions result in what Benedict Anderson (1983) calls "imagined communities" that call for a simultaneous *homogenization* of dominant ideals and *marginalization* of non-dominant ideals.

When examining Disney's *The Lion King* this becomes significant because of the underlying, if unintentional, messages for *subaltern* children. There are several defining moments in *The Lion King* that posit an attempt to construct accepted political beliefs and social behavior. While these *parameters* are constructed, dissenting beliefs and behavior are made to appear as evil and *conniving*. In this essay, I suggest that the plot line is characterized by three "C's": Conformity, Contestation, and Consolidation. Combined, the three "C's" reflect Mufasa's (the patriarch and father of the young lion king) lessons to his son and heir apparent Simba: They reflect the circle of life. Thus, these C's suggest a *pseudo* natural composition of state building at various stages: establishing the state, repressing *dissidence,* and defending the *status quo* through *reaffirmation* of privilege for the elite.

The first of these C's—conformity—is reflected across species and gender. The opening scene of *The Lion King* depicts different species traveling long distances to greet Simba the newborn lion cub and heir to the throne. This *convergence* of beasts and their subordination to the newborn prince denotes an acceptance of a hierarchal social positioning. Animals at the bottom of the food chain gladly accept their suppressed state. The *juxtaposition* and calm peace among the different wild species, some of them natural enemies, further suggests the mission of *The Lion King:* an attempt to control or otherwise regulate diversity. Here the implications are that diversity is good only when groups who represent difference are content with their respectively unequal and suppressed social positioning. In the movie, as in U.S. society, social positioning derives in part from cultural and racial difference.

A second example of conformity is Mufasa's statement to Simba that "everything that exists, exists in delicate *equilibrium:* the circle of life." In doing this Disney "imagineers"

———
Excerpts reprinted with permission of The Regents of the University of California from "Deconstructing Disney: Chicano/a children and Critical Race Theory (Spring 2000), UCLA Chicano Studies Research Center. Not for further reproduction.

(animators and creators), through Mufasa, construct a pseudo "objective" reality suggesting in *social Darwinist* fashion that social hierarchy and the mechanisms that maintain it are a part of nature and that Simba's eventual place atop that hierarchy must be closely guarded, thus, a *"delicate equilibrium"* (Harding & Haraway, 1996). This event sets the rules and establishes parameters for the rest of the film. It foreshadows events to come such as *contestation* and eventual *consolidation*.

Gendered conformity is also apparent in several instances. One example of this includes Simba's "rough-housing" with his young female friend and eventual spouse Nala. As they play she outwits him and physically overpowers him. All the while Nala teases Simba that she (a girl) is smarter and stronger than he (a boy). Despite these "innocent" affirmations, both concur that it doesn't matter, since in spite of this, Simba, not Nala, will be king one day. Another example of this type of conformity is the reluctant *acquiescence* of the lionesses to Scar, Simba's villainous uncle. At one point in the movie Scar manipulates Simba into believing that he is responsible for Mufasa's death and convinces Simba to flee and never return. Scar, who is next in line to the throne, becomes king by forging an alliance with the lions' natural enemy, the hyenas. While the lionesses are visibly in disagreement they do not act on their beliefs until Simba's return. Thus, while the females of the species do not hide their displeasure, they nonetheless remain loyal to the supposed natural order and submit to male authority and privilege.

The nature of Scar's disloyalty to the lions and in short to the kingdom/nation is significant for several reasons. This event represents the first real challenge to the supposed natural order. Scar's defection and the hyenas rise to power highlight the second "C"—contestation. Initially lions and hyenas conflict over territorial rights. This dichotomy is represented in light of the beautiful, fertile, and lively kingdom-nation that belongs to the lions and the *obscure* "shadowy place" that is the domain of the hyenas. The "shadowy place" reminds the audience of the presumed inability of non-whites to run their own states. Scar, the dark and *sinister* lion, allies himself with the savage, thug-like hyenas to conspire and take over the kingdom. As Robert Gooding-Williams (1995, p. 377) reminds us, in this sequence, *The Lion King* suggests:

> *that the impoverished life of America's inner cities is itself the product of a communicable* malaise *embodied by inner-city residents.* Enfranchise *poor blacks and Latinos, Disney's movie intimates, and this malaise—a sort of biological and perhaps racist version of the Moynihan Report's* "tangle of pathology"— *will spread inwards from the polity's* periphery, *entirely consuming its vital resources.*

The imagery in the scenes of the alliance between Scar and the hyenas depict darkness and flames. Thus, the attempt to assert themselves and to contest the "natural order" of their domination is represented within satanic and hellish contexts. The message to marginalized children is evident: don't question authority, don't question socially constructed parameters, accept your *submerged* position in society. To violate this message is to place oneself in the position of these villainous creatures. To plot against the state may result in condemnation to hell or may be seen as an act of the devil. In this manner Disney's pedagogical significance is combined with a social imagineering that teaches children to accept their suppressed status in order to ensure a peaceful coexistence with those members of society who occupy dominant positions.

The *appropriation* of this imagery further suggests the *conscription* of conscience and its internal administrator—guilt—by Disney's social imagineers. The role of conscience as a self-regulatory mechanism and its contribution to a distinct form of Anglo-Saxon *republicanism* has been evident since the formation of the United States (Takaki, 1990, pp. 3–10). Intangible characteristics were and continue to be *racialized*. As the so-called "founding fathers" were devising the birth of the nation the ideas of reason and other mental capacities that included conscience were believed to be in the exclusive possession of whites. Thus, non-whites were *infantalized* and believed incapable of possessing such mental capacities. In a similar way Disney creators attribute criteria for a social and civil backwardness to the racialized and gendered species who occupy the lower social positions in *The Lion King*. It is made to appear that those who challenge the established order lack a moral sense of conscience.

Thus, after having established the rules of the game in the form of racial, gender, and class constructed parameters, Disney's social imagineers relay a devastating message for children who attempt to challenge those rules. In this case, children are scared into assimilating "normal" American principles and at the same time warned of the devastating individual and social consequences for non-assimilation or non-acceptance of unequal social positioning.

The emphasis on assimilation encourages a particular conservatism in that it almost forces children to want to belong to the "natural order" even if it means that they have to sacrifice privilege and power. The important thing is that children avoid devastation that results from revolt so that the "delicate equilibrium" of the "circle of life" is maintained. Hence, regardless of how much power one has or lacks, social order results in a form of security. On the other hand, Disney's social imagineers also project an alternative to the *conservatism* of assimilation. The *neo-liberalism* espoused in *The Lion King* encourages children who are aware of their compromised positions to accept their fate, be patient, and they will eventually reap their reward. This is best exemplified by the reluctant acquiescence of the lionesses to the revolutionary Scar/hyena alliance and regime.

Every character, minus Simba, who is without or with relatively less power and asserts him/herself is portrayed as evil and sinister. Conditions worsen for everyone when these characters assert themselves and attempt to improve their conditions through the acquisition of power. Their assertion of power results in social decay as reflected in the drought and famine that follow the Scar and hyena inspired takeover/revolution. Disney's message here is that social decay and the decline of the industrial world as we know it result from the *ascendance* of historically marginalized groups into power. Disney takes this message a bit further suggesting that acquiescence to authority is moral and a violation of this results in social chaos and eternally punitive consequences for the individual. In turn the individual is left to determine his/her own fate by dealing with his/her own conscience.

The third "C"—consolidation—is represented by the rehabilitation and restoration of the old order through the reaffirmation of traditional ideals. Sex and species privileges are combined and reclaimed as social forces. The hyena social structure is matrilineal, or female dominant. Hyenas also represent a different species, which in the context of U.S. society represents different ethnicities or "outgroups." Thus, when the hyenas assert themselves and take power from the patriarchal lions, Disney's social imagineers assert that the consequences are mismanagement and chaos.

The consolidation of old views is represented in Simba's return as an adult to reclaim "his" kingdom/nation. This portion of the plot also takes on biblical proportions and can be equated with the return of the prodigal son or even the re-emergence of Jesus Christ himself. Simba's return as the savior results in the final suppression of the hyena insurrection as order is restored and as good wins over evil. Simba, with celestial help from his father Mufasa, becomes the savior/king. The lionesses, upon Simba's return join in the counter-revolutionary or restoration efforts on behalf of the kingdom/nation. Thus, while they were in opposition to the Scar/hyena rule, the lionesses waited for the return of their male king before acting on their political beliefs. Once the insurrection is repressed and order is restored, the drought and famine end. A storm comes and vegetation grows back. The gloomy atmosphere that was representative of the Scar/hyena regime is replaced by scenic color and contentment among all in the film. All species, whether happily or begrudgingly, once again accept their subservient positions to the lions. Nala and Simba have a cub together and the opening scene resurfaces. All species from distant places travel to greet and pledge their allegiance to their eventual king. All species submerge themselves once again so that the delicate equilibrium can be maintained.

The three "C's" reflect the delicacy of equilibrium found in the race, gender, and class based hierarchical social positioning, which *indubitably* is projected as the criteria of kingdomhood/nationhood, which Mufasa preached to Simba early on. In the end, the circle of life is about the trials and tribulations waged by power struggles among competing factions and the ability to maintain social privilege through the guise of proper comportment and social order. Such behavior is encouraged by the infusion of threatening consequences for those who dare to question authority and the established cultural, social, and economic parameters.

Political consequences for dissent are reflected in the *Lion King's* message that non-conformity is to be met with damnation or other repercussions reflective of criminality. Children who see *The Lion King* are exposed not only to society's conformist rules but to the consequences for violating them. To have "impure" thoughts reflects the *subversive* potential of the individual. When the individual self-regulates and experiences guilt for having had those thoughts, we assume that the natural order of things has once again proven successful since the individual has stayed "in bounds" and out of trouble. In this regard, Disney's "social imagineering" of rules and acceptable behavior circumvents the potential to be critical of inequality and lack of fairness in American society.

References

Anderson, B. (1992). *Imagined communities*. London: Verso.

Gooding-Williams, R. (1995). Disney in Africa and the inner city: On race and space in The Lion King. *Social Identities, 1*(2), 377.

Haraway, D. (1996). Situated knowledge: The scientific question in feminism and the privilege of partial perspective. In Keller & Longino (Ed.), *Feminism and science* (pp. 249–263). Oxford: Oxford University Press.

Harding, S. (1996). Rethinking standpoint epistemology: What is "strong objectivity?" In Keller & Longino (Ed.), *Feminism and science* (pp. 235–248). Oxford: Oxford University Press.

Hobsbawn, E. J. (1992). *Nations and nationalism since 1780*. New York: Cambridge University Press.

Takaki, R. (1990). *Iron cages: Race and culture in 19th-century America*. Oxford: Oxford University Press.

Writing Prompts

1. Discuss what the author means when he writes that "the mission of *The Lion King* is an attempt to control or otherwise regulate diversity."

2. Briefly explain two of the three C's: conformity and consolidation. For example, Gutiérrez says through one of the C's—"contestation," people of color accept subordination in *The Lion King*.

3. According to Gutiérrez, how do people form different social positions?

4. Why do you think the lionesses, although opposed to Scar and the hyenas, await Simba's return before acting on their "political beliefs"? Is that, in any way, a reflection of the ways in which human beings behave? Why, or why not?

Viva *Chocolat*

Gerard Meraz

The five time, Oscar-nominated film *Chocolat* (2001), starring Juliette Binoche, Judi Dench, Alfred Molina, Lena Olin, and Johnny Depp, was not just another period love story. The film's *synopsis* tells the story of a striking woman who comes to an old-fashioned French town and opens a *chocolaterie* that inspires the citizens to "abandon themselves to temptation and happiness" *(Chocolat)*. In return, she finds love and peace. Upon closer inspection, from a cultural studies and Chicano/a Studies perspective, *Chocolat* becomes a feminist, Xicanisma (Castillo 11), a tale of identity, tradition, and liberation.

The lead character Vianne (Binoche) is a Chicana. She is the daughter of a French pharmacist who traveled to Central America to research medicinal plants. One night he experiences the powers of chocolate and falls in love with a local native woman who is a *shaman* or *curandera*. Her particular role as shaman is to travel the countryside following the North wind dispensing medicinal and spiritual cures to troubled souls. They marry, move back to France, and have Vianne, their *mestiza* daughter. Once Vianne is old enough to travel, mother takes daughter on the path of her people. Leaving her husband behind, she travels the countryside and helps *heal* souls via the powers of their delicious chocolate-based *culinary* creations. According to the film, Mayan *cacao,* or chocolate, was used "in their sacred ceremonies (that) held the power to unlock *yearnings* and reveal destinies" *(Chocolat)*. For example, Vianne gives a village woman cocoa beans that helps re-ignite her husband's *libido* and to another woman (Lena Olin's Josephine Muscat), Vianne gives not only chocolate but advice that empowers her to leave her abusive husband.

Vianne's *mestiza* background is a beautiful back story in and of itself, but the social political implications of her upbringing and how she raises her own daughter refers to a historical identity that is at the core of Chicano/a Studies. In Ana Castillo's work, *Massacre of the Dreamers: Essays on Xicanisma,* she describes how "Xicana" identity is based on a *matriarchal paradigm.* Matriarchates were first popularized in 19th century feminist discourse in the work by Matilda Joslin Gage, *Woman, Church and State: A Historcial Account of the Status of Woman Through the Christian Ages: With Reminiscence of The Matriarchate* (1893). According to Gage,

> *This priority of the mother touched not alone the family, but controlled the state and indicated the form of religion. Thus we see that during the Matriarchate, woman ruled; she was first in the family, the state, (and) religion. The tribe was united through the mother; social, political and religious life were all in harmony with the idea of woman as the first and highest power. (14)*

Using feminist and anthropological sources Castillo brings forth how women organized many native societies of the pre-Columbian era, and how an individual's position in his/her society was based on his/her mother's position, which was usually as leader or healer/spiritual guide (Castillo 222). Castillo *posits* that today's Chicanos/as are continuing or re-learning Amer-Indian *matrilineal* traditions, such as *curanderismo* (145). One of Chicano/a Studies central themes is to what degree can Chicanos/as maintain traditions, be they pre-Columbian or post colonial, and to what degree must they *assimilate* to the current dominant culture and changing social *morés?*

Assimilation was not part of Vianne's life with her native Mayan mother, and it is debatable if her second-generation daughter, Anoch, will adapt to the dominant culture. In the film, Vianne's *adherence* to her people's traditions makes her an immediate outcast. She is a single mother; she is not Catholic and refuses to attend church even for "appearance sake." She opens her chocolate shoppe during lent, and she stocks the shoppe with Mayan art and pottery that seem almost *satanic* in contrast to the Catholic Church across the town square. This refusal to assimilate or cast aside her traditions takes its toll on her daughter Anoch. She is tired of traveling from town-to-town, carrying her grandmother's ashes in an ancient looking *urn* every time the North wind blows. Anoch wants to settle in this town and live a "normal" life. Vianne is torn between her loyalty to her people's way of life (*matrilineal* tradition) and her daughter's happiness (negation of tradition).

Vianne's liberation and the happy ending of the movie shows her deciding to stay in town and abandon the traveling chocolate-dispensing *curandera* life. The life-transforming scene shows Vianne dragging Anoch down the stairs carrying bags and the urn containing ashes of Vianne's mother. As Anoch is crying, kicking, and screaming, the urn is dropped and the ashes scatter all over the stairs. As Anoch apologizes, and picks up the ashes, Vianne realizes the pain she is causing her daughter, by clinging to an *irrevocable* past. Vianne openly weeps in shame and sorrow. The next scene shows Vianne awaking to the sound of the wind. She opens her bedroom window and lets her mother's ashes fly away. Like many Chicanas who break from traditional or *stereotypical* roles, Vianne realizes that she does not have to continue living her mother's ways. She decides to keep her chocolate shoppe, which has liberated so many lives, and now liberates herself from her role of traveling from town to town.

In informal discussions about this essay and its thesis, many politically and socially aware Chicanos/as also acknowledge the Chicana role of Vianne. Vincent Gutiérrez, a screenwriter, noted the symbolic importance of the décor Vianne uses in her chocolate shoppe, which he currently sees "decorating many of my colleagues' businesses and homes" (Telephone Interview). Lorena Salazar, a special education graduate student, admires how Vianne tackled the *patriarchal* system that ignored the suffering of women. She likens Vianne's struggle to artists/activists she admires such as Lorna Dee Cervantes, Cherríe

Moraga, and Barbara Carrasco, "who use beauty of words or art to empower women. In Vianne's case she used chocolate recipes handed down by her *curandera* mother" (Personal Interview). Vianne's chocolate embodies a healing power that transforms men and women, so they can experience and express love.

In reading the various reviews and praises this film *garnered,* not once do film critics refer to Vianne's native culture, or indicate that she is mestiza. Critic Roger Ebert at the very least mentions the ancient battle between the old and new world when he wrote, "*Chocolat* is about a war between the forces of *paganism* and Christianity, and because the pagan *heroine* has chocolate on her side, she wins" (Internet). Much more disturbing, and one reason why this essay was written, was because the various Latino/a groups who usually protest any perceived slight against *La Raza* in film, also missed this beautiful representation of an aspect of our culture. Vianne is a fully developed lead character, who not only helps others find personal liberation, but she also grows and transforms herself. One wonders had they wanted to make a film about a Chicana who did what Vianne does in the film, would the character have been so rich and positive. Chicana/o roles in today's cinema have progressed just slightly above the negative stereotypes that were common just 10 years ago. Hookers, maids, thieves, cops, "the bad guy," "the victim," or the character *swooning* over an Anglo object of desire or salvation are the current roles being played by our major Latino stars. Thank you "Viva *Chocolat*" for showing that Chicanos/as can be positive lead characters. If only major film companies would do this consciously and with Chicano/a actors.

Works Cited

Castillo, Ana. *Massacre of the Dreamers: Essays on Xicanisma.* New York: Penguin Books, 1995.

Chocolat. Dir. Lasse Hallstrom. Perf. Juliette Binoche, Judi Dench, Alfred Molina, Lena Olin, and Johnny Depp. Miramax, 2001.

Ebert, Roger. "*Chocolat.*" *Chicago Sun-Times,* December 22, 2000. *http://www.suntimes.com/ebert/ebert_reviews/2000/12/122202.html*

Gage, Matilda Joslin. *Woman, Church and State: A Historical Account of The Status of Woman Through the Christian Ages: With Reminiscences of the Matriarchate.* New York: Truth Seeker Company, 1893 {Scanned at Sacred-texts.com, March-April 2002. John Bruno Hare, Redactor.} *http://www.sacred-texts.com/wmn/wcs/wcs00.htm*

Gutierrez, Vincent. Personal Interview. 2 May, 2003. Northridge, California.

Salazar, Lorena. Personal Interview. 27 April, 2003. Los Angeles, California.

Writing Prompts

1. What is the significance of chocolate in the film *Chocolat,* according Meraz? Explain his argument. Do you agree?

2. Do you see a parallel between Vienne's traditions she inherited from her mother, and those of Chicano/a and Mexican culture.

3. Why did Vianne finally let go of her mother's ashes? What is the symbolism in this scene? Analyze and explain.

4. Meraz reveals that the film does not point out the connection Vianne has to indigeous culture. Why does he find this disturbing?

Salma's *Frida:* A Visual "Feast," But Not without Its Disappointments

Roberta Orona-Cordova

The release of the long-awaited bio-pic of Frida Kahlo finally arrived on the big screen in the fall of 2002. Interest in Frida was sparked in the Chicano/a community on November 2, 1978, through the "*Homenaje* de Frida Kahlo," at the *Galería de la Raza,* in the Mission District in San Francisco. Then, in 1983, the most widely read biography of Frida Kahlo, *penned* by Hayden Herrera introduced Frida Kahlo to many more national and international readers. Therein began a frenzied interest in Frida: ". . . in the past 20 years, Kahlo's paintings have appeared on everything from cocktail napkins to baseball caps" (Schwartz). Admirers find fascination with her life, her art, her sexual relationships with women, and with men, her politics, her drug and alcohol addiction, and her love-hate relationship with her husband, Mexican muralist, Diego Rivera.

> *(Frida) had it all in terms of politically correct victimization: She was half-Jewish, Hispanic, leftist, bisexual, female artist, who suffered a crippling accident, was oppressed by a* phallocratic *husband, and made love to a Russian exile (Leon Trotsky). What more could one ask of a culture heroine today? (Schwartz)*

For many, to know Frida was to admire her and all she stood for as a woman ahead of her time. For Chicana scholars and artists, Frida became a cultural and feminist role model. During the early days of the Chicano/a Movement, Chicanas sought independence in their scholarship, creative writing, and their art. They found an *affinity* with Frida, for their lives followed similar patterns: breaking away from rigid Catholic traditions and expectations that *subjugated* women; the most obvious was the *dichotomy* between the virgin and the whore—and according to early Church influence, a woman is either one or the other. Like the rebellious Frida, Chicanas rebelled too, thanks to the feminist movement in the 1960s and the Chicana liberation movement, which was a renaissance for women who, at the time, were in universities and art schools, and following graduation, successfully started professional careers.

Frida lived in old-fashioned, traditional, Catholic Mexico (1907–1954). Patriarchy ruled and women adhered to static and assigned roles, yet there were exceptions, and Frida Kahlo was one of them. She was independent in thought and practice; yet contradictory in that she was willfully dependent on Rivera, a man she loved unconditionally in spite of his *candid* confession he could never be faithful to anyone *(Frida)*. "I cannot love him for what he is not," she told Betrand Wolfe, Rivera's biographer (qtd in Herrera 108), and although he caused her great suffering throughout their 25-year marriage, she remained loyal and by his side until her death at the age of 47. (However, Frida was not physically loyal either, for like Diego, she too had her own affairs.)

During the decade of the eighties, *notable* names like Madonna, theater and film director Luis Valdez, directors Gregory Nava *(Selena)* and Brian Gibson *(The Josephine Baker Story)*, attempted to produce a film about Frida. Then in the latter part of the nineties, starlets Jennifer Lopez, Salma Hayek, and community activist and actor Edward James Olmos became the front runners (Muñoz F1). It was, however, Salma Hayek's astute producing abilities, her personal friendships with leading stars (who usually "carry" films themselves), willing to take minor roles, and her *relentless* determination, plus a genuine affection and passion for Frida Kahlo, that she was able to produce the movie with financing from Miramax Films. According to Salma, Frida's "colorful spirit inspired me; her passion made me passionate" *(Frida, Bringing* 17). Salma sought to capture this passion for Frida by focusing on the relationship between Frida and Diego "No es una película didáctica para mostrar la situación política de México—La película es una historia de amor" (Hayek qtd in Loaeza 7D). (It is not a film that is intended to teach or show the political situation in Mexico. The film is a love story.)

Finally, worldwide audiences are able to see the movie and to enjoy the beautiful appearance (the look) of the film, or to "feast" on the visual and vibrant imagery the film offers. "The first language of this film is visual which was Frida's" (Hayek qtd. in Sandoval), and most assuredly, the film conveys the color, grandeur, and landscape during Mexico's *renaissance* after the Revolution of 1910.

> *The real star of Frida, the much-hyped film biography of Mexican artist Frida Kahlo is not Salma Hayek, the beautiful Arab-Mexican actor who handles the lead role, but Mexico—in all its legendry, folklore and intensity of colour and passion. (Schwartz)*

Salma Hayek is a powerful, new force in Hollywood, and a Mexican one. Just as one admires Frida, there is much to admire in Salma Hayek as well. She managed to bring together leading actors, and with her intelligence, charm, and beauty (which is quite persuasive in a town that thrives on youth and good looks), she convinced the production company she could carry this film. The success of the film is to her credit; and without a doubt the picture is visually exquisite (thanks to director Julie Taymor's imagination).

A friend of Frida's in Mexico had this reaction after seeing the movie: "We forgive Salma for being so beautiful. The film is beautiful, too. The way the paintings come to life has everything to do with how Frida was and her special sense of humor" (Custodio qtd in Ferris). Salma deserves much of the credit for it was her project (as co-producer), that won the long, drawn-out race to bring Frida Kahlo's story to the big screen. Salma, a woman with beauty, and a Mexican woman with brains, imagine that!

In all its grandeur, beauty, and *sheer* entertainment, the film is lacking in two areas: performance and story, the latter dependent on the screenplay, although performance and story are *intertwined*. Salma's *Frida* (and Julie Taymor's) film is rich in color, texture, and technical experiments, however, those who studied Frida's life are able to see beyond appearances (though clearly appealing). The film's visual "look" delights audiences, and Salma's beauty matches the beauty of the film, but her beauty in fact masks her less than successful performance.

Salma, as Frida, fails to reach the depth of Frida's complex emotional life. A journalist with *The Denver Post* agrees with the point of view in this essay: ". . . she never takes us inside the torment of the mature woman. She always seems to be too impertinent, flippantly defiant" (Rosen). It appears Julie Taymor is not an actor's director, for she was unable to elicit an actor's performance. The "exterior" Frida is on the screen (her paintings, her indigenous costumes, her interesting life with Mexican and international *intelligentsia*). However, Salma's acting does not demonstrate a powerful performance; she does not successfully show the suffering Frida experienced because she had over thirty operations, beginning after the tragic accident in 1924 (Gomez Arias, Personal Interview), and throughout the rest of her life. Noted screenwriter William Goldman offers some insight: "What works in a film is the actor's emotion" (in Brady 97). Actors must convey thoughts, ideas, and specific emotions, so viewers feel the rawness of what a character feels. They must make it look as if they are not acting. Salma did not portray real emotions of the character in key scenes. When she *was* emotional, she played a scene "over the top" (*melodramatic* or overly dramatic). Melodramatic acting is typical in telenovelas. Coincidentally, Salma started her acting career appearing in soap operas in Mexico.

Should a film be laden with dark, sad episodes showing Frida's suffering, which was a large part of Frida's life because of her *debilitating* illness? In part yes; however, capturing and showing her physical and emotional suffering had to be cleverly portrayed through the performance, and without melodrama. Apparently, the challenge was too great for Salma Hayek. Frida lived an incredible rich, full, creative life, in spite of physical setbacks. *Viva la Vida*, the title of one of her last paintings, appropriately represents Frida's spirit and attitude about living life to the fullest.

Clearly, there was much more to Frida's life than her illness. The film represents this through its "*fantastical* imagery" (*Frida, Bringing* 7), of Frida's work, but not Frida's interior life. Julie Taymor depended on Frida's paintings to do this for the actress. Yet, a film story must speak the truth of the interior life of its protagonist. An actor's performance must be believable. There are those viewers, however, who applaud Salma as an actress in this role; needless to say, she has her fan club. A UCLA film school graduate praises Salma: ". . . she really was the only Hollywood celebrity that could play the role. She prepared for the role, did a great job. Her acting was subtle and playful" (Contreras, Personal Interview). Salma, however, did not act from her heart, from her passion that she no doubt has for Frida, nor did she begin to touch on Frida's pain. Perhaps Salma was overwhelmed by this bigger than life character; or she (Salma) relied on the paintings to reveal much of Frida's story. Salma admits, "This is the most complicated role of my career" (Ferris). *Frida* was an "actor's movie"; one many female actresses saw as an opportunity to deliver a great performance. Salma as Frida, however, was far from a performance that merited an Oscar nomination. A movie reviewer for *The San Diego Union-Tribune* is one of many who agree: ". . . while viewers may leave the film somewhat more impressed by Kahlo, few will think: 'Wow what a performance'"(Elliott). There are many viewers who applaud Salma's performance, including other film critics.

However, given that the film received mixed reviews pro and con, Salma's acting suggests that her supporters were unable to see beyond the creative visual presentation and "inside" the performance. The film excelled in style and lacked in substance: "Frida may contain an Oscar-nominated performance from Hayek, but everything about it smells of *conventionality* and a mistrust of the material" ("Frida Misses the Point"). One cannot help but ask—Is "Hollywood" a political circle where producers lobby for nominations?

Equally troubling is the shallow screenplay. Imagine, large sketches of self- portraits of Frida, and pictures of colorful scenes, one-by-one, hanging from a clothesline, and four credited writers, plus Edward Norton (who wrote a polished draft), each one-at-a-time, fill the gaps with words to complement and to compliment the visuals, but the movie script did neither. A film critic with *The Buffalo News* also finds the script disappointing: ". . . it's curiously dutiful and biopic bland," and he adds, "Producers and directors in consort are supposed to pull together all versions of a script into one compelling story. It just didn't happen here" (Simon). Is it the fault of simply too many writers over a period of several years writing and rewriting the script? Did it lose vitality, creativity in story, passing through many hands? Another film reviewer supports Simon's critique of the script: Taymor was attracted to the film because of "the visual spectacle that is Frida Kahlo's paintings. I doubt it was the *stolid, perfunctory* screenplay of this film. . . . Its flatness ultimately defeats a film that's always a treat to look at" (Rosen). Clearly, Rosen applauds the visual spectacle, for one cannot deny the strengths of the film.

When writing a script, a veteran screenwriter knows dialogue should not reveal too much in a line(s). Good writing is most often hidden in the *subtext*. Contreras, again, begs to differ: "The writing flowed really well. The film moves fast. Many lines in the script I really enjoyed. The script captured lines that were Frida's own lines" (Interview). The screenplay is based on Hayden Herrera's biography of Frida. The writer(s) drew from the textbook, however, quoting Frida line for line in a film is not subtle, but direct. Telling too much "face-to-face" is described in screenwriting technique as dialogue that is "on the nose," and must be avoided at all times (Gutiérrez, Personal Interview). A few examples below will demonstrate some problems with the script that may be responsible for Salma's overall weak performance.

Avoid chit-chat, and too much exposition (overwriting).

Many of the scenes in the script are poorly written. At times responses are trite and simplistic; for instance, the first time Frida approaches Diego he is painting a mural at the Ministry of Public Education located near the central plaza in downtown Mexico City. Frida enters the courtyard and asks Diego to come down from the scaffold to "critique" her paintings. He answers, "Who are you? What do you want?" (*Frida:Bringing* 54). This is an example of writing that is on-the-nose and trite. Frida responds by saying, "I have something important to discuss with you!" (54). In good dialogue, a character never answers the question directly, unless the character has a clever response. Diego claims, "I'm working," and Frida says, "I'll wait" (54). Here is an example of boring and unnecessary chit-chat. It is also an example of a throwaway line, and there are too many of them in the script. In general, this scene, which marks the beginning of their relationship, demonstrates many weak aspects of the writing. There is too much exposition, an excellent example of overwriting that drags and slows down the movement of the story. For instance, when Diego says to Frida, "I'm working," she clearly sees he is working. Does he need to tell her this?

There are other problems with this scene. For instance, the exchange takes too long to arrive at Frida's goal, which is for Diego to validate her talent. Writing "lean and economic dialogue means writing short, uncomplex sentences—made up of words from a small vocabulary," says William Miller in *Screenwriting for Film and Television* (181). Short, uncomplex sentences must have meaning. Also, dialogue that works effectively is more economic, direct, with quick responses. Each word, each line must advance the story; it has to be in the script/story for a reason. If it does not contribute to the goal within the scene, then it definitely should not be in the script. Another function of dialogue reveals character. When Frida first approaches Diego to ask for his opinion about her paintings, this is her first opportunity to show (or remind) Diego who she is, not only as a painter, but as a feisty, young, intelligent woman.

Consider an alternate scene—same location (in Orona-Cordova 20–22).
Suggestion: Read the entire scene in *italics* **first; then go back and re-read it, and
examine the comments in boldface.**

*Diego sits high on the edge of a scaffold, painting a mural at the Ministry of Public Education.
He is eating a taco. Diego touches up one section of the mural.*

He bites into his taco without losing a brushstroke. **(Too busy to stop and eat.)**

*Frida stands below the scaffold. She begins to SING "Las Mañanitas" (the Mexican birthday
song).* **(The element of surprise is effective.)**

*Diego's brush moves in rhythm with the song. Diego hesitates, listens, then turns and looks down
at Frida.*

Frida stops singing.

Diego: Only a stranger remembers my birthday! **(She is not yet part of his life.)**

Frida: It's me who asks for a gift from you. **(Subtext: a gift of approval and encouragement.)**

Diego: Give this child some taquitos. **(Diego shows a playful sense of humor.)**

Frida: I'm not a child. I'm a painter. **(An indication she wants to be taken seriously.)**

Diego: If you are a painter, what gift do you need from me? **(A clever answer from a famous
painter, who knows what she wants.)**

Frida: Your opinion, Maestro. Please come down. **(Simply suggests: What do you think?)**

Diego CHUCKLES. He hands the paintbrush to one of his assistants

AT THE BOTTOM OF THE SCAFFOLD.

Diego studies Frida's paintings in silence: an eternity for Frida. **(This creates tension.)**

Diego: And this . . . a self-portrait? **(Suggests: Why do you paint yourself? Also, here is an
opportunity to introduce her first self-portrait.)**

Frida: I painted that for my boyfriend. **(She tells the truth.)**

Diego: Your boyfriend? **(Subtext: Diego is interested in her.)**

Frida: Yes, to get him back. **(Alex, who was in the accident with Frida, and survived without serious injury, hesitated to continue the relationship.)**

Diego: Did you? (**Suggests: Did you seduce him back?**)

Frida: Only to lose him again. (**She lets Diego know Alex is not in her life.**)

More silence.

Diego: You have great promise. (**After playfully digging for details about her, he gives her the gift of approval.**)

Frida: Come to my house in Coyoacan next Sunday, and you will see many more. (**Frida wants to be with him, as much as she wants him to approve of her work.**)

Diego: There's no time. (**Subtext: I'm a busy man.**)

Frida: You won't regret it. (**She teases him.**)

Diego: You promise me a masterpiece? (**He teases back.**)

Frida: I promise you nothing. (**Diego sees the playful feisty side of Frida.**)

Diego: Why then, would Diego Rivera give up a perfectly fine day for painting? (**Subtext: Why would a famous man like me take time off to be with you?**)

Frida: Because you can't resist me! (**Flirtatious words of seduction and an excellent example of punctuating a scene with a clever remark.**)

Diego CHUCKLES. He inspects Frida's paintings again. He turns one last time, smiles and nods his head as if charmed.

In the scene above, Frida and Diego banter back and forth. The dialogue moves fast and rhythmically; messages are hidden in the subtext. They both play with words until he gives her the *gift* she wants, and she offers him the challenge of another potential sexual conquest. This writing provides the actress more opportunity to demonstrate a subtle and powerful performance. Lines in the movie script are ones she recites in rote fashion.

Never announce a scene, or tell what is about to happen.

This scene takes place prior to their first love tryst. Diego and Frida walk toward a large building, late one night. Diego stops in front of a doorway and starts to insert a key in the door. Frida says, "What is this? Your studio?" (*Frida: Bringing* 67). Here is an example of a radio line—actors talk like this when they read a script for a radio play. This is also considered "announcing a scene," e.g., telling more than is necessary. Diego invites Frida in; she is suspicious: "Hey listen, if you think I'm going to sleep with you just because you've taken me under your wing, you're wrong" (67). The American expression in a Mexican setting sounds unnatural, artificial. In addition, it is too obvious. Diego wants Frida to feel safe, but she knows his reputation with women. To reassure her, Diego promises they will only be friends (yet everyone knows Diego has sex mostly with his "friends"). Frida desires him also; she extends her hand as if to "shake on it," but instead **she** kisses **him.** The street lamps suddenly brighten, which offers a nice effect and suggests there is electricity between them. The scene ends here and, fortunately, showing her assertiveness when she kisses Diego, and the nice touch of the bright lights help "save" the mostly flat, overwritten dialogue. (For full text, see *Frida: Bringing* 67–68).

Show, do not tell, is a cardinal rule in screenwriting, and challenges the actress to show emotion, more than announcing how she feels.

There are many more scenes one can analyze in the film, however, one more example suggests that Salma missed an opportunity to win the much coveted Oscar for Best Performance by a Leading Actress.

In this next example, Diego begs Frida to forgive him after he is caught having sex with her sister. Diego approaches a glass door at Frida's house and studio. He knocks hard hoping she will let him in. He admits, "I'm a beast, yes. I, I, I'm an idiot, but it, it meant nothing Frida, nothing" (112). Frida looks at Diego momentarily and tells him "There have been two big accidents in my life Diego. The trolley and you. You are by far the worst" (112).

Frida's remark is quoted over and over again by several of her biographers, including Hayden Herrera's account of Frida's life (107). Frida ends the scene by announcing: "You are by far the worst!" Do audiences need to be told that he is a betraying, dirty bastard? (Is there a better way to put it?) Imagine what she is going through after the betrayal and when he comes begging forgiveness. A repentant Diego stands before her, a glass door separating them. Drawing from inside, from her anguish, instead of from a direct quote, Salma had another opportunity to show real emotion. This is a critical and powerful moment and calls for little, or, better yet, no dialogue. Silence is golden. Consider another way to act and show her anguish instead of announcing it. *A long, hard stare penetrates the glass barrier, like a dagger stabbing Diego with her pain. Her gaze is chilling, and Diego, silenced, shrinks inside.*

Emotion is the life-blood of a performance. An actor must make audiences feel what he or she feels. Frida's pain must be excruciating here. An actor must have confidence in viewers; allow them to feel what the actor feels. Do not *tell* them what to feel. When viewers are told what to feel, they lose the emotion; they listen and hear words. This is a significant turning point in the love affair between these two great artists. Betrayal. Frida knew Diego was a philanderer, but he went too far.

Salma's performance in the scene above, and in many other scenes, was, unfortunately, surprisingly disappointing. She missed the chance to turn this role, this character inside out; to expose many layers of Frida's interior life; to re-live intimate and poignant episodes in her life through a fine performance. Salma depends over and over again on Frida's self-portraits to reveal that emotion.

The story of Frida Kahlo is an epic story. The historical backdrop of her life, her time was one of the richest in politics, education, art, music, folklore, and culture in all of Mexican history. Mexico was deeply involved in an exciting renaissance; and Frida, Diego, and their *avant-garde* circle of friends represented and reflected that period, particularly Frida and Diego's love and appreciation of indigenous culture. The grandiose panoramic landscape of Mexico City at this time was painted in the film; perhaps Taylor devotes too much attention to the visual, and not enough to Frida the woman, the multi-layered and complex emotional life of this great and unique woman. Frida's art speaks for itself; Salma, however, fails to paint a true portrait of Frida Kahlo.

Writing Prompts

1. Briefly describe the historical backdrop in Mexico during the period depicted in the film, according to Orona-Cordova. Consider additional research on the period.

2. How does the title of the essay reflect the theme?

3. Write a critique of the scene written by Orona-Cordova.

4. Analyze a scene from the film, and write a response—pro or con. *Frida* is available on DVD and VHS.

5. What is more important in a film: the story or creative technical and visual effects? Explain. Give examples from the film.

Works Cited

Brady, John. *The Craft of the Screenwriter: Interview with Six Celebrated Screenwriters.* New York: Simon and Schuster, 1981.

Contreras, Diana. Personal interview. 14 April 2003.

Elliott, David. "Artful *Frida;* Movie That Hayek Pursued for Years is a Gift to—and from—the Mexican Artist." *The San Diego Union-Tribune.* 8 Nov. 2002, Lifestyle: E-3. 6 May 2003 Lexis-Nexis Academic News.

Ferris, Susan. "*Frida* Opens to Tough Mexican Critics, But an Eager Public." *Cox News Service.* 20 Nov. 2002. International News, 6 May 2003 Lexis-Nexis Academic News.

Frida: Bringing Frida Kahlo's Life and Art to Film: A New Market Pictorial Moviebook, Including the Illustrated Screenplay. New York: Newmarket Press, 2002.

Frida. Dir. Julie Taymor. Perf. Salma Hayek, and Alfred Molina. Miramax 2002.

"Frida Misses the Point." *Morning Star.* 28 Feb. 2003: 9. 6 May 2003 Lexis-Nexis Academic News.

Gomez-Arias, Alejandro. Personal interview. 8 Jan. 1988.

Gutierrez, Vincent. Personal interview. 25 May 2003.

Herrera, Hayden. *Frida: A Biography of Frida Kahlo.* New York: Harper and Row, Publishers, 1983.

Loaeza, Guadalupe. "Todo por el amor de Frida." *El Mexicano* 18.

Miller, William. *Screenwriting for Film and Television.* Maryland: Allyn and Bacon, 1998.

Muñoz, Lorenza. "Perhaps, Finally, a Frida Kahlo Fillm." *Los Angeles Times.* 30 Aug. 2000, sec. F: 1+.

Orona-Cordova, Roberta. *Viva la Vida: The Story of Frida Kahlo.* UCLA Thesis. 9 Dec. 1990.

Rosen, Steven. "Writing Miserable in 'Frida' Mexican Artists' Tale Paints Shallow Picture." *The Denver Post.* 8 Nov. 2002, Weekend: F-01. 6 May 2003 Lexis-Nexis Academic News.

Sandoval, Ricardo. "*Frida* Opens to Good Business, Mixed Reviews on Artist's Home Turf." *The Dallas Morning News Service.* 21 Nov. 2002 Lexis-Nexis Academic News.

Simon, Jeff. "Paint by Numbers: Bland Biopic Doesn't Capture Kahlo's Spirit." *Buffalo News.* 8 Nov. 2002, Gusto: G4. 6 May 2002.

Swartz, Stephen. "Frida's Just a Crutch for Old Lefties." *The Australian.* 19 Dec. 2002, Features Column Op Ed: 11. 6 May 2003 Lexis-Nexis Academic News.

Words to Learn

"Mainstreaming the Dream: *Spy Kids, The Messenger*

Collective Unconscious—relating to Jungian psychology based on the accumulated knowledge from all preceding generations held in common by humankind for the present and all future generations

infinitely—boundless, endless

divergent—to branch off in different directions from a common point

wield—to use power in an influential way

exploitation—the promotion of an agenda at the disadvantage of others

composition—the arrangement of various parts of a work of art when completed becomes a unified whole

semblance—a likeness, appearance

proportion—a quantity of something that is part of the whole

honed—to sharpen one's skills

undercurrents—a feeling, opinion, force, or tendency that is felt to be present in somebody, but that is not openly shown or expressed and often differs markedly from the person's outward reaction

sensibilities—the capacity to perceive or feel

delectable—absolutely delightful, very pleasing, or very attractive

culminations—the highest, most important, or final point of an activity

bastion—somebody or something regarded as providing strong defense or support, especially for a belief or cause, or a place where there are such people

iota—a very small amount of something

stealthy—the action of doing something slowly, quietly, and covertly, in order to avoid detection

immerses—to become completely occupied with something, giving all your time, energy, or concentration to it

calaveras—Mexican skulls usually used as a decoration during the Day of the Dead

lineage—the line of descent from an ancestor to a person or family

permeates—to enter something and spread throughout it, so that every part or aspect of it is affected

unsavory—not pleasant or agreeable

rough-edged—something that is unpleasant or not smooth

innate—coming directly from the mind rather than being acquired by experience or from external sources

echelons—a formation in which individuals or units are positioned behind and to one side of those in front to give a stepped effect and allow each a clear view ahead

No Substitution: The Play vs. the Film *Real Women Have Curves*

gender—the characterization of masculine and feminine

solidarity—harmony of interests and responsibilities among individuals in a group, especially as manifested in unanimous support and collective action for something

emancipate—the act or process of setting somebody free or of freeing somebody from restrictions

aspiration—a desire or ambition to achieve something

patriarchy—a social system in which men are regarded as the authority within the family and society, and in which power and possessions are passed on from father to son

persecuted—to make somebody the victim of continual pestering or harassment

instincts—a powerful impulse that feels natural rather than reasoned

empowering—to give somebody a sense of confidence or self-esteem

voluptuous—curvy and sensual in appearance

desvergonsadas—Translation: "You should be ashamed of yourself."

monologue—a passage in a play or motion picture spoken by one actor, or an entire play for one actor only

self-determination—the ability or right to make your own decisions without interference from others

reconcile—to make two or more apparently conflicting things consistent or compatible, or to become consistent or compatible

la bendición—Translation: "The blessing." In many Catholic Latino families, mothers provide a blessing to their children before they leave the house. The gesture done by the mother is the sign of the cross toward her child, ending with the child kissing her/his mother's hand.

Social Imagineering in Disney's *The Lion King:* The Three "C's"

homogenous—to be uniform or of one kind, often resulting from a process of "homogenization." This is significant because diversity and true multiculturalism are seen as negatives and the doing away with these results in a "homogenous" culture

nationhood—a sense of common ideals and ideologies tied to political sovereignty of a state or government

co-optation—taking from another and using as one's own

homogenization—the process of changing criteria or characteristics that are often identified as being "different" to make uniform or singular

marginalization—the process of pushing a social group to the margins or exteriors of society

subaltern—the ideologically, politically, economically, culturally, racially, etc., marginalized

parameters—rules or boundaries

conniving—to have the qualities of being scheming, manipulative, or devious

pseudo—fake, pretend, artificial

dissidence—to be a nonconformist or the act of rebelling

status quo—the existing state of affairs

reaffirmation—to confirm or reiterate

convergence—the act of coming together

juxtaposition—to be side by side

equilibrium—the state of being equally balanced

Social Darwinist (from social Darwinism)—meaning the applied belief, from Charles Darwin's theory of "survival of the fittest," that human beings are separated into presumed superior and presumed inferior classes. According to this theory the supposed "superior" survive at the expense of the supposed "inferior."

contestation—the process of contesting or challenging

consolidation—the process of bringing together

acquiescence—to give consent to something or to "go along" with something without much resistance

dichotomy—division into two parts.

obscure—lacking light; dark

sinister—wicked, evil, dishonest

malaise—a vague awareness of moral or social decline

enfranchise—to give entitlement to or as in this case, to give full citizenship rights to members of historically marginalized groups

tangle of pathology—term coined by former U.S. Senator Patrick Moynihan in reference t o his belief that African Americans could not succeed in American society   b e c a u s e they were presumably caught in a "tangle" of pathology (abnormal variation from a sound or normal condition)

periphery—on the margins or outskirts

submerged—to be placed underneath

appropriation—the act of taking for one's own or exclusive use

conscription—the enrolling or drafting of something

republicanism (with a small "r" and not with reference to the "republican party")—meaning to have the principles of self-governance as a result of learning and practicing what is considered to be right over what is considered to be wrong

racialized—the process of attributing racial characteristics to something or someone, often in negative light

infantalized—to characterize a person, usually an adult, as having the same qualities (usually in reference to mental capacities or social behavior) as an infant or child

conservatism—the principles or practices of being conservative, and thus to oppose change in institutions or methods.

neo-liberalism—the political philosophy advocating personal liberties for members of the privileged classes, often at the expense of institutional guarantees of fairness for those of the under-classes.

ascendance—the rising of something

indubitably—that which can not be doubted

subversive—tending or seeking to overthrow or destroy something that is considered normal

Viva *Chocolat*

synopsis—a summary of the plot of a book, movie, or television show

chocolaterie—a store that sells chocolate products

liberation—gaining equal rights for a particular group by setting its members free from traditional socially imposed constraints such as those arising from sexual or ageist stereotyping

shaman—somebody who acts as a go-between for the physical and spiritual realms, and who is said to have particular powers such as prophecy and healing

curandera—a Mexican medicine woman

mestiza—a woman who has parents or ancestors of different racial origins, especially a woman in Latin America of both Native American and European ancestry

healed—to repair or rectify something that causes discord and animosity

culinary—relating to food or cooking

yearning—a very strong desire, often tinged with sadness

libido—in some theories, the psychic and emotional energy in somebody's psychological makeup that is related to the basic human instincts, especially the sex drive

matriarchal—used to describe a society in which power and property are held by women and handed down through matrilineal descent

paradigm—an example that serves as a pattern or model for something, especially one that forms the basis of a methodology or theory

posits—a fact, assumption, or suggestion for consideration

matrilineal—used to describe the line of genealogical relationship or descent that follows the female side of a family

curanderismo—the practice of Mexican-Latino medicine usually by women

assimilate—integrate somebody into a larger group so that differences are minimized or eliminated, or become integrated in this way

mores—the customs and habitual practices, especially as they reflect moral standards, that a particular group of people accept and follow

adherence—devotion

satanic—relating to Satan or the worship of Satan

urn—a sealed vase in which the ashes of somebody who has died and been cremated are kept

irrevocable—not able to be revoked, undone, or changed

stereotypical—oversimplified standardized image or idea held by one person or group of another

patriarchal—relating to a culture in which men are the most powerful members

garnered—to collect or accumulate something such as information or facts

paganism—not Christian, Muslim, or Jew, especially a worshiper of a polytheistic religion

heroine—a woman who is admired or looked up to for her qualities or achievements

swoon—to be overwhelmed by happiness, excitement, adoration, or infatuation

Salma's *Frida:* A Visual Feast, But Not without Its Disappointments

homenaje (homage)—special honor or respect shown or expressed publicly

Galeria de la Raza—Gallery of the People

penned—to write or compose

phallocractic—decisions made by men or to favor men

affinity—a natural attraction, liking, or feeling of kinship

subjugated—to make subservient; to enslave

dichotomy—division into two usually contradictory parts or opinion

candid—characterized by openness and sincerity of expression; straightforward

notable—characterized by excellence or distinction

relentless—steady and persistent

renaissance—the humanistic revival of classical art, architecture, literature, and learning

sheer—completely; altogether

intertwined—to join or become joined by twining together

intelligensia—the artistic and intellectual elite

melodrama—a drama, such as a play, film, or television program, characterized by exaggerated emotions, stereotypical characters, and interpersonal conflicts

debilitating—to weaken the strength and energy

fantastical—strange or strange in form, idea, or appearance

conventionality—the state, quality, or character of being predictable

stolid—having or revealing little emotion or sensibility; not easily aroused or excited

perfunctory—acting with indifference; showing little interest or care

subtext—the underlying personality of a dramatic character as implied or indicated by a script or text and interpreted by an actor in performance

avant-garde—progressive leaders who introduce new techniques in art and style

Contributors

L *alo Alcaraz* was born of Mexican parents in San Diego, California. As he grew up, he faced the challenge of growing up in two cultures. He was not considered Mexican through the eyes of Mexicans because he was born in the United States. Yet, he was not considered American by American people; because he was between cultures, he was called *pocho*. Today he accepts his *pocho* status. He calls himself "King of Pocho." Lalo has a master's degree in architecture from the University of California, Berkeley. His work has appeared in the *LA Weekly*, and he has written TV scripts for the comedy group, *Culture Clash*. His "La Cucaracha," a syndicated comic strip is now in newspapers such as the *Houston Chronicle, Chicago Tribune*, and the *Los Angeles Times*.

Víctor Carrillo resides near downtown Los Angeles and works as a lecturer for Chicana/o Studies and Educational Leadership and Policy Studies Departments at California State University, Northridge. He started writing poetry 20 years ago.

Yreina D. Cervántez is an assistant professor in the Department of Chicana/o Studies at California State University, Northridge. She earned a B.A. in Fine Arts from the University of California, Santa Cruz and an M.F.A. from the University of California, Los Angeles. She is recognized for her unique sensibility and versatility in her artwork that includes drawing, painting, watercolor, printmaking, and murals. Ms. Cervántez has received numerous awards for her achievements. She has also participated in national and international exhibits.

Elena Contreras is a teacher who is especially committed to the educational advancement of underrepresented students. She also mentors Chicano/a students in graduate-training programs.

Diana Marie Delgado was raised in the city of La Puente. She received her bachelor's degree in creative writing from the University of California, Riverside and will begin Columbia University's M.F.A. writing program in fall of 2003. She has published a poetry chapbook, entitled *Holding Nothing Like It's Something*.

Karin Duran received her doctoral degree in Library and Information Management at the University of Southern California, and is currently a librarian in the Oviatt Library at California State University, Northridge. She is a faculty member in Chicano/a Studies, and the department's resource librarian. Her responsibilities for the Chicano/a Studies Department include library instruction, development of instructional materials, collection development, participation in faculty governance and department management through strategic planning, committee work, and development of policies and procedures

Dora Daniels volunteers as a Sunday school teacher at her local church. She makes her living working as a courtesy clerk at a grocery chain; and during her free time, she attends school where she is earning credits toward a high school diploma.

Lorenzo Flores. An encounter with Con Safos in 1970 inspired Lorenzo T. Flores to write about the Chicano experience. He earned his graduate degree in creative writing at Antioch University, Los Angeles. He is a founding member of the Institute for Chupa Cabras Studies. "Toppy" hopes to publish several pieces, one of these days. Currently, he is a professor in the Chicano/a Studies Department, and teaches Chicano literature, freshman composition, and speech.

Deena J. González is an active scholar in Chicana/o Studies. She was the first Chicana to receive a Ph.D. from the University of California, Berkeley, history department. She publishes works about ninetieth-century women's history, on contemporary gender and sexuality, and on race and ethnicity. She has received numerous awards for her scholarship, including an Emmy for Historical Consultant as part of the *The U.S.-Mexican War Series*, PBS (KERA/Dallas), Best Historical Programming, 1999.

Maria C González is an associate professor of English at the University of Houston. Her book, *Contemporary Mexican-American Women Novelists: Toward a Feminist Identity*, traces the development of Chicana novelists. Her current work is an institutional history of Chicana/o literary studies. She teaches courses in American literature, Mexican-American literature, and feminist and queer theory.

Gabriel Gutiérrez graduated from the University of California, Santa Barbara. His specialty is Chicano/a History—Nineteenth and Twentieth Centuries, and United States History. He is an assistant professor at California State University, Northridge, where he teaches History of the Chicano, Chicano/a Culture, and critical reasoning.

Vincent A. Gutiérrez graduated from film school at the University of California, Los Angeles, with an emphasis in screenwriting. Soon after graduation he sold his master thesis screenplay *Lowrider* to MONAREX, a German-based production company. It was soon produced as a feature-length film with a new title, *Heartbreaker.* The film is distinguished for being one of the first Hollywood movies ever directed by a Chicano, Frank Zuniga *(The Golden Seal; Mustang)*. Over the years, Gutiérrez has written over 27 screenplays, most for various production entities including ABC, CBS, Columbia Pictures, and Esparza/Katz. Presently, he teaches in two departments, Chicano/a Studies and Cinema Television, at California State University, Northridge.

Xocoyotzin Herrera is an ethnomusicologist in the department of Chicana/o Studies at California State University, Northridge, where he teaches courses in regional Mexican music. He is also a multi-instrumentalist, and forms part of the Conjunto Hueyapan, a family musical ensemble who specializes in traditional music from Veracruz, Mexico, known as *son jarocho.* As a musician, Herrera has many recording credits to his name and has performed in numerous prestigious venues throughout the United States, Mexico, Europe, China, and Korea. He has composed works that can be heard on *Showtime's Resurrection Blvd.,* and *The Shield,* which airs on Fox. Currently, he is preparing new material for an upcoming film and television project.

Michael F. Jacobson is the executive director of the Center for Sciences in the Public Interest, a nonprofit consumer advocacy group. Dr. Jacobson helps educate the public through his award-winning Nutrition Action Health Letter, the largest-circulation health newsletter in the country

Elizabeth Rodríguez Kessler left Houston, Texas, where she had lived most of her life. She moved to teach at the University of California, Northridge, in the Department of English. She has a Ph.D. in English from the University of Houston and has taught for thirty-three years in public and private settings. Her writing includes personal memoirs, poetry, and short stories, as well as academic articles, a monograph, and a multicultural composition text, *Hands Across Borders: A Multicultural Reader for Writers.* She is currently working on a critical text concerning the roles of Latina women in society.

Lawrence Littwin former associate dean of the College of Social and Behavioral Sciences at California State University, Northridge (CSUN), has written extensively about politics and religion in Latin America. As coordinator of CSUN's participation in the series of international conferences on the U.S.-Mexican border: "The Frontier: A New Cultural Context," Dr. Littwin worked with a bi-national team of U.S. and Mexican scholars investigating migration within Mexico and from Mexico to the United States. His own research focused on the human rights of immigrants. Dr. Littwin is currently Professor Emeritus of Political Science.

Oriel María S. Bernal grew up in Honduras, Central America. She came to the United States in the summer of 1998. Since then, Oriel has studied at California State University, Northridge. She strongly believes that we must use our education for creating positive social change. Her academic goal is to graduate in 2004, then enter a master's and doctorate program in literature. Throughout her four years at CSUN she has held positions of leadership in several organizations on campus including the Central American United Student Association.

Bruce Maxwell has been active as a freelance writer, editor, and publisher since 1989. He has written, edited, and co-authored Quarterly Books and Workman Publishing, launched Silver Hammer Publishing, an electronic publishing firm; written articles for numerous national magazines and newspapers; written and edited a group of newsletters about state and local political issues; presented seminars about how to access government information on the Internet, and BBSs; and written extensive content for a corporate Web site.

Gerard Meraz was an early contributor to URB magazine via a column called DA EAST-SIDE. He is a graduate student and part-time instructor in the Chicano/a Studies Department at California State University, Northridge. His master's thesis topic focuses on early DJ culture in East Los Angeles. His future plans include writing a book on DJs in Los Angeles, and starting a DJ school.

Theresa Montaño is an assistant professor in the Chicana/o Studies Department at California State University, Northridge, and is president-elect of the National Association for Multicultural Education. Her emphasis is in critical pedagogy, anti-racist/multicultural education, bilingual education, and social justice teacher education.

Juana Mora was born in Jalisco, Mexico, and immigrated to the United States in 1960. She is the first member of her family to attend college. She attended the University of California at Santa Cruz where she completed her B.A. in linguistics. She later received a Ford Foundation Fellowship to attend Stanford University. Dr. Mora earned a Ph.D. in Education at Standford University in 1984. She specializes in research on alcohol consumption and related problems among Latinos in the United States. She is currently a full professor in the Department of Chicano/a Studies at California State University, Northridge.

Cherríe L Moraga is the author of the now classic, *Loving in the War Years*. She has produced several award-winning plays, including *Shadow of a Man, Heroes and Saints,* and *Watsonville: Someplace Not Here.* Her two most recent books include a collection of poems and essays, entitled *The Last Generation,* and a memoir, *Waiting in the Wings: Portrait of a Queer Motherhood.* In 2001, she published a new volume of plays, entitled *The Hungry Woman.*

Javier Morelos was born in the San Fernando Valley. He is studying journalism and Chicano Studies at California State University, Northridge. He enjoys writing poems and short stories and thinks that knowing how to write well is the key to success in college. He hopes to put his journalism training to use writing about issues that affect Latinos and gays.

Naomi Quiñonez is a Los Angeles born and raised poet, educator, and a community activist. A recent Rockefeller Fellow, she has published two collections of poetry: *The Smoking Mirror* and *Hummingbird Dream.* She received her Ph.D. in History/American Studies at Claremont Graduate University and is currently a professor in the Chicano Studies Department at California State University, Fullerton. Quiñonez publishes and lectures extensively on the history and cultural production of Mexican-origin women in the United States.

Gerald Resendez earned a B.A. at St. Mary's College in Moraga, California. He has an M.A. in Romance Languages and Literature from the University of Southern California, and completed further graduate studies at UCLA in Romance Languages and Literature.

He started teaching at an inner-city school in Los Angeles in 1959. He extended his love of teaching to college students in 1969 when he participated in the struggle to establish the Chicano/a Studies Department at California State University, Northridge. He teaches classes on Chicano culture, literature, and religion.

David Rodriguez is the Associate Chair of Chicano/a Studies Department at California State University, Northridge. He earned a PhD in Political Science from the University of California, Riverside. His book *Latino National Political Coalitions: Struggles and Challenges* is an examination of the Chicano, Cuban and Puero Rican national coalition experience, and its relationship to the Latino/a community. He teaches courses in politics, theory, critical thinking and culture.

Barbara Morales Rossi was born in El Paso, Texas, and raised by young parents, who divorced when Barbara was a teenager. She "came out of the closet" when she was eighteen, and her mother announced to friends and neighbors that Barbara was a lesbian. Her mother asked, "What took so long?" At 29 years old Barbara moved to Los Angeles, graduated with an Associate of Arts degree from Santa Monica College in June 2003. Today she is a full-time student at the University of California, Santa Cruz, majoring in United States history.

Trinidad Sánchez, Jr., wrote the bestseller, *Why Am I So Brown?* and *Poems by Father & Son.* He travels widely, lecturing and reading. Presently, he is the coordinator of the Fatherhood Project for Rocky Mountain SER Head Start in Denver, Colorado where he lives with his wife, Regina.

Valerie Talavera-Bustillos is an assistant professor of Chicano Studies at California State University, Los Angeles. She graduated from the University of California, Irvine, and completed her Ph.D. at the University of California, Los Angeles. Her research focuses on the educational experiences of the Chicana and Latino populations through qualitative observations. She integrates resistance theory, critical race theory, and Chicana feminism in her work to better understand the cultural dynamics involved in the Chicana/Latino experiences within the educational system.

Fabiola Torres-Reyes was born in Los Angeles, California, in 1971. Ms. Torres-Reyes is a product of Mexican parents who taught and inspired her to work hard. She has lived her life demonstrating that their love and moral teachings have nourished her soul and dreams. Now they are proud parents of a university lecturer at California State University, Northridge, and Glendale Community College.

María Victoria is a full-time student majoring in film and photography. Her primary goal in life is to carry the message of recovery to those people suffering from alcohol and drug abuse. She participates in various 12-step programs and facilitates women's groups, helping them to manage their addiction.